SPEAKING THE GOSPEL TODAY

SPEAKING THE GOSPEL TODAY

A THEOLOGY FOR EVANGELISM

REVISED EDITION

Robert Kolb

CONCORDIA PUBLISHING HOUSE · SAINT LOUIS

Contents

Preface

Ten years ago the first edition of this little volume appeared in an America that was beginning to show the signs of wear and tear. At the beginning of the '80s greed and ego were being enshrined as the chief values and virtues of the United States, according to popular wisdom. Every effort was being made to beat back the feeling of malaise which had resulted from Watergate, the Arab oil embargo, and Vietnam. But success was short-lived. The feeling of malaise had been well founded. Precisely the values of greed and narcissism led, directly and indirectly, to the continued decline of family life and the rise of crime, the decline of that which holds all societies together, the rise of the internal foe which tears them apart.

The past decade has witnessed an acceleration of the deterioration of life on this continent. Faltering social structures and failing social values are driving people to search for personal identity and for a larger meaning for life in ever-new ways, as the proliferation of Christian and non-Christian sects reveals. There is therefore an ever-increasing urgency for believers in the Christian Gospel to bring its life-restoring message to their neighbors. The church must always be about addressing the ageless message of the Scripture to the changing age in which it is called to serve.

Christians have seldom lived in as exciting an age as this. For the world falling apart around us cries out for the sense of identity and security which Christ gives, and which He has given us to share. A litany of complaints about the world in which we live, from within the church and outside it, can easily lead to unseemly boasting or to self-defeating defensive maneuvers among Christians. Instead, believers have the opportunity of rising to the challenge of sharing the secret of God's love in Christ, who died and rose for such an age as this.

Speaking the Gospel today requires, first of all, the ability to listen to the world around us and then to convey the biblical message of God's restoration of our human identity through Christ to the people He has placed around us. Speaking the Gospel today calls for a simple reading of the Scripture within the context of our own circumstances at the end of one century and the beginning of the next. Speaking the Gospel in any age demands that connections be made between God's Word and the world as it has shaped itself, in its goodness as His created order, and in its sinfulness as His fallen creation. Bridges must be built between the Word of the Lord and those who are deaf to its message. Theology exists as a discipline in order to interpret God's Word in the Scripture for the changing human scene. Theology is the original cross-disciplinary field of study, the original inter-disciplinary exercise in human learning. For the theological task demands listening to voices from every field of human endeavor in order to bring God's Word to all the corners of His world.

This book once again attempts to model the way in which the insights of theologians, the observations of other disciplines, and the pulse of popular culture can be brought together to inform the bridge-builders, the baptized children of God, on ways of constructing the bridges over which they, as the Holy Spirit's agents, can bring the dying into new life in Christ.

As I wrote twelve years ago in preparing the first edition of this book, "It is my hope that reading this book may strengthen the conviction of those who realize that theology cannot exist apart from its application to the lives of others and above all to those who are outside of the faith, in need of the Gospel's transforming power. I hope that this book may convince those whose chief interest is evangelism that the skills of Christian witness are nothing if they do not convey the biblical message accurately and effectively."

To God alone be glory.

Robert Kolb
Concordia Seminary, Saint Louis
Epiphany 1994

8

INTRODUCTION

The Art of Christian Conversation

Christians are reborn with silver tongues in their mouths. It is just natural for Christians to talk. God's reborn people can fail to feel the urge to speak of Jesus Christ no more than children can suppress the joy of the heart or restrain themselves from sharing a secret.

That is because Christians are created and then re-created in the image of God—God, who loves to talk. He began all reality as we know it by saying, "Let there be ..." (Gen. 1); He spoke, and from His words all creation was given life (John 1:4). When He wanted to fashion for Himself a special people, He called Abram out of Ur of the Chaldeans and sent him on his way with no more than a promise and a blessing (Gen. 12:1–3). When He intervened in human history most decisively, to perform His work of re-creation, He came as the Word made flesh (John 1:1, 14; cf. Heb. 1:2). Again, He called people from their fishing nets and tax tables to form a new people for Himself. He commissioned them to bring others into the family of God by making them disciples, and he described that process of making disciples in two steps: baptizing and teaching. Baptism is new birth into the family (John 3:3–6); teaching is the process of growth and maturing which brings God's children to maturity in the practice of their humanity (Eph. 4:12–16). Baptism enacts the commission of our Lord to bring people to repentance and to the forgiveness of sins (Luke 24:47). He has sent his people forth to pronounce judgment on those who defy God, and He sent them on a mission to pronounce forgiveness and freedom upon those who realize that their gods and their lives are broken (Matt. 16:19; 18:18; John 20:23). His commissions placed words on the tongues of his followers, words of repentance and of life. Believers, made in His image, can hardly help but talk about their God.

9

THE BEGINNING OF THE CHRISTIAN ANSWER

Yet when believers begin conversations with those outside the faith, they find that the initial agenda of this dialog is set by the experiences of life which have imposed questions that yearn for answers. For the traumas and tribulations, the tragedies and tricks of human experience mock our plans for living and make us ask:

In view of the mess the world is in, how in the world can there be a god?

Can life really be meaningful in the face of the onslaught of death?

If I join your church, do I have to be in church every Sunday?

Is there really a "last day" coming, and if so, when will it get here?

Sure I was baptized once, a long time ago, but what good has that ever done me?

Is there any way in the world not to be lonely?

Can you give me a ticket to set me free from my guilt and shame?

Can you be a Christian and have an abortion?

Some questions may seem profound, and others trivial. Some people may feel secure enough to be a bit bolder and more honest, with themselves and with the Christian witness, but others may bear burdens and bruises so severe that they dare not articulate the dilemma of human living with anything but a shallow and tentative groping for the believer's reaction.

Whatever the question and however it is phrased, the initial Christian reaction must always be another question: *Why do you want to know?* For Christian conversation can begin only when the Christian knows *why* the other person is asking about life. Human creatures formulate their questions about life from one or the other of two stances: from *a stance of security,* based on a sufficiently firm trust in someone or something to enable them to get along without recourse to trust in their Creator; or from *a stance of brokenness,* perhaps even despair, in which the old bases for decision-making have been so challenged and shaken that they are no longer viable. In this case life must find a new basis, or cease.

No other response to the claims of the Creator is possible for the human creature who has found a basis for life other than the Creator, another source for identity, security, and meaning. Either sinful creatures are comfortable with the new gods which they use to cope with trouble, or they are insecure and broken by those troubles which their new gods can no longer overcome.

Thus, it is vital for the Christian witness to determine whether the hearer wants to know about life's meaning because Michael is interested in defying death out of his own resources and on his own terms, or whether he is terrified by the prospect of death itself. Effective Christian witness cannot proceed until it is known whether Mary wants to earn a place in the heavenly choir by singing in the local church choir every Sunday, or whether she fears her failure to worship in the past has closed the doors of the church and heaven to her forever. It is absolutely necessary to know whether John wants to calculate the timing of judgment so that he can yet schedule the delights of defying God, or whether he yearns for the day of liberation. It is crucial to know whether Beth is looking for a license for an abortion which would be convenient for her, or whether she is seeking forgiveness for an abortion which has brought her guilt and self-hatred.

Christian witnesses must know the agenda behind people's questions. They must ever ask: *Why do you want to know?*

QUESTIONS AND ANSWERS IN CONTEMPORARY SOCIETY

That question and its answer, of course, do not end Christian witness. They do not even simplify it. Rather they lay the basis for an effective application of God's messages to those who have not been listening. For God has placed two messages in the believer's mouth: *a message of wrath and judgment* for those who doubt Him and defy Him, for those who trust in objects of His creative hand to give them identity, security, and meaning; and *a message of mercy and forgiveness,* of liberation and new creation for those who have come to realize that their gods were not gods at all.

Once this basis has been laid, we believers may proceed with the task at hand. If the person with whom we are talking is secure with his gods, we must formulate an approach which will bring him to recognize their insufficiency. If the person with whom we

11

are talking is broken and has recognized that her gods cannot provide security, meaning, or a viable identity, then we must formulate the message of God's mercy and love for His straying human creatures so that it is plausible to her. To accomplish its task, our expression of the Gospel must reveal that Jesus Christ bestows identity, provides meaning, and is Himself the security for His people. But in the bewildering variety of human predicaments and sins of our day the believer confronts in each witnessing situation a new challenge for formulating God's message carefully and precisely. Thus, to identify the broad category (secure or broken) into which the hearer fits is only the preliminary step. The believer must then analyze how best to bring the wrath or mercy of God to the other person in such a way that God's Word will work most effectively.

The task is even more complicated in 20th-century America, which boasts of being a pluralistic society in which innumerable flowers of thought can be cultivated. In defiance of God, in the frantic search for a replacement for Him, we and our neighbors internalize this pluralism. We are bombarded by competing truth claims and absorb both their alternative arguments and the culture's suggestion that all systems of thought have some merit, some piece of a wider truth. Therefore, "the confrontation of the various reality-defining agencies takes place within us. The results may be personal monstrosities like 'Christian atheism' or nature worship advertised as Christian hope. ..."[1] Even believers must examine their own views of life and deal with the implications American pluralism has for their own faith and their witness to that faith.

Believers are also tempted in two directions as they approach those outside the faith in this pluralistic society. On the one hand, we think in the categories of the religion of Western culture, if not always, strictly speaking, in biblical categories, and we may mistakenly take for granted that everyone else in our society has charted reality in the same way in which we and our European ancestors have. Therefore, we conclude, they will assuredly understand us if we speak to them in our own age-old categories.

On the other hand, we can easily exaggerate the degree to which people around us have become secularized or "de-religionized." North American culture at the end of the 20th century still poses and articulates many human problems in at least quasi-reli-

gious terms. Human experience often forces people without religious backgrounds to pose questions and to conceptualize problems in religious categories, even if they do not always use traditional Western religious terminology. Yet contemporary believers
must remember that increasing numbers of our neighbors in all age
brackets—even among the elderly whom we regard as naturally
religious—demonstrate not only little if any biblical knowledge but
also little if any interest in specifically "Christian" or "religious" concerns at the conscious level. They may hurt emotionally, but they do
not attribute this to sin, nor do they look for deliverance from God
in the Flesh.

They do not understand "justification" as more than the attempt
to give a ready excuse for something they know they should not
have done—but they do want to "justify" themselves. They do not
even pose the question of how to become righteous in God's sight.
But at its root the question regarding the good life—how can I enjoy
my humanity fully? why is life so loused up? how can I get myself
out of this mess and straighten myself up? is the root question of
all people. The 16th century search for a gracious God remains,
but cloaked under the contemporary absorption in self and the
quest for identity. Biblical tradition does provide the answers to
such versions of the root question of humankind since the fall,
whether "God" appears in the current formulation of that question
or not.

Furthermore, living with the Bible ringing in our ears has created a cultural gap between us and the people "just like us" across
the street or at work who have no sense of the biblical rhythms
and songs we march to. The Scripture has its own thought patterns,
and they must bridge the gap into the world around us if they are to
lead those caught in that world of death into the light of life.

Thus, as believers ask "Why do you want to know?" they must
listen carefully so that they can proceed with their task of applying
the message of God's wrath or the message of God's mercy to the
person with whom they are speaking. Believers must imagine what
it is like to see life from the other person's perspective. Believers
must try to think themselves into a life lived in the midst of that
person's home, onto a path walked in that person's shoes. Only
then can Christian witness proceed to speak for God.

CALLED TO SPEAK FOR GOD
TEMPTED TO REMAIN SILENT

The Christian witness presumes to speak for God because God has called His people to speak for Him. He has commissioned us to pronounce judgment and deliverance in the appropriate situations to appropriate hearers. Children of God, as human creatures, possess what educators call "spontaneous communicative tendencies," one cluster of which "leads us to talk to other people about our interests." Other such tendencies lead us to applaud or commend others, to express disapproval of their performances, and to supply the answers for which someone else is groping.[2] Just as some educators complain that so much of the spontaneous, positive inclinations of childhood are too easily and too quickly suppressed in the growing child, so believers often find that the spontaneous desire to tell others of the wonders of God's love is choked off easily and quickly.

Many possible reasons for this might be cited. Some Christians fail to recognize that God has called and commissioned them as the agents of His re-creating power, those who are to speak that Word of His which transforms human lives. Others would like to say something and know that they should from time to time, but they are overwhelmed by the size of the challenge. They think that to begin to talk about life and life's Author, they must be ready to give more answers than they know and solve more problems than they are able. Feeling incapable of defending their God adequately, they shrink from embarrassing Him.

The fact is, believers do not have the choice of witnessing or not. They only choose whether to witness better or less effectively. If people know that we are Christians, they are always and easily noticing and evaluating what Jesus means to us. If they do not know we are Christians, they do get to know quite quickly, as we become acquainted, what is of ultimate worth to us, what the ultimate source of our identity, security, and meaning is. So it is; that's God's design for human creatures.

There can be no doubt that God wants His Christian people to speak His Word; above all, to bring that Good News of new life in Jesus Christ to those who are writing their own bulletins and guidelines for a life which is dying. This living voice of the Gospel in

14

our mouths is the very power of God for the salvation of fallen human creatures (Rom. 1:16), and He has placed this power into the hands of all His disciples (Matt. 16:19; 18:18; John 20:23). The 16th-century reformers spoke of this commission as the "priesthood of all believers."

Many of their modern followers regard the chief significance of their priesthood as their privilege to go to God as individuals directly and not to have to rely on anyone else to perform the services of priest, or intermediary, for them. But Peter defines the chief significance of being priests of the King and members of His nation and people as their calling to declare the wonderful deeds of Him who called them out of darkness into His marvelous light (1 Peter 2:9). The Latin word for priest, *pontifex,* literally means "bridge-builder." God has made us His people so that we might build a bridge between the revelation of His saving will for us, His re-creating Word, and the people of our day and our society. He has entrusted His Word to us, as He gives it in the Scriptures in which He breathed and in which He has set the authoritative form of His Word, so that we might proclaim it and apply it to the people of our culture in terms which effectively translate that Word for them. That process begins when we translate the Scriptures from the original Hebrew, Aramaic, and Greek into, for instance, modern English. As believers approach unbelievers, that "translation" process must be extended; therefore, the ability to transmit the biblical message effectively to those who find its ancient context and its explanation of life quite foreign will demand the cultivation of skills and knowledge that come only through hard work. The study of the Word includes an ongoing reading of the biblical text, and an imaginative yet disciplined searching for its contemporary implications and applications. The biblical text is not some wax nose that may be twisted by the reader's whim. The biblical writers used human language to convey specific meaning, and through the study of that language and the world in which it was uttered we can determine quite well—in most cases quite precisely—what it was that the prophets and apostles were given by God to convey to their hearers and readers. But the message of the seventh century before Christ or the first century of the Christian era can be translated into the thought world of 20th-century North Americans. When it is, it brings

15

the same power to kill and to make alive that it bore at the time it was first formulated in human language. Through the insight of faith the Holy Spirit guides and aids the process of translation. The insight of faith is built upon, and grows through, engagement with the Word.

Knowing the biblical text is not enough for effective Christian witness. The task of bridge-building demands a knowledge of our immediate neighbors, and believers must use the tools of modern academic disciplines, which are also products of God's creative hand, to gain an understanding of the world around us. Christians must recognize that those who practice these disciplines always let their work be influenced by their own presuppositions and world views. We dare not be deceived into thinking that there is some "objective" truth in every whim of every social scientist. Nonetheless, whatever ideologies may influence modern practitioners of psychology, sociology, or anthropology, for instance, these disciplines still offer us the means to grasp certain categories in which our contemporaries think, as well as some accurate glimpses of the ways in which human creatures function.[3] These insights are useful and necessary, both for our analysis of why life is not working for the person to whom we are witnessing, and also for our formulation of the message of God's gift of new life in Christ for that person.

Witness to the love of God in Christ Jesus is, we must remember, not primarily a sharing of information but introducing one person to another. Acquaintances can be sparked even by those whose command of the details of this man's life and message is limited. When believers do not know as much as they would like to about this Jesus whom they are introducing to others, they should practice tag-teaming. They should start the acquaintance with Christ and then call on others to help the friendship grow.

Nor does witnessing require the perfect life—any more than it requires the perfect answers. In fact, we witness in our vulnerability. The failures and frailty of our own faith and life demonstrate that God is in charge, also of our witness. The person beset by troubles wants to have some sense of solidarity with us while he or she is under the assault of evil. Such a broken person, who is ready to hear the Gospel, can be turned away by someone who appears to be a "super-Christian." Super-piety intimidates. We illustrate and testify to the love of God when the raggedness of our life shows and the struggle of faith becomes evident from the start.

ACTUALIZATION, NOT ACCOMMODATION

The life which the voice of the Gospel takes on in our own speech must always spring from and be disciplined by the voice of God in the Scriptures. We must make scriptural words as clear and understandable as possible to people who do not share Luke's experiences or Isaiah's view of the world. But there is also a danger here. The Christian bridge-builder is most often tempted to balance the bridge on the side of the culture in which we live. The Christian priest is always liable to be lured into trying to explain the biblical message so clearly in the terms of the rationality of our culture that the message of the Scriptures becomes twisted and out of focus at best, or, at worst, is totally denied and lost.

Most heretics in the history of the church have been people of good will who fell as they bent over backwards trying to refashion the message of God in their own cultural terms. Helmut Thielicke's distinction between our actualization of God's Word and our temptation to accommodate it to the cultural world view around us must be kept in mind. Actualization of God's Word is the readdressing of His message to the circumstances of our day; "the truth itself remains intact ... the hearer is summoned and called 'under the truth' in his own name and situation." Accommodation, by contrast, "calls the truth 'under me' and lets me be its norm. It is pragmatic to the extent that it assigns truth the function of being the means whereby I master life."[4]

Christians rely on the guidance and counsel of the Holy Spirit in this matter, but they must also remember that the Holy Spirit does not work magically. He guides and counsels through intensive study both of the Word and of the culture in which He has called us to serve. He guides and counsels through fellow believers who are engaged together in the study of the content or teaching of the Word and its application and proclamation in their society.

In North America we reserve the title "theologian" for those who have done advanced work in the academic discipline of theology.

In some parts of Europe the title is awarded to anyone who has completed the basic course of study for the clergy. But in one sense every Christian is called to the lifelong study of theology or Christian teaching. Often North American Christians have found "doctrine"—the word simply means "teaching"—intimidating, divisive, or boring. This assumption may have some historical basis in the abuse of Christian teaching in the life of the church; it has no basis whatever in God's plan for the re-creation of human creatures in His own image. For He re-creates as He created: through His Word. His Word is not babble; it has content. Its re-creating content, the Gospel, is not just a magical formula or a signpost pointing to an otherworldly super-reality. His Gospel is His very power for saving, for delivering, for re-creating His people, even as it comes in ordinary human language—as ordinary as Jesus of Nazareth, the baby in diapers, the man who wept and grew weary. The content of God's Word in ordinary words is of utmost, life-giving importance.

Genuine biblical teaching, doctrine, is not correct if it is merely flawless in content. It must also be accurately presented, aimed precisely at the situation of the contemporary hearer. It must be as effectively spoken by us today as it was effectively delivered to the prophets and apostles two millennia and more ago.[5] The practice of theology, the conveying of Christian teaching, is not beyond the reach of the "average" Christian. It is neither the sole province of professionals nor an optional activity for any Christian witness. God instructs His people: "earnestly desire the spiritual gifts, especially that you may prophesy" (1 Cor. 14:1). Prophesying meant for Saint Paul that human hearts may be convicted—the work of the Law—and that they might be edified and comforted (1 Cor. 14:24–25, 31). All Christian witnesses must spend time in the same process of determining the content of the Scripture and how to apply that content to the lives of their neighbors. It is tempting to opt for a "cheap faith" which wants to drop the name of Jesus but does not want to exert the mental energy to be able to confess His name effectively and advertise winsomely the benefits which He delivers to us. That kind of "cheap faith" may avoid the mental sweat required to mine the biblical treasures and to process them for useful presentation in our time. It also avoids the thrill of hearing the Word proceed from itself in all its power and all its care and concern for broken human creatures.

To be sure, good theologians will not parade everything they know in front of their hearers to intimidate the hearers or to inflate their own egos or reputations. They will avoid speaking over the heads of their hearers. But it is impossible for humble believers to "know too much" or to be "too well-prepared" in their command and understanding of God's Word and His creation. Increased knowledge provides an increased range of perspectives from which the believer may view the situation of the unbeliever. That will improve Christian witness, for it makes it possible for the believer to present the Word of God more clearly and in the precise form in which it can be most effective.

C. S. Lewis dared to write on the psalms, he told his readers, because "two schoolboys can solve difficulties in their work for one another better than the master can," and therefore he writes "as one amateur to another."[6] It must be remembered that Lewis, no Hebraist or Old Testament scholar, was nevertheless a very well-studied "schoolboy," an amateur who was extremely sensitive to the psalmists' texts, to the world in which they were composed, and to the world in which he was sharing the fruits of his study.

Such study stands behind all Christian witness which is any more than a sharing of ignorance or mere emotion. This volume is written to assist readers in the task of Christian witness. Its survey of Christian teaching aims at providing insights and models for the believers' use of God's Word and for the application of His message to the lives of their audience in North American culture at the end of the 20th century. The Great Commission texts (Matt. 28:18–20; Mark 16:15–16; Luke 24:45–49; John 20:21–23; Acts 1:7–8) serve as the basis of this book: God is at work through His commissioned disciples, making disciples by restoring His fallen but chosen people to Himself through the call to repentance and the forgiveness of sins. The outline of the book rests on the confession that God is Father, Son, and Holy Spirit, and the conviction that God's message is twofold: a message of wrath against all evil and sin, and a message of mercy and liberation, of forgiveness and new life.

1

Through Him All Things Were Made

Jesus confronts us with His claim. "All authority in heaven and on earth has been given to Me." His disciples worshiped Him, but some doubted (Matt. 28:17). To them He issued His claim that He exercises all authority in the universe. He is able to do that because He is the Author of the universe, the Author of life.

As Christians we take for granted that God exists and that He is the Author of life. All Christian witness aims to acquaint a fellow human creature with another person, the person of God. Helping two persons get acquainted requires sharing information, helping each to know more about the other. But this process is never merely a sharing of information. It is the creation of a relationship. Not all people in our culture begin conversations with us presupposing that God exists, that He exists as a person, or that He is the Author of life. Christian witness does not begin by laying out a broad philosophical basis upon which the discussion of biblical viewpoints and values may be discussed. Christian conversation really begins most often where the person with whom the believer is talking wants it to begin, usually where he or she is hurting or questioning or feels ill at ease. Believers will be certain that they themselves have a clear understanding of the presuppositions of their faith. Christian witnesses will recognize their own presuppositions so that they can analyze possible differences in presuppositions which could, in turn, cause much of what we say and hear to be misunderstood in the course of conversation. This first chapter reviews the biblical presupposition that God exists and is the Creator. Its contents have less immediate relevance for the way in which witnessing proceeds face to face than will chapters 2 and 3. Nonetheless, it is of utmost importance that believers recognize the presuppositions, here in the doctrine of creation, on which their faith rests. In addition, they must recognize the presumptions which they carry with them from the Scriptures as they begin their conversation with an unbeliever.

The biblical doctrine of creation has a number of important implications. These include, first, a series of observations about our understanding of human relationships, above all with God, but also with nature, other human creatures, and self. Second, Jesus' claim to the authority of the Creator offers insights into the proper definition of piety, or proper human living. Third, the words of our Creator signify a source of security which frees us from demanding that our every question about life find a completely satisfying answer in our own terms. Finally, the doctrine of creation reminds us of the goodness of the created, material world around us, and it leads us to recall how God uses selected elements in the created order to accomplish the re-creation of fallen human creatures.

JESUS OF NAZARETH: GOD, PERSON, CREATOR

The authority which Jesus of Nazareth exercises is "the power which decides, ... the invisible power of God whose Word is creative power."[1] This authority belongs in the first instance to the one who "cannot be asked concerning the relationship of power and legality" in this authority "since He is the source of both."[2] This authority is the right to destroy even human creatures (Luke 12:5); it is the responsibility to fix the seasons (Acts 1:7). The one who has designed and determined all things, upon whom all things are dependent, speaks and acts with authority.

Jesus claimed that authority, and His followers acknowledged that He was indeed the Creator of all things. "All things came into being through Him, and without Him was nothing made that was made; in Him was life," one of those disciples, John, confessed (John 1:3–4). God created the world through His Son (Heb. 1:2); this man, the image of the invisible God, is the One in, through, and for whom all things were created (Col. 1:15–17). In Him all the fullness of God was pleased to dwell (Col. 1:19). Therefore, Jesus of Nazareth announces to His followers that He exercises authority as the Author of life.

People have had trouble understanding this since the time of God's revelation of Himself in this human creature from Galilee 2,000 years ago. One problem arises from the fact that we encounter one of us, another human creature, claiming ultimate authority for life and the universe. That problem will be treated later as we discuss the Gospel.[3]

GOD IS

Some independently-minded North Americans have a problem believing that there really is one who deserved to exercise that kind of authority at all, that there is a god of any kind in the universe. From time to time during the past century the death of God has been widely heralded. While some Americans around 1900 could confidently predict that the 20th-century would turn out to be the "Christian" century, Karl Marx and a host of others have come just as close to making this a century of atheism, or at least of its official advance. Yet the assertion that there is no god can only be made through verbal and philosophical sleight of hand. For human life cannot be lived without a source of security, a sense of meaning, and a personal identity.

Whatever it is that supplies identity, security, and meaning for the atheist functions in the same way as do gods of whatever kind or name for those who claim to be religious. Our god is whatever we put our trust in,[4] whoever or whatever he, she, or it may be. That entity may be some formal religious system or ancient philosophical tradition. It can be a lust or longing for meaning and security in—as was the case for Willy Loman—"being liked, being well-liked," a longing which, unfilled, led inevitably to the death of the salesman.[5] A god may even be rodeo riding. Alvin Toffler describes a cab driver for whom rodeo riding "not only engages the cab driver's passion; it consumes his time and money. It affects his family, his friends, his ideas. It provides a set of standards against which he measures himself. In short, it rewards him with something that many of us have difficulty finding: an identity."[6] People must fashion a

basis for their own security, for meaning in life, for identifying themselves. If the world is "dedivinized" so that God is no longer remembered in any way as the normative authority and the source for life
in the world, then, according to Helmut Thielicke, "redivinization
begins. ... This does not mean a return to the vanquished religions.
It means post-religious ideologizing. ... The world [or any part of it
we may choose as our 'designated divinity'] is decked out in the
attributes of God."[7]

Carl Gustav Jung observed that patients in the second half of
their lives without exception fell prey to mental illness because they
"had lost what religions of every age have given their followers." He
concludes, "none of them has really been healed who did not regain
his religious outlook."[8] Jung did not assert the primacy of one religion over another; he merely insisted that human beings must be
able to make sense of their lives and feel safety in their way of life—
or their inner being collapses and often brings their outer being
falling in on top of it.

Those who try to deny that there is One who deserves to exercise the authority of the Author of life deceive themselves. Believers dare not mock that self-deception as they begin their witness.
Just because the fool says in his heart, "There is no God!" (Ps. 14:1;
53:1), that does not mean that foolishness is easily dislodged or
that it need not be taken seriously. We approach the unbeliever
"with gentleness and reverence" (1 Peter 3:15). The Christian witness will help the other person analyze the true significance of what
it means to have someone to put his or her trust in.

GOD IS PERSON

Someone—or something? A second problem which plagues
some contemporary North Americans regarding Jesus' claim to
authority as the Author of life revolves around the personal nature
of God. Some people feel so insecure about their own persons or
have experienced such harm in interpersonal relationships that they
cannot imagine that anything truly good could come from any person. For whatever reason, there are those who recognize something
greater than the human creature but who try to reduce that "greater-
ness" to a power, to "the force," or to the divine universe itself,

24

according to the pantheistic view. For them, to fit the concept of a higher power, or the highest force, into a person seems to be a case of the human tail wagging the divine dog. Surely, it is argued, we anthropomorphize by trying to limit the divine to the form in which we find ourselves, the form of a person.

But in the Christian faith the dilemma is more extreme than merely the "problem" of anthropomorphic language used to describe the ultimate authority in the universe. We confess that God does not just describe Himself with human-like terminology. We confess that God took human form and became this human creature who announces His exercise of all authority in heaven and on earth. God anthropomorphized Himself. Actually, it is the reverse of our conceiving of God as a person because we are persons. We are persons because we are created in the image of God.

For people who assert their independence of God, it is convenient to package Him in impersonal form. We suspect that the personal is finally superior to the impersonal. If we can place the ultimate power into some impersonal capsule, we might still be able to master it. But doing so drives people into that contradictory language which ascribes personal characteristics to "the force" and even prays to it. They may depersonalize God into nature, but they must then repersonalize It into "Mother Nature." To understand our own persons, how we came to be, and where we are going, we need to know the person of God who is the Author of our persons and the Creator of the world. As believers, we cannot insist that those who trust in the force or rely on the regularity of nature must already understand this. We recognize that human fears and ambitions may construct a convincing case for depersonalizing God, thereby keeping Him in a place suitable for their own designs on life. The first task of the Christian witness is to persuade his or her neighbor that those who depersonalize their Creator depersonalize themselves.[9]

God revealed His personhood—and His personality—in conversations with His people from the beginning. He did not reveal a concept of God to Adam or to Abraham. Instead, He revealed His name, and He attached His name to His actions, in the midst of the experience of His people. A name "eludes any concept. ... In itself it tells us nothing." A name "expresses the fact that this person cannot be reduced to a common denominator or equated with anyone else."[10] God told Moses, when he inquired what the name of God is, "I am who I am" *(Yahweh)* and He identified Himself as the One in whom Abraham, Isaac, and Jacob had put their trust. This Yahweh gave Moses a promise of deliverance from Egypt and of His continuing presence with His people (Ex. 3:7–22). That is the kind of person the God with the name Yahweh is. He alone is God, for He created the universe and exercises authority in it. We may call Him Yahweh, in the manner of those who want to get familiar with everyone immediately on a first name basis, or we may respectfully call Him "the Lord," in the manner of His Israelite children who whispered even that name in the way that respectful and loving children of another age whispered "Mr. Smith" of their fathers. But He does have a name, and the Lord, Yahweh, has taken on a human name, Jesus, of Nazareth, Mary's son, just as He has taken on human flesh and blood and bones. He is a person; He has a name—or, He has a name; He is a person.

JESUS IS CREATOR

Some people are also provoked by Jesus' claim to exercise all authority because they recognize behind this claim the person of the Creator. Whatever other powers may exist in the universe, Paul says, God the Father is the One from whom are all things and for whom we exist, and our Lord Jesus Christ is the One through whom all things are and through whom we exist (1 Cor. 8:6). His claim to be Creator discomfits us. "That the Bible should speak of the beginning provokes the world and irritates us," Dietrich Bonhoeffer noted: "For we cannot speak of the beginning; where the beginning begins, our thinking stops, it comes to an end."[11] God alone remains. There is a person, not an explanation, at the end of our search for our origins. His being there confounds our attempts at mastery over life and things. Figuring "it" out will not be able to grant us power, for behind every "it" of creation stands the power of its Maker, who is also our Lord. We like to think of ourselves as human beings, beings with an autonomy and independence all our own. The Scriptures present us as human creatures, creatures who have their origin in the hand of God.

That our life has an author deprives us of the hope of gaining absolute authority, and we resent that reality. We flee from a doctrine of Creator and creature. Even when we insist on creation, we desire to dodge the implications of being creatures of the Creator. C. S. Lewis is correct when he writes, "In reality, creation, in any unambiguous sense, seems to be a surprisingly rare doctrine; and when stories about it occur in Paganism, they are often religiously unimportant. ..."[12] Pagan creation stories abound, but often they have little effect on their people's view of themselves and the way their world works. The teaching of the Scriptures is unambiguous: we are creatures, and He is our Creator. Without this teaching firmly at the base of Christian witness something in it is bound to go askew.

God created the universe in a once-for-all event. He *continues* to function as Creator, or, perhaps better, as Sustainer, exercising His loving care for His creatures each day. He did not wind the world up, as a watchmaker might wind up a product which he knew to be dependable, and depart from His creation, as the 18th-century Deists depicted His relationship to the world. God is actively involved in keeping His creation functioning. "Thou didst form my inward parts, thou didst knit me together in my mother's womb," the psalmist confessed to God (139:13); Job knew that, too (31:15; cf., chapters 38 and 39), and the Lord reminded Jeremiah of that fact (1:5). Natural birth, as a creative act of God, illustrates that He normally provides and preserves through the structure He has fashioned, through the "natural" or "normal" functions of His creature. He is not bound, of course, by our observations of how His structure should work. The "laws of nature"—as *laws*—were passed by human observations. They predict probability, as natural scientists in this century have come to recognize. God's love stands always ready to deliver His care and concern through the improbable or even the impossible, if need be.

No concept of miracle, God's extraordinary ways of demonstrating His love and expressing His concern for us, should be permitted to obscure God's daily, usual, normal, and natural love and concern for His human creatures. Indeed, He works from time to time in ways which we cannot explain, miraculously, but His miracles are no more marvels of His love than is the everyday functioning of the structure through which He opens His hand and satisfies the desire of every living thing—giving food and all else we need in due season (Ps. 145:15–16). The Creator cares for and about His creatures. Those who feel themselves thrown up as driftwood on the shores of life need to hear and experience the care of God through us.

THE DUST OF THE EARTH
AND THE BREATH OF GOD

The Creator designed us and determined our place in creation. Because He is Creator, because our origin rests in Him, we are dependent on Him and on His design for our lives, for the life which He has bestowed upon us and has structured for our welfare.

God Took the Dust and Breathed

God's design for His human creatures was executed by taking dust from the earth and breathing into that dust the breath or spirit of life (Gen. 2:7). That breath animated—gave soul to—the physical material which God chose as the substantial base for this creature, the human creature. That breath animated a creature which reflects God Himself in the midst of the whole creation. The human creature was made in the image and likeness of God (Gen. 1:26). Theologians have debated the precise definition and significance of the image of God in the human creature. Some have argued that it is human holiness or righteousness in our relationship with God. Others have maintained it is the ability to think rationally and act volitionally. Still others define the image as one's natural tendency to love God, and to care for His creatures. Some also insist it is sovereign freedom.

The text of Genesis 1:26–27 suggests that the image of God is connected with the dominion the human creature is to exercise in relationship to creation. However, that dominion, which we shall shortly define more sharply, cannot be properly exercised if our relationship with the Creator and our faithfulness to His design for that dominion are not functioning properly. Whatever specific definition is given to the term "image of God," it assures us that we exist by God's decision and design and that we have a special role and place which other creatures do not have.

Yet we are one with them as creatures. We arose from the dust of the earth.

> Darwin and Feuerbach[13] themselves could not speak more strongly. Man's origin is in a piece of earth. His bond with the earth belongs to his essential being. ... Of course, the ground from which man is taken is still not the cursed but the blessed ground. From it he has his body. His body belongs to his essential being. Man's body is not his prison, his shell, his exterior, but man himself. Man does not "have" a body; he does not "have" a soul; rather he "is" body and soul. Man in the beginning is really his body.[14]

In a materialistic age and culture, where often trust is placed only in what is empirically manipulable through physics or chemistry, the biblical emphasis on the material aspect of human life offers a significant entree to the thought world of many outside the faith. Materialism rejects whatever cannot be proven by the current canons of empirical, natural scientific assertions regarding reality— in short, whatever cannot be grasped and enjoyed by visual and tactile senses. To the materialist the Christian can testify that, indeed, the material is good, for the Creator brought it into being through His good Word, and He pronounced the material (light, water, vegetation, animal life, and all the rest) good. The materialist errs fatally by ignoring that the material flows from the mouth of the Creator, and by focusing life on the product rather than the Producer.

Christians in contemporary North American culture have a difficult time saying and realizing this truth because for centuries our culture has tended to view the material as second class at best and evil at worst. Long before the message of the Hebrews of both Old and New Testament periods was grafted onto the world view of the Mediterranean and European peoples, our intellectual and cultural ancestors had formulated an understanding of the material and the spiritual which could not share God's enthusiasm for His visible, material creation.

> Elements of Greek philosophy set spirit and matter against one another. It [this philosophy] allows the uniqueness of the human being to consist in the fact that spirit (reason) governs the sensual,

material part (body) and can even set itself free from bondage to the human body. But the Old Testament gathers together all humans and animals into one unity and calls it "all flesh." This would have been an impossibility for Plato or Aristotle. ... [15]

There are, of course, some good reasons for assuming the superiority of the unseen to the seen, the immaterial to the material. Apart from His time on earth as a human being, as Jesus of Nazareth, God has not revealed Himself in material forms since the Old Testament theophanies, even though He regularly reveals His power and/or His goodness in tangible, visible ways. God is spirit (John 4:24). When the mighty evil of death strikes a human creature, the material lies before us, cold and stiff, and whatever it was which gave life to those physical remains is not apparent anymore, and we call that intangible "spirit."

It perhaps makes some sense to decide that whatever is unseen and intangible about us—the heart, as we often say, not meaning the cardiac muscle—is superior to the material part of our being. But God observes that His material creation is good (Gen. 1). He also notes that the imagination of the human heart is evil (Gen. 8:21) and that every kind of rebellion against God and every destructive urge against our neighbor arise out of that heart (Matt. 15:19).

The entire Gospel of Jesus Christ met a challenge in the ancient system of thought labeled *Gnosticism,* and gnostic ideas still challenge and pervert the message His disciples bring to the world at the end of the 20th century. Gnosticism fed on the world view of the Platonic and Neoplatonic philosophy of Christ's age, as well as other religious and philosophical schools current in the Mediterranean world.

Although a variety of Gnostic systems emerged to plague the early church, some general outline of this misinterpretation of reality can be sketched. The Gnostics believed that they formed a spiritual elite, who had the secret, special knowledge which would deliver them from evil. They conceived of matter as inherently evil, or at least troublesome, especially to that spark of spirit which is the soul of the individual, unfortunately imprisoned in human flesh. The spark of spirit was viewed as a part of the ultimate being, the "great soul" beyond the universe. Thus, salvation meant escape from the material. Salvation meant divinization, a return to that great soul which is god and which draws its alienated splinters from this evil world to itself. The Gnostics therefore rejected the individual and the concrete, as well as the importance of the material or created order and all that is a part of it: human history, nature, and even interpersonal relationships.

Defining the human creature as primarily a bit of the spiritual, divine substance plays havoc with the biblical teaching of creation in a number of ways. It cuts off the possibility of history as a vehicle for the revelation of God's will, a position antithetical to biblical revelation. It teaches that salvation is essentially a return to divine status rather than, as the Scriptures repeatedly make clear, a return to a perfectly functioning human life. It renders impossible the proper perception of God as the Creator and of ourselves as creatures.[16]

Dust of the earth and the breath of God—the composition of the human creature—points toward two of the four relationships into which the Creator sets us as He originated His human creatures with nature and with the creator God. (The other two are the relationships with other human creatures and with self.) Lewis' observation that relatively few cultures have taught a strong doctrine of creation is certainly applicable to the ancient Mediterranean world which has so vitally influenced European and American thought.[17] The ancient Greek gods had lost credence by the time of Socrates, Plato, and Aristotle, and no great divine figure replaced them in decisive fashion. The philosophical underpinnings of Western thought were set in place without the presence of a strong creator figure actively in charge of a universe which He had fashioned for himself.

In that intellectual environment the human being becomes the primary and supreme element in any human view of the world. The intellectual descendants of Plato could define the human being primarily in terms of a soul which had as its right an eternal existence. Immortality was not a gift of a creator but rather the essence of the human being, who as an immortal being possessed an autonomy, independence, and integrity which not even a god could threaten. The immortal soul did not owe its origin to a creator, and therefore no god could claim absolute power over it. If God were to appear in the purview of this soul, God would be standing on the same plane as this being, a bit taller perhaps, but on the level with the immortal soul. The human being then stands on its own two feet over against God, fists clenched, ready to negotiate.

This picture of the relationship between the human creature and the Creator has often penetrated Christian thought throughout the past two millennia in spite of the fact that it contradicts biblical teaching. The creature of God rests in the Father's hand, on the Father's lap, rather than taking a stance over against Him. The life of the human creature is recognized as a gift of that Father, not as an inalienable right, and the center of that life is recognized as its Creator. "If God is not at the center of life, He will not be on the margin, either."[18] The primary relationship which determines human life is the relationship with the Creator, the vertical relationship with Him who is above us because He fathered us. All other human relationships malfunction if that relationship is not in good order, that is, if it is not righteous, or harmonious.

The relationship of child to father is determined by the origin of the former from the latter. In the Scriptures the person who has the task of naming another being holds authority over that being (e.g., Gen. 2:20, 23). God calls us by name, and our relationship is then inevitably one of the creature's dependence on the Creator. This dependence is not a concession which we grant God but rather a corollary of the authority which belongs to the Author of life. God determined that our relationship to Him be one of harmony— the Hebrew word is *shalom*—a relationship in which all is right, or righteous, because God provides for us and we can trust Him completely, depend on Him totally, rely on Him for every need. The peace which the human creature was designed to enjoy in the presence of the Creator is the peace of being at home, where, to paraphrase Robert Frost, God has committed Himself to having to take us in even though we do not deserve it. Being at home with God means relaxing without fear; it means feeling whole and complete, safe and secure, even though "you somehow haven't to deserve" it.[19] This peace remains stable because we can count on God. This harmony sets us at perfect rest because God remains our providing and protecting Father. God is righteous in this relationship because He shelters us in His steadfast love. We are righteous in this relationship because we "fear, love, and trust in God above all things."[20]

Dominion

God set His human creatures in relationship with the rest of creation as well as with Himself. The human creature recognizes that nature is not a mere datum but an achievement, an act of God and a gift from God. Any thought that natural forces are independent sources of power which might command our worship is foolish when we understand that our own Father fashioned nature as well.[21] This is especially true when we recognize the nature of our relationship with the rest of creation, with nature. God labeled it "dominion" (Gen. 1:26).

That term has caused a great deal of confusion in our culture. Combined with a view of the human being as an autonomous, independent being whose world centers in himself, that biblical term has resulted "in Europe, and later in America [in] the combining of

Greek and biblical views, ... " in "a notion of dominion which in turn has given rise to technology and industrialization and finally to environmental destruction on a global scale. Nowhere in the civilization of these countries have people really felt at home in the biblical picture of the world with its deep sense of unity between the human, the animal, and the vegetative."[22]

In so far as that judgment is correct, it reveals a tragic misunderstanding of the meaning of dominion, or lordship, in Scripture. If we are autonomous, independent beings, then perhaps the exercise of lordship could simply mean domination, with the right and privilege of exploitation attached. But human creatures in the image of God cannot exercise lordship *over* that to which God gave them dominion; they are created to exercise lordship *under* the creation.

That is God's style of lordship. He supports and uplifts as He functions as our Lord. He provides the foundation and underpinning for our life and for the existence of the whole creation. When He exercises lordship, He lords it *under*. To our unrighteousness He comes in human form to bear our sinfulness on His back. He demonstrates His lordship in service and care and love. His lordship provides the only workable pattern for the dominion He designed as our relationship with the rest of His creation.

The dominion of autonomous human beings, exercising a lordship independent of the Creator and of His commission of dominion, has wrought a ruin in creation which has turned upon us, its perpetrators. "Non-human nature—trees, flowers, and animals—are the victims of human wrongheadedness. They groan continuously under the dominion of destruction."[23] Such a dominion perverts the design of God and offends the Creator, who wants us to lord it under His other creatures. His design gives us the world around us as "the instrument of our activity, the tool [with] which each one of us, at the position in the front line assigned to him, participates in the work of determining the future configuration of the world."[24] We exercise dominion according to the pattern and will of our Creator, who has given us responsibility for, and stewardship under, His other creatures and holds us accountable for our exercise of dominion under them.

Human Community—the Warp and Woof of Our Existence

Among those other creatures, though not specifically mentioned in Genesis 1:26, are other human creatures. As God was bringing His universe into existence and had fashioned Adam in His own image, He noticed that "it is not good that the man should be alone," and He thus created human community (Gen. 2:18). He structured life so that we are our brother's keepers (Gen. 4:9). "Existence is also essentially coexistence."[25] The rugged individualism so highly prized on the North American continent stems from a view of the human being standing on his own two feet, existing as an autonomous, independent soul over against God. The longing for "personal" religion untrammeled by concern about the neighbor often stems from this rugged individualism. Many a person boldly asserts, "I have my own religion." Indeed, we stand alone as individuals in our vertical relationship with our God. Yet even that relationship arises out of communication with other people and is sustained only in the midst of God's community of believers, according to God's design. The vertical relationship with our Creator and Father intersects by His very design with a network of relationships which He designed within the human community.

Designed in the image of God, the human creature was created to love and care for other human creatures just as God does. Luther could call us "masks of God,"[26] for, as he pointed out, God comes through us to carry out His will for those around us by providing for their needs and showing them love in our actions. Behind us, through our hands and tongues, God works, for we whom He created in His own image function as His agents. He hides His care and concern in our acts of love. John's words, "we love because He first loved us," (1 John 4:19) were written after God had revealed His love in Christ's cross, but Jesus came to restore us to the pattern of living which had been ours in Eden. Human creatures love in the first instance because God created them that way. After the fall into sin we love because God has come in the flesh to re-create us and recall us to that pattern.

God Calls Us to Serve in Four Situations

At creation God also set in place for us the structure in and through which we are to care for one another. He instituted four situations in which human life takes place: the situations of home, occupation, society, and congregation (the family community, the economic community, the political community, and the worshiping community). God structures and conducts His government of the world through human actions in these situations. Within each of these situations God assigns specific responsibilities.

In the home we exercise responsibilities of spouse, parent, child, and the various assignments of relationships within the extended family. Occupational responsibilities embrace all economic functions as well as the social functions of friendship and mutual support in the workplace. Societal responsibilities may be divided into the formal and the informal; the formal include participation in state functions and duties, from voting and paying taxes to activities in public action groups and political parties in a democracy, while the informal encompass all contacts with neighbors, near and far. Congregational responsibilities begin with the common calling to worship and the Word, both in evangelization and edification, and extend to the formal and informal responsibilities which God's people bestow on pastors, teachers, evangelists, elders, committee members, and ushers. God's structure was twisted but not destroyed when the human creature fell upon it, and human life is possible only when this structure continues to function, even though it does so imperfectly. It functions better at the hands of some societies than others, but family life, public economy, and political order are necessary for human survival. Equally necessary is some kind of public ideology or religion. Apart from the presence of Jesus Christ this last situation is totally perverted (in contrast to the partial perversion of the other three apart from Him). But even unbelieving human creatures can exercise responsibilities as parents, workers, and political officials, in what is called "civil righteousness."[27]

We ought to avoid trying to determine a universal hierarchy for the exercise of these responsibilities, but it must be noted that the fundamental situation in which Adam and Eve found themselves immediately is the situation of the home. Family life is fundamental to the working of the other three, and the other three grow out of the needs of the family. The responsibilities of congregational life do have an eternal dimension which those of basic economic activity do not have. Neither set of responsibilities is more worthy or valuable in God's plan for human living. The proper functioning of His structure depends on our performance of responsibilities in each situation according to the talents and abilities which He has given to us, for use in the great variety of relationships which we have with other human creatures. When we carry out these responsibilities, which are both gifts and assignments from God, we are acting rightly in our horizontal relationships and are thus righteous in the horizontal plane.

The Gift of Self

Intimately connected with our horizontal and our vertical relationships is our relationship to self. God created human creatures to be at peace within themselves. His command to love the neighbor as one loves oneself (Matt. 22:39) offends some Christians, who have cultivated the belief that the sinful human creature must hate creatureliness as well as the sin that perverts it (a subtle remnant of Gnosticism, perhaps). But that love or respect for self is part of God's design for His human creatures. At the same time, it is vital to recognize the source of that self-regard. Proper self-regard, which bestows true harmony on our lives, comes alone from our perception that God is Father and Creator and we are His creatures. Martin Luther could confess that we receive every temporal blessing, not just the blessings which flow from Christ's cross and empty tomb, "without any merit or worthiness" in us.[28] With this statement he was emphasizing that we human creatures have no prior claim on God. He was under no compulsion to call us into existence. His favor and mercy toward us began with His decision to create and to provide. This kindly disposition remains as mysterious to us as does His kindly disposition which accomplishes our forgiveness and re-creation in Jesus of Nazareth.

It is dangerous to answer the question "What is the value of my person, or any other person?" with the same answer which serves for the question "Do I have any claim on God?" We must ask *why* the questioner wants to know whether he can consider himself a worthwhile being. Just as I cannot understand myself without understanding myself as God's child, so I will never have the "self-esteem" for which our society is so deeply concerned if I do not recognize the basis for it in God's esteem of me. My worth stems from His treasuring and prizing me as His child. All other bases for self-esteem fade before they bloom. God treasures us as His own creation. His history of intervention into the midst of human life, climaxing in His own incarnation, demonstrates that He will spare nothing to put His steadfast love into practice (Rom. 8:32). He does not do that for a creature whom He regards as of little or no value. He depends on us to convey His love and concern within the structures He constructed so that human life might find support from God through human creatures who exercise God-given responsibilities.

We are of value to Him in our horizontal relationships as well, even though we can in no way merit His favor through the exercise of horizontal responsibilities. He simply expects that of us. We must recognize in our fallen state that we betray His plan for us and disappoint Him with our failings and rejection of Him and His plan. We must also recognize that He has re-created us in Jesus Christ to return to trust in Him alone and to be restored to a more perfect care and concern for those whom He places within our sphere of responsibility. Individuals who do not feel comfortable with themselves, for whom that God-given harmony within has vanished, do not feel comfortable with God or with other people, either.[29]

In preparation for Christian witness the believer will remember that we cannot be restored to that inner harmony without some experience of harmony between self and God. Yet we are caught in a vicious circle, for it is difficult to imagine that God can love, or that love is possible, without some experience of what love means on the human level. The Christian witness then must very patiently articulate God's love in Christ and draw out its implications for the hearer's harmony with self. The Christian witness must cultivate a sense of God's love which enables the restoration of God-designed confidence, for if God loves me in Christ, in Christ I am a valuable person once again. This message can be conveyed only on the basis of the repeated expression and demonstration of the believer's care and concern for the hearer.

Peace with self, other human creatures, nature, and above all with God Himself permeates the perfect human life, as it is lived harmoniously in the network of relationships which God created when He took dust and His own breath and made Adam as a child for Himself, and when He took his rib and made the basis of human community, Adam and Eve.

WITHIN FREEDOM AND RESPONSIBILITY

Countless tomes have been written through human history trying to define what it means to be human. To conclude our discussion of the biblical view of the human creature we must turn to a basic factor in nearly every North American definition and in many fashioned by other cultures as well; namely, that human beings are born free. This is a fundamental principle which we have inherited from the Greeks: "Plato and Aristotle depict the citizen as the completely free man with full command over himself, his own master. ... Though free, he puts himself under the law, as the only means of securing the *polis* [city, i.e. community] against the despotism of the tyrant on the one hand and mob rule on the other."[30] The autonomous, independent being submits himself to the law of his own free will, and he remains the focal point of his own universe. This observation makes some sense within the horizontal relationships of our lives, so long as we ignore the primary vertical dimension of human existence. Plato found his supreme being too far removed to have anything much to do with human freedom. Aristotle's unmoved mover had to be dealt with in human freedom since the human soul and the mover had no relationship which could diminish that human freedom.

North American Definitions of Human Freedom

Those who fashioned the ideas of North American culture in the 18th century combined biblical and philosophical ideas, with a decided preference for the Platonic and Aristotelian values which had formed the heart of the Enlightenment in Europe. This rationalistic approach to human living has forged a political system of amazing durability and equity, considering the lifespan and success in dispensing justice of most political systems. Nevertheless, it has brought corrosive effects to the Christian faith, and not just through various forms of virulent secularism which take certain Enlightenment principles to their logical conclusion in the vertical dimension of life. Above all, the Enlightenment has misshaped the understanding of the biblical message, in different ways, among the heirs of both the classical liberal and the fundamentalist approaches to the Scriptures. Nowhere can this be seen more clearly than in the Christian definition of human freedom in decision-making in the context of our vertical relationship to God. Even some who most stoutly defend a doctrine of creation somehow can argue that sinful creatures can pick themselves up and deliver themselves, body and soul, to a waiting (!) and gracious Creator.[31]

Christians, too, have inhaled the spirit of individualism and share with unbelieving fellow citizens the presupposition of an inalienable right to "be me," to "do it my way," to "do my own thing" at any cost. Yet our society is also experiencing the bankruptcy of trying to make life work outside human community. This in turn has led to doubts about the definition of human freedom in the absolute terms implied in our guaranteed "right to the pursuit of happiness" for self. Moreover, this comes at the time when it seems possible to attain maximum individual autonomy and freedom through economic prosperity and technological breakthrough on a massive scale. Apart from any Christian concern Alvin Toffler insists, "The Super-industrial Revolution also demands a new conception of freedom—a recognition that freedom, pressed to its ultimate, negates itself."[32]

In the struggle to examine the meaning of human freedom an opposite voice has arisen. Certain behavioral scientists argue that human freedom is nonexistent, an illusion and a sham. Although even B. F. Skinner, who could offer the description of the human being as "beyond freedom and dignity," does not deny human freedom completely, some determinists depict the human being as the puppet or victim of environment or genes or both.[33]

Biblical Definitions of Human Freedom

If we think of freedom as the absence of any conditions, confines, or constrictions which limit, define, or determine existence, then it is clear that the belief that God created and we are His creatures denies the possibility of our being free. To be created, have a beginning, and be the product of another's hand destroys any possibility of living without conditions. In designing and determining the creature's life and life-plan the Creator places conditions for that life in His act of determination and in the structure of His design.[34] As creatures we are indeed "free to be me," but we are not free to define me. That is the prerogative of the Creator. He has created us free to fulfill His design, His definition, of what it means to be human and to be untrammeled and unhindered in exercising the responsibilities which He has given us in His creation.

This freedom is prepositional freedom. Prepositions designate relationships. Human freedom is first of all freedom *for* service to God, which means freedom for meeting the needs of other human creatures, nature, and self, within the harmony of God's design or structure for human living. Freedom finds a corollary in Eden in the freedom *from* all evil, from everything which might threaten God-given harmony. Adam and Eve were not conscious of that freedom, but they did enjoy it as they exercised the freedom for service to God and His creation. Since the fall into sin these natural freedoms have been so twisted and perverted that it is impossible to imagine what the exercise of freedom for God and the enjoyment of freedom from evil truly mean. For a third kind of freedom—it is horrible to confuse it with genuine human freedoms—also lay within the grasp of Adam and Eve. It is the freedom *against* God, the ability to doubt God's creative and loving Word. This ability does not deserve the name "freedom," for it is not only an ability which opposes God but also one which destroys true humanity. It enslaves and binds. Freedom to act against God is the very opposite of the freedom to act in behalf of Him and His creatures. The latter is true human freedom.

It is clear from our belief in our Creator that even in Eden the human creature could not exercise a freedom which would disrupt our harmony with God without destroying an essential part of ourselves. In our vertical relationship we are by nature free only to

41

choose which way of praising our Father is most appropriate. Also in the horizontal relationships of life we may freely choose only among ways to serve as God's masks in a proper way. If we break through God's structure for these relationships and disrupt our natural harmony with other human creatures, with nature, or with ourselves, we have destroyed a vital part of what it means to be human by God's design. Freedom against God is exercised against the Author of life. Freedom against God is bondage and death. Yet within the structure of life as He fashioned it, within the situations of His design and in our exercise of dominion under His creatures, we were created free indeed!

The determinists are unable to sustain their own argument against human freedom and responsibility, Francis Schaeffer observes.[35] A consistent determinism is so enslaving that the urge for a sense of freedom and responsibility breaks through in spite of both a desire to suppress it and a well-argued case against its viability. We may sing, "whatever will be, will be," but in the face of what we do not want, we at least feel the urge to rage against the dying and fading we have tried to avoid by ascribing them to fate, genes, or environmental powers beyond our control. The believer cannot say, "whatever will be, will be," but insists instead, "whatever God wills, will be."

Free to Be Responsible

At the same time we recognize that two distinct questions may lie behind the query, "Am I responsible, or is God responsible, in this case?" We respond, "Why do you want to know?" If the question seeks to establish whether God is truly in command of His world, when so much seems to indicate that evil is about to triumph, the believer answers, "Our Creator and Father has the whole world in His hand." If the question, however, is one of human responsibility and action, the believer assures the questioner that God works through us, to whom He has given responsibilities for the welfare and well-working of His world. If we are functioning as we were created, we hold ourselves responsible for reflecting His love and applying His merciful care to those around us.

God has bestowed freedom for service, or responsibility, upon His human creatures. We cannot escape that sense of responsibility which is inextricably bound up with the freedom for service. To "turn the tide of our aggressions and of the moral struggle in which much of the world population is engaged," the psychologist Karl Menninger prescribes for American society "a revival or reassertion of personal responsibility in all human acts, good and bad."[36] A healthy,[37] properly functioning and integrated human personality, he notes, must take responsibility for its good actions, for from such responsibility comes that sense of confidence which enables the person to live with self and others.

An honest appraisal of our lives demands that we also take responsibility for the evil which we perpetrate by mistake or by design. At the same time we experience that our responsibility for ourselves, for our good and our evil deeds, provides us with a limited freedom and limited powers. Every child finds that he must "ground himself in some power that transcends him," that "he lives on borrowed powers."[38] Common sense suggests that either we are responsible for our lives, or some greater person or power is. However, our experience insists *both* that we must feel and bear responsibility for ourselves *and* that our sense of living on borrowed powers points to the responsibility of another. That experience may not ascribe total responsibility to God and total responsibility to ourselves, as the Scriptures do, but an honest appraisal of life does imply what the biblical writers affirm when they attribute our well-being to God and yet demand responsible action from us.

Responsible action includes an appropriate response to our creating Father. The origin of our relationship lies in Him. That relationship is a given when our existence begins, and we can only react. Responsible action also includes living with God's structures for our horizontal relationships. Toffler continues the argument cited above: "Freedom cannot be absolute. To argue for total choice (a meaningless concept) or total individuality is to argue against any form of community or society altogether. If each person, busily doing his own thing, were to be wholly different from every other, no two humans would have any basis for communication."[39] Community and communication, Toffler presumes, are inextricably linked to the heart of being human. The heart of human freedom lies also in this responsibility to care for other human creatures and for nature as well as for self.

> Man is free by the fact that creature is related to creature. Man is free for men, *Male and female he created them.* Man is not alone, he is in duality. And it is in this dependence on the other that his creatureliness consists. Man's creatureliness is not a quality, something that exists, something that is, any more than his freedom. It can only be defined in man's being over against the other, with the other and dependent on the other.[40]

Within this community, in the context of His design for human interaction, the Creator has given us the freedom to exercise responsibility for the rest of His creation. The Greek concept of a sovereign free will at the heart of an autonomous, independent being stands opposed to the biblical concept of a creature designed to exercise responsibility within the Creator's design as that creature rests in the hand of the Father. The former view must posit as the only alternative to an absolute human freedom (which leads to individualism) a determinism which suffocates individuality. The believer rejects this set of alternatives because neither has a place for God.

The logic or rationality of our culture has been so conditioned by the former view that it is difficult for North American Christians to think biblically regarding freedom and responsibility as gifts of the Creator to His human creatures. Biblical thinking comes easier if we take into account our experience of a sense of personal responsibility, and a sense that at best our responsibility cannot accomplish the best. This experience must then be combined with the logic of the teaching of creation, based upon its fundamental principle that the creature originates from the absolutely free hand and design of the Creator. The sense of our experience, perceived through a twisted human reason, cannot affirm the biblical position that the human creature is completely responsible and that God is completely responsible. Apart from God's Word we can at best only cast a glimpse in the direction of this accurate analysis of the way we are.

Either with God or with Satan

It is important to recognize that the human creature dare not be depicted as being poised originally halfway between good and evil, between God and Satan, with a sovereign free decision to make in choosing between the two. Rather, the human creature, resting in the hand of God, was exercising freedom for service to the Creator and enjoying freedom from evil, and then decided to exercise that mysterious and inexplicable pseudo-freedom against God. The creature leaped from the hand of God in revolt against Him, and the proper freedoms were destroyed and damaged—destroyed in the vertical relationship with the Creator and damaged in our practice of responsibility in relationship to other human creatures and nature.

> Given freedom cannot become caprice. It cannot be a neutral thing with no values. It must be handled with gratitude to the one who has given it. This is why such freedom can never be license to sin (Rom. 6:1, 15), without being snuffed out or degenerating again into bondage. ... We have freedom only as paradoxically we have become the servants of God (Rom. 6:16). ... Freedom to misuse is in the strict sense perversion, a fall into the impossible (Gal. 5:4). For sin, wherein we fall victim to being, to the powers, is not a possibility that freedom can choose if it is to be true to itself (Gal. 5:13). It is true to itself only when it is always conscious of its debt to Him that granted it, so that it is a committed rather than an uncommitted freedom, committed to Him who gave it its authority.[41]

"Real freedom is the open possibility of self-realization."[42] That self-realization, or realization of the harmony which God implanted in His human creatures, is possible only within the Creator's design. True human freedom exercises responsibility according to that design and finds there the dignity and worth of the creature who exercises dominion under the rest of creation for God.

The doctrine of creation begins with the fundamental premise for the rest of theology, that God is our creating Father, and that we humans are His creatures, resting in His hand and living according to the design which He determined would give us peace, *shalom,* harmony, and wholeness in our relationships with Him, His nature, His other human creatures, and the self which is both I and His.

THE PIOUS OR HARMONIOUS LIFE

From what has been said about the relationship between the Creator and the human creature, it becomes apparent that the North American cultural view of proper human living, the pious life, is incomplete. For we usually think of piety as an external display of moral values in the horizontal relationships of our lives. From a biblical point of view piety begins in the vertical relationship, and as a result of the right relationship between God and the human creature that creature lives righteously or piously in relationship to others. Genuine harmony between me and other people or between me and nature can exist only if I feel no need to exploit and to dominate the rest of creation for my own security, in a search for meaning for my life, or in an effort to establish the worth of my own identity. As long as I recognize that He who claims authority over everything in heaven and on earth is my Father, I will know that I am secure in His hand; I will know that my identity and the meaning of my life are bound up in His love for me and His high regard for me as His mask.

Since I no longer need to worry about my security, I can live in proper fashion, righteously, in my horizontal relationships, without any need for a plan for my own self-defense: I can always cope with anything potentially threatening, because I can count on God's being right behind me. I no longer have to search my own soul self-consciously for meaning and identity since I am conscious that God has given me the identity of His child and has given me meaning in my exercise of responsibility and dominion in relationship to other human creatures and nature.

Thus, the pious life is not just following God's design for human living but doing so because we are confident that God is following us, protecting and covering us, ready to catch us when we fall. The righteous life is trust in the Creator which is active in love.

DILEMMAS AND ANSWERS

Another implication of Jesus' claim to exercise all authority as the Author of life is that He does so in the midst of and in the face of all the confusions and questions of our experience. Adam and Eve did not know all that God knows, about Himself or about His creation, before the Fall, but they were not faced with the questions which haunt their descendants who struggle with the evil which has been unleashed by our doubt of God's Word and our defiance of His lordship. The tragedies and tribulations of daily life under the curse raise a host of questions about our security, about the meaning of our lives, about our own identity.

Human societies have had to resolve these questions in some fashion sufficiently satisfactory to allay besetting and immobilizing fear, so that their people might cope with the threats of evil well enough to get on with the business of the society. These societal systems of coping have taken the form of narrative myths or rational philosophies. In each case a view of life is developed in order to hold life together, to forge a meaningful construct for life which will enable people to deal with reality in most situations. In every case each ideology or "system of 'ideas,' concepts and convictions, of interpretative patterns, motives and norms of action … mostly governed by particular interests produces a distorted picture of the reality of the world, disguises real abuses and replaces rational arguments by an appeal to emotion,"[43] even though, in the case of philosophy at least, the expressed purpose of the system is to rise above emotion to the purely rational.

Christians have not always realized this, but the biblical doctrine of creation takes away the necessity of having a firm answer for every question, at the same time the Scriptures refuse to give answers for the complex of questions which revolve around the ultimate human problem, the existence and origin of evil.[44] The Scripture offers a person in every dilemma, but not an answer or explanation for every dilemma.

If I am in charge of my life, I have to provide all the answers for every question which life raises. If God has charge of my life, I can rest in His hand even if all the answers are not apparent and some of the questions are sorely vexing. For questions posed by evil, however vexing, should never be the focus of the believer's life. In the midst of every trouble and trial God remains the focus of my life.

In Christian witness the believer dare not boast of being unconcerned that he or she cannot provide answers for certain questions, for Christian witness takes place in situations in which an unbeliever is searching, sometimes desperately, for answers to questions. The Christian has confidence in the answers which God has provided for every human dilemma through His intervention in human history as Jesus of Nazareth. The believer will study diligently to be able to deliver the answers which God has given for human dilemmas by engagement both with the text of Scripture and by keen observation and analysis of the setting in which the testimony of the Gospel is to take place. For Christian witness in the midst of daily human living a certain kind of courage is required. Believers must be bold enough to "be there" for the neighbor even when we bring no satisfactory answers with us to his or her problems. More than answers, such people need the presence of a friend who will stand by them. More than explanations, they need the care and concern of our heavenly Father expressed in our love, as mute and wanting as it may seem.

Believers are not unnerved and immobilized by the realization that they cannot answer every question or solve every dilemma which they will encounter as they witness to the love of God. They are certain of God's Word for sinful human creatures and are confident in the power of that Word, even in their own lips. That confidence frees them to be bold enough to admit that they cannot answer some questions which the unbeliever will pose. Some of those questions they will refer to fellow believers who may be able to answer them. Some questions they will cope with through their own loving care and concern, when explanations fail. All such questions the believer will refer to the hands of the Creator, who holds life together even when our rational constructs break apart.

REBIRTH THROUGH SELECTED ELEMENTS OF THE CREATED ORDER

A final premise which we draw from the doctrine of creation arises out of our conviction that God's perception of the visible, material creation was correct when He pronounced it good (Gen. 2). We will expand our treatment of this premise in Chapter 3 since it does have to do with our rebirth as human creatures in harmony with our God, our salvation. As a part of our understanding of the goodness of the created order we must affirm that God has worked His re-creative work through selected elements of that created order. He did not merely talk about salvation in these elements, but He effects the new creation through specific elements of the material or created order and its visible or audible manifestations.

First, He began with the flesh, blood, and bones of Jesus of Nazareth, the Word who is God, who came as God in the flesh with the power to restore human creatures to being children of God (John 1:1, 12–14). Second, the re-creating power of Jesus is conveyed by His Gospel, the human language which saves (Rom. 1:16). Saving human language is found in the Scriptures, which God breathed through His chosen writers for the purpose of giving us what we need to know to be saved through trust in Christ Jesus (2 Tim. 3:15). Saving human language is found in the living voice of the Gospel as we speak it out of the Scriptures into the lives of those in our society. Third, God has linked sacramental elements with His Word. In Baptism water and the Word save us (1 Peter 3:21), and in the Lord's Supper bread-body and wine-blood with the Word are given to us for the forgiveness of sins (Matt. 26:28). Finally, God has chosen His reborn human creatures to take human language and sacramental elements to deliver the power of the incarnate God to others for their salvation. God acts to restore His fallen human creatures through these four material vehicles, all of which have to do with His Word.

GOD'S GENERAL REVELATION

God naturally communicates with His creation. He created the universe by speaking (Gen. 1), and He has continued to talk with His human creatures through human language in the Scriptures and in the mouths of His people ever since. He refused to reveal His essence, His glory, even to Moses, because His face would bring death to His human creature. But He did reveal His goodness, His promise to be gracious and show mercy to His people, with a personal appearance to Moses (Ex. 33:17–23), and through Moses' words to His people. The words which God entrusted to Moses included more than a proclamation of His steadfast love and faithfulness, His forgiveness. It included a message alien to God's conversation with His people in Eden, a message of wrath and judgment upon iniquity (Ex. 34:6–7).

God spoke with His people in Eden, and even God's design and structure for the creation communicated clearly with His human creatures. Then, however, the mutual expressions of love which must have filled Eden gave way to the curse which Adam and Eve brought upon the human creature. Nonetheless, echoes of God's original conversation with His human creatures can be heard from outside us and from inside us.

General Revelation in Nature and History

The structure of creation continues to communicate a message about God to those who refuse to acknowledge His lordship and to listen to His Word. This communication from the structure and design of the creation is called general revelation. From inside ourselves and from the outside God's design still speaks to us. Nature itself offers evidence that God has spoken (Rom. 1:20; Ps. 19:1; 50:6), and theologians have argued that both its existence (the cosmological argument) and its functioning and purpose (the teleological argument) reveal that God exists and that He provides for His creatures.

History also has been used to argue that God is in control of the course of the nations and the rise and fall of the peoples of the earth. However, many theologians as well as philosophers have long found such arguments less than universally convincing or logically irrefutable. Furthermore, as 20th-century people have removed themselves more and more from direct contact with nature into a world totally touched by human hands, nature seems less impressive than it once did as a witness to the existence of a power beyond the human sphere. For humans have tamed the atom, and while they have not eliminated the threatening, destructive urges of nature, they have blunted their impact with everything from sea walls to crop insurance. The testimony to God is there in nature, but it is more difficult than ever for contemporary people to perceive it since we live to such a great extent in a world so totally shaped by human hands.

The significance of history can also be misunderstood because of the human perception of its unfolding. The combination of modern technology and age-old human tendencies toward evil have suggested to many in our time that history proves that no God worthy of the name can exist. A German acquaintance, a Marxist, told me that her atheism did not grow out of her adult conversion to dialectical materialism. It had been born instead when she was nine years old, when a half-decade of praying to the almighty God that her father might return from the Russian front had produced no returning father. Her experience with that particular evil of this century pales by comparison with those whose lives have undergone Buchenwald or Hiroshima, Dresden or My Lai, starvation and civil war in Biafra or Bangladesh—or even the vicious violence of neighbors against each other in Belfast or Brooklyn. The observation of an American soldier who returned from Vietnam to sadden his deeply religious parents by confessing, "You can't sell me on the idea that there's a God who cares. Not after that,"[45] makes sense to many when they view human history, especially contemporary history, up close.

God's work and Word appear in nature and in human history, but the human creature fails to perceive what God is saying. We no longer understand ourselves in our creatureliness, and our evil disposition has so bound us to other sources of security and meaning that we cannot in our sin-ridden nature hear the Word of the Lord.[46]

General Revelation in Conscience, Reason, and Emotion

From within, the human creature receives a general revelation of God through moral, rational, and emotional senses. The structure of our lives, set in place at creation by God, still squeezes us when we grow too big for our britches. Every human creature is badgered and bothered by some sense of right and wrong (Rom. 2:14), even though the content of human views of right and wrong are conditioned by culture and by individual experience. It is noteworthy that while conscience does function to point us on the right path, we usually speak of it as a "guilty conscience." The overwhelming preponderance of the conscience's message for us is that we are at odds with life, with the ultimate power, with God.

Theologians have also argued that a properly functioning reason will convince us that there must be some kind of god, whether personal or impersonal, for there must be something or someone "than which nothing else is greater." This ontological argument for God's existence is not beyond logical challenge, but it does appear to make some sense; the psalmist points out that whoever says there is no God is a fool (Ps. 14:1; 53:1). However, he did not say that fools might not be common in one culture or another. Nor does the admission that there must be a god bring one to the proper recognition of the Creator, Yahweh, the God of Abraham, Isaac, and Jacob, who has revealed Himself as Jesus of Nazareth.

Emotion also provides the basis for some to feel, and to argue, that there must be a god. Early in this century the German theologian Rudolf Otto identified a common human emotion, the feeling of awe at powers greater than anything human, through his study of native tribal religions around the world.[47] From within—perhaps as a result of fears arising from the struggle with forces outside us—arises a sense of something divine, some greater powers to be reckoned with. This sense expresses itself in both fear and hope, whatever its sources or rationale. Hope itself points to some kind of deliverer or deliverance from outside us, and hope can combine with our rational processes to construct a guess about what form that deliverer or deliverance might take. Such hope in the face of declining prospects for North American society can create, for example, gods from outer space who will come (or return!) to right what we have ruined and cannot repair.

Emotion combines with rationality in a different way in the thought of the great proponent of logical positivism, Ludwig Wittgenstein. His friend and interpreter, Norman Malcom, observes that "Wittgenstein did not reject the metaphysical; rather he rejected the possibility of stating the metaphysical" because he believed that truth is apprehensible and comprehensible only when it can be tested empirically and stated in terms of mathematical logic.[48] Wittgenstein posited a truth beyond what could be charted empirically but refused to believe that this truth could venture beyond the emotional or the mystical. Wittgenstein's categories served as his source of security, meaning, and identity, and although he knew that there must be more to life than mathematical categories, he could find the evidence for that only in the "inexpressible."

In varying degrees mystics throughout human history have sought God by sinking or rising toward Him within their emotional constructs. However, the God who reveals Himself through His Word can be reached only through that Word, not through mystic urges and surges as human emotion chases its own tail in search of God. From within us the general revelation concerning the Creator provides no more satisfactory approach to the Father than that from outside ourselves.

General Revelation and Christian Witness

The Christian witness must further ask whether it is worth the investment of time and energy trying to bring unbelievers to a plateau of belief in some higher being or power as a temporary end in itself. The answer to that question may vary in specific situations. In some there is a danger that certain arguments for belief in God which seem to "make sense" to the Christian will fall apart logically under the scrutiny of the unbeliever. Every subculture has its own unique "rational" system, and Christians often fail to perceive how nonsensical "Christian common sense" sounds to others, who have been forced to construct their own brand of "common sense" by the exigencies of a sinful world.

Furthermore, arguments from general revelation can backfire. Even when they do "convince" the unbeliever, they still provide at best an ambiguous benefit. For instance, if I am trying to save a friend walking in an open field from an impending electrical storm, it is of questionable value to lure him to the shelter of a nearby tree rather than hurrying him into a building which is somewhat farther, for the lightning may strike the tree. If a person recognizes that the rising storm of life is about to engulf him or her, and we hustle this person into a belief in the hidden God of general revelation, that belief may provide sufficient security to arrest the progress toward trust in the revealed God who claims authority in the person of Jesus Christ.

To be sure, some atheists and agnostics will begin to progress toward that relationship of trust through arguments of general revelation which contribute to the destruction of old security systems and sources of meaning. Others will respond directly to the claim of God in the flesh and come to a belief in a god through trust in the God who created the universe. The believer must cultivate a sensitivity which guides the approach to the individual unbeliever. Careful listening is the order of the day at the beginning of all Christian conversation. The need for careful listening never is superseded as the conversation continues.

GOD'S REVELATION IN HIS MIGHTY ACTS

God has revealed Himself in many and various ways, and He

culminated His special revelation of His love by speaking through His Son, through whom He had created the world (Heb. 1:1–2). God did not inspire abstract philosophical ruminations; He moved His chosen spokesmen to speak of the Creator's concrete actions in human history (2 Peter 1:21). When the Lord was communicating with Elijah, He was not in the wind, the earthquake, or the fire. He spoke in a still, small voice, in human language (1 Kings 19:11–12). This means that God's revelation of Himself eludes those who seek Him through their own minds, from within. This revelation comes only to human creatures as the Holy Spirit creates in them the ability to listen to the Word of the Lord and His intervention in human history (Rom. 1:16; 10:14–20).

Without a strong, creator-god in their mythical systems or in the doctrines of their leading philosophers, the ancient Greeks could not understand a history with a beginning in the Creator's hand and an end determined by His Word. Instead, they viewed time as circular or cyclical rather than linear, and they believed that fortune's course recurs in an eternal swirl. For the Gnostics, then, redemption was conceived as escape from this wheel of fortune, from entrapment in time and history—as well as in humanity. The Christians opposed this view with an understanding of redemption as liberation from defiance of God and a return to a relationship of service to Him as restored human creatures. That restoration, the early church announced, had been accomplished in God's most dramatic and decisive intervention into human history, His enfleshment as Jesus of Nazareth.[49]

The Hebrew faithful had lived in confidence that the Lord had created and was preserving them. They rejoiced and praised His name because He had called them to be His own people, and they called Him the God of Abraham, Isaac, and Jacob. They exulted regularly that He had smitten the firstborn of Egypt and brought Israel out from among them with a strong hand and an outstretched arm, for His steadfast love endures forever (Ps. 136:10–12; cf. numerous passages, e.g., Ps. 78:50–53; Neh. 9:9–15; Is. 63:11–14; Hag. 2:5). The mighty acts of God provided for His people and protected them; His mighty acts revealed His steadfast love.

But His mighty acts do not interpret themselves. The significance of the exodus might be interpreted as an act of the Egyptian gods who cared nothing for the followers of Moses but were very angry with their own pharaoh. The voice of the prophet of the Lord must proclaim the steadfast love of the Creator if the intentions which He has as He acts mightily are to become apparent. The people of the Lord interpret both His mighty acts and the design and structure for the relationships that He created between Himself and the human creatures (and between the human creature and nature, other human creatures, and self) on the basis of the Word which He breathed authoritatively through the prophets and apostles whose message we have in the Scriptures. Francis Schaeffer refers to God's mighty acts and to His design for the world in the following way: the Bible "teaches certain things in didactic statements, in verbalizations, in propositions," and it "teaches by showing how God works in the world that He Himself made."[50] However, it is important to note that the understanding of the latter is also dependent on a correct appraisal of the acts of God, and that appraisal rests in verbalizations and propositions. The significance of this mode of revelation is that it does not reduce God to a set of insights or ideas, to mere information. The Christian faith is not just one more ideology. We share the faith by introducing the person of our God, by telling His story, the story of who He is and what He does. As is the case in any acquaintanceship, information is important; it is the way to getting acquainted with the person. But friendship is always based on more than mere information; it is based on trust. Christian witness tells the story of our God, using biblical information to make the acquaintance, build the friendship, establish the trust.

GOD'S REVELATION IN HUMAN LANGUAGE

Thus, it is important to recognize that we should not play "information" and "trust" against each other as we think about the ways in which we share the faith. Some contemporary Christians often express concern that the Christian faith not be understood as merely a belief in certain propositions or verbal formulae. To be sure, it is of utmost importance that we recognize that the trust between us and our Father embraces our entire being. Trust is not a trust in words for their own sake, and it certainly is more than a mere knowledge of the words and an acknowledgement of their veracity or accuracy. However, the trust which the believer has in God rests upon God's revelation of Himself in His Word. His Word speaks to us first of all in His own flesh, the incarnate Word, Jesus of Nazareth. Yet we know and are acquainted with Jesus as the Word of the Lord only through the human language which God uses to convey the Good News of the mighty act of the incarnation, of the revelation of God's disposition toward us in Jesus. The verbalizations and propositions of the prophetic and apostolic witnesses to the acts of the Creator and the Re-creator form the foundation not just for the knowledge which is a part of Christian life, but for the household of faith itself (Eph. 2:20).

God's Word as Proposition and Power

God approaches us through propositions because He has created us beings whose nature it is to communicate and whose communication is fundamentally—though certainly not exclusively—verbal:

> ... what marks man as man is verbalization. We communicate propositional communication to each other in spoken or written form in language. Indeed, it is deeper than this because the way we think inside of our own heads is language. We can have other things in our heads besides language, but it always must be linked to language.[51]

To be sure, art and music can express human emotion without verbalization eloquently and adequately—from me and to me as an individual. In either case I remain in charge of that expression, whether given or received, because I, and I alone, interpret it. If the community is to have a role in my appreciation of another's artistic expression, or if the community is to receive from artistic expression a precise explanation of what I have in mind as I express myself artistically, then human language must come into play. My emotional expression in artistic form will make an impact on your emotions without words, but I cannot share with you the *meaning* of my experience, what I view as its significance, apart from verbal communication. We may even have a community of expression in playing a duet or in a symphony, but our meanings—and our feelings as distinct from their expression—can become common only through verbal "sharing." Words create community. Common experiences build community by sharing meaning through verbalization.

All other doctrines or teachings, about political or social theory, about aesthetic or moral values, about chemical or biological truths, are and remain teachings *about* something. Only the teaching of God's Word can take the human creature as its direct object. Christian teaching addresses and claims me; it transforms and re-creates me. It does concern what we would like to know about life, certainly, and it does give us information. But it also brings the very power of God, the power of His forgiving and creative might, into the midpoint of our lives, and it brings us into the midst of the power of God's forgiving and creative might. Doctrines about this or that are able to give us important details and knowledge, but Christian doctrine gives us that and more. It gives us life. In its most natural, most effective expression, God's Word is conveyed to our hearers in direct address, in "I-thou" language, when we say, "I forgive you, in the name of the Father, the Son, and the Holy Spirit." That proposition packs power.[52]

Thus, the propositions of the biblical message dare never be viewed as "mere propositions." For when God speaks, His words convey His power. They work. They effect change. His Word is active, creative, re-creative. His Word is a sovereign Word.

The message of the Scriptures does come in normal human words. God did not inspire some special religious language, which offers a secret code for unlocking the mystery of the universe in gnostic fashion. The creative breath of God took the dust of common, everyday Hebrew, Aramaic, and Greek when He formed the propositions of His authoritative biblical revelation.[53] Anyone who understands these languages can read the Scriptures and apprehend what the writers were saying. God's Word in human language is propositionally rational. Human reason in its linguistic dimension is a creature of God and in the Scriptures it is His servant.

This does not mean that the significance of the biblical message is comprehensible to the sinful reader who apprehends the meaning of its words. Nor does it mean that sinful human reason can approach the biblical message with its tools of logic and cultural common sense and force a meaning from or upon the Scriptures.[54] It does not mean that the words of common everyday language which the Holy Spirit breathed through the prophets and apostles will make sense to those who read them or hear them lifted from the page of Scripture. The significance of the biblical message indeed offends the hearer whose ears are plugged by a disposition which is turned against the Creator. God alone can re-create the disposition, the relationship, which He originally designed for His human creatures and Himself. He does that through the Word made flesh. He effects that through His Word in human language: written, oral, and sacramental.[55]

Two points must be kept clearly in mind. The Word of God comes in thoroughly human form, yet it remains totally divine. This is true of Jesus Christ, and it is true of the written and spoken human language which conveys God's message for us. God's revelation in Jesus, as in the words which convey His significance for us, must be apprehended through God's gift of human reason. It can be comprehended as God's truth and His power only when human reason functions in a servant role, subject to the lordship of God. Propositional rationality facilitates the proper conveying of the message. The rationality of our culture's logic and our community's common sense will try to break out of the servant's role and to dominate and thus pervert the Word of the Lord. The Word of the Lord brings judgment upon our reason when it attempts to manipulate God's address to us.

His Word is power, in personal form first of all, to be sure, but in propositional form as well. Even in its human, propositional form it does remain the sovereign Word of the Lord which can be submitted to human judgment no more than He can be. For that Word created human judgment and continues to sustain all human functions.

God's Word Interprets Human Experience

God reveals Himself in language which is rational and propositional. The first implication of this proposition is that the language of Christian theology can be used to interpret and make sense out of human experience. That sense may not be apparent to every human creature, but within the context of faith and its acceptance of even the mysteries of God's dealing with the world, the biblical message has definite meaning. This Christian conviction stands in contrast to the existentialist judgment that life cannot make sense, that is, that no universally apparent system of meaning can make sense of human experience. The existentialist answer to evil, anti-rational as it may be, nonetheless grasps life and forces it into submission through the creature's act of will; it resists submitting the creature to the Creator. Although existentialism as a formal philosophy has faded in popularity in North America over the past decade or two, a garden-variety kind of existentialism influences the lives of many, who wish to assert the power of their own wills against a society gone mad, against a world filled with confusion and conflict. The absurd is ever with us, and the counsel of despair which the existentialist wishes to fling against it continues to have its absurd appeal.

This confusion and conflict make it difficult to perceive any sense to life in the midst of the dark night of Nazism, or the savagery of attempts to suppress revolutions from Hungary, Czechoslovakia, and Lithuania to Bangladesh and Biafra, or the snuffing out of young life by bullets or booze on the streets of an American city. But in quieter corners of the earth, even in the 20th century, the order of God's design drops strong hints of itself, and at their worst the destructive forces of evil desires harnessed to advanced technology defy that order in such a way that they force their victims to deny that disorder is proper.

The believer will then dismiss that retreat from the proper exercise of God's gift of reason by both the atheistic existentialist, who glories in the absurd, and by his intellectual first-cousin, the Christian fundamentalist who boasts that he would gladly make the intellectual sacrifice of believing absurd propositions simply for the sake of defying reason—a sacrifice which the Creator of rationality has indeed not asked His human creatures to make. Both end up where the rationalist ends up, for both focus on one's own power to determine the truth through one's own dominance on the basis of the exercise of the mind or will. This will defies God and boasts of one's own powers to make a leap of faith, toward the void or the absurd. God's revelation remains in mystery at some points, but it remains

His, not ours to twist into a springboard for proving ourselves. Human rationality remains His tool, and every perversion of it—both the denial of its proper role and the exaggeration of its capability—offends its Creator.

God's Word Grows in the Lives of His People

Second, since God restores His relationship with His fallen human creatures through human language, it is important for believers to know His Word and to keep growing in their knowledge of it. Indeed, the infant church was growing throughout the period Luke describes in the Acts of the Apostles, but Luke's refrain focused on the motor of the church's growth, the growth of the Word of the Lord in the lives of His people (Acts 6:7; 12:24; 19:20). The biblical writers did not fling words at the church to be shaped into whatever meaning and significance might occur at first glance to their heirs in different cultural settings. They and the Holy Spirit meant something quite specific with their words, and that meaning, not some bright idea which floats in our heads, is the Word of the Lord. Through the use of linguistic, historical, and archaeological studies we can determine quite closely in nearly all instances what the prophets and apostles meant as they wrote in the context of the Hebraic culture which God chose as the setting for the revelation of His love. We dare not let our ideas of what God should have said influence our perception of what He did say.

Third, as noted in the introduction to this volume, the Christian witness must realize that God's power resides in the human language which He has given us to speak. Propositions about God carry the power of God. These propositions from God grasp our entire being, emotion as well as reason, with this power, which He has placed in our hands. Christian witnesses can step forward to speak in full confidence that God is working through their words, as they retain and forgive sins (John 20:23).

GOD'S REVELATION IN WRATH AND MERCY

Within God's design and structure for human life remain echoes of God's conversations with Adam and Eve which even fallen

61

human creatures today can hear, however indistinctly. "The fundamental of human experience is the distress which man experiences in his conscience when he is aware on the one hand of the promise inherent in his life and on the other hand of the judgment and threat also present. ... From this tension in his being man cannot set himself free."[56] God's Word makes explicit this human experience: God speaks a message of wrath and a message of mercy to fallen human creatures. The tension, the contradiction, between these two messages cannot be compromised out of existence. Believers must live with this tension in their own lives, and as they witness to others they must live with the tension in the lives of others.

God's message of wrath and His message of mercy differ in several significant ways. First, God's wrath makes itself felt through general revelation as well as the revelation in the Word made flesh and in Scripture. God's message of mercy is apparent only in Jesus Christ and the biblical witness to God's faithfulness in human history. History and nature do give occasional hints of God's goodness, but these hints become explicit only when interpreted through the Word.

Second, the content of God's two messages differs quite obviously, for one condemns and the other forgives. God's message of wrath seems to offer a promise of redemption if the human creature can overcome that wrath through his or her own righteousness; from God's design for our horizontal relationships we gather that goodness wins reward and badness wins punishment, and the promise of reward for goodness holds out some hope for personal redemption. Such a presumption denies God's role and right as Creator (Rom. 9:9–33) and, in addition, does not do the sinner any good at all. For these foolish hopes are dashed when put to an honest test, and but one hope remains, namely, that redemption is possible beyond the realm where our own goodness exercises power. God's message of mercy assures us that it is, from the realm where God in His mysterious counsel has decided to rescue and restore His chosen people. The message of wrath seems to hold out a promise, but because no one could attain the conditions it stipulates, its final address to sinners comes as a threat. The message of mercy does not threaten at all and has no conditions; it is pure promise, undeserved yet certain.

Third, His Word of condemnation is addressed to the sinner who is sufficiently secure with old gods to continue to resist the Lord and His Word. His Word of mercy is addressed to the sinner who recognizes the insufficiency of old sources of identity, meaning, and security and to the creature whom He has already turned to Himself and returned to Edenic trust in His goodness.[57]

The message of wrath is based upon the evaluation that God's Law makes of our lives on the basis of His design and structure for human life. Because it springs from this Law it can only evaluate, and because it is evaluating a perverted humanity, it must judge— and condemn. In contrast, the re-creative Word of mercy is

> deed-word, event, surprise. It does not just tell us something about a general nature of God. It is the experience of God's Yes. It is really God's Yes over against his judgment. It is an act of mercy. In it God is no longer against me. He is no longer the one as whom I must see him outside Christ. The gospel is the wonder of this turning in God. It is the achievement of this turning.[58]

God speaks to us and our world as we and it are. We are in revolt against Him, having proclaimed the end of His authority as Author of life in our lives; we are still within His power of re-creation, rescue, and restoration. In this plane of existence the people of God will never move beyond the tension between our captivity to our own doubt of God's Word and defiance of His lordship on the one hand, and, on the other hand, God's plans for us and His power to accomplish them. Some human creatures remain secure in their own security systems and must have them destroyed. Others are trying to live in the broken wreckage of identities which would no longer function because these people became honest enough to evaluate life without God in sober and frank fashion. God must speak to each kind of person in a different way because each kind of person is so radically different from the other. Even believers, caught in the struggle between their own desire to find security and meaning on their own and the power of God's forgiving and restoring will for them, must hear both God's message of wrath and His message of mercy. In Christian witness we must weigh where the burden is falling. For instance, when we repeat our Lord's words from John 3:16, "that whoever believes on Him should be saved," we make God's love conditional upon our faith, if we understand the passage literally. The burden can fall upon the hearer's faith, and it can crush a hearer's weak faith. We must always evaluate where the burden is falling, upon the hearer or upon Christ. Is it crushing or re-creating?

Christians are often tempted to mingle and merge God's two Words, ignoring the radical contrast between the two kinds of people that we see around us and that we experience within ourselves. That confusion of God's Law and Gospel wreak havoc on the message, the witness, and the hearer. Often what results is that neither message is expressed clearly. The seriousness of God's condemning wrath is blurred by promises of shortcuts to conforming to His design for human life and thereby winning the rewards which His Law holds out for those who keep it. Or the mercy of God is so tightly guarded that conditions are attached to it which transfer the focus of our proclamation from the merciful God to those who fulfill the conditions.[59]

The two messages of God, and the proper Christian proclamation of each of them in a fashion which preserves the integrity of each, are the subjects of the rest of this volume. The message of His wrath is a message alien to the will and design of the Creator; its work of condemnation is a task which He does not like to do. He likes to create and to forgive. His message of salvation gives Him joy just as it gives us joy and life. The proclamation of this Good News and the Gospel's transforming effect which re-creates sinners into disciples is the primary task of the Christian witness.

THE EPISTEMOLOGY OF THE GOSPEL

It is crucial that we recognize the nature of God's message of mercy and how we may best cultivate its comprehension. As noted above, God will not reveal Himself in all His glory to His human creatures, not even to Moses himself. God in all His Self is hidden from us. Religions of all kinds have speculated about that hidden Self of God and forged a myriad of descriptions of that Self. All these religions give us pictures shaped in our own images, as Feuerbach cynically—but correctly—observed.[60] God's revelation of Himself in Jesus Christ does not qualify as one of these religions, for in Jesus Christ the hidden God becomes the revealed God. (It is interesting to note that the pictures of the hidden God which we shape in our own image all depict Him primarily as a demanding rather than a giving, creating, and providing God, thus reflecting our own fallen nature. Often, the gods constructed by human imagination are angry gods, reflecting our own anger with ourselves, who never attain the standards we have set for ourselves.)

The hidden God has revealed Himself in human flesh. The revealed God is hidden in human flesh. The true God has hidden Himself in the crib and on the cross and in His crypt. He reveals Himself in a promise wrapped in swaddling cloths, in diapers, and nailed to a cross.[61] The glory of God comes to rest in a baby and a corpse—a corpse, to be sure, which came alive again, but in an event which defies verifiability at the hand of empirical testers, who believe, or presuppose, that every believable event should be repeatable under the watchful eye, and dominance, of the human experimenter. Even the resurrection, which early Christians testified had happened on the basis of their encounters with the risen Jesus, has little significance for such people. So long as they are secure in a false ideology, or fear abandoning the presuppositions which have governed their lives for a long time, they can find excuses to set aside the documentary attestation of the New Testament writers and their successors. False gods must be cleared away before unbelievers can recognize the validity of that documentary evidence, and even then Christian witnesses must proceed further to lead their hearers to recognize that the resurrection of which the New Testament writers spoke offers life to the people of the 20th century.

We dare not disregard the importance of the logical proofs and arguments which our cultural common sense provide for the believer's address to the world. But we must carefully demarcate the proper use of these proofs from the proclamation of the promise itself. The proofs may clear away the conceptual constructs which have housed the sinner in the security and comfort of a perverted meaning for life stemming from a false identity conceived outside of a relationship with the Father. The proofs may also support and clarify the promise once the Re-creator has transformed the sinner's disposition and returned him or her to trust in Himself. (The danger, of course, in this case is that the trust rests more on the proofs than the promise.) Always at the heart of God's transforming message of mercy is His revelation of Himself in the glory of suffering, in the splendor of the cross, in the triumph of death. Glory, splendor, and triumph lie concealed in the likes of suffering, cross, and death.

This Word of promise, the Word of the cross—a cross burdened with all the evils and sins of human history, yet an empty cross which sprouts new life—summarized the message which St. Paul proclaimed. He described it as a word of folly to the perishing but a word of power and salvation to those whom it has brought to trust in the Creator (1 Cor. 1:18, 21). Paul pointed out that the people of his day demanded signs (some kind of visible, empirical proof) or wisdom (some kind of rational demonstration) if they were to believe, but God addresses them with the folly of the cross, and there He displays His power (1 Cor. 1:22–26). Paul disclaimed the use of philosophical persuasion so that the cross of Christ might retain His power as the focus of our faith and so that the Holy Spirit's demonstration of God's love might not be obscured by a human persuasiveness which draws attention and trust to itself (1 Cor. 1:17; 2:3–5). The only sign He gives is the sign of Jonah, the sign of Jesus' death and resurrection, a sign which will not satisfy the wise men of Israel (Matt. 12:39). God offers His people the signs of the life of Jesus, which led them to believe that He is the Messiah, the Author and Giver of life (John 20:30–31), signs which climax in the foolishness of the cross and the triumph of the resurrection.

It is difficult for contemporary North Americans to entrust much of the burden of life, much of their existence, to mere promises, not just because human promises seem so often and easily broken but especially because the epistemology of our culture insists to a large extent on proofs. We believe that solid, indisputable knowledge cannot come on the strength of a promise.

Three common, generally quite meaningless, expressions in the North American idiom help us understand the prevalent approaches to knowledge in our culture. "Well, it's this way, you know" issues an appeal to a rationally obtainable bit of information or insight. "You know," although today most often an appeal for support from lack of knowledge, implies that there is a principle behind my point which rational thought should make obvious to you and me. "Well, it's this way, you see" invites one to look; by testing empirically with our senses, you and I should be able to determine the truth of what I am saying. "Well, it's this way, you hear" is neither an appeal to a common rationality nor a suggestion which can be tested empirically. It is the voice of authority, making a statement which elicits trust, not because the statement makes sense or can be tested but because the speaker commands authority. "This is the way it is, you hear" is the gift of a parent to a child.

The first of these approaches to knowledge was highly prized by the rationalistic Enlightenment of the founding fathers of the United States, and North Americans have always prided themselves on being a common sense kind of people. But the rising success of the natural sciences in improving human life carried the popular epistemology of the 19th and particularly the 20th centuries away from a strict rationalism into empiricism. Today many North Americans believe that a superior kind of truth comes from empirical testing, and that any other system of knowledge has no, or at least an inferior, claim to validity, authority, and truth.[62] This popular view ignores the weakness of this positivistic approach to knowledge, such as the necessity of its presuppositions—which cannot help but play a role in determining the outcome of the search for knowledge—before empirical testing can take place. The presumption of investigators that their instruments convey reality through the lenses of the microscope or the screen of the spectroscope, for example, and the theoretical framework into which they fit their data, do play a role in determining the results produced by their experiments. Furthermore, it ignores the fact that human creatures appropriate reliable knowledge for various aspects of human living in various ways.[63] There is certainly nothing inappropriate about the use of empirical testing for obtaining knowledge about God's creation. Rational seeking of knowledge is also a tool given to us by the Creator. Both are designed for functioning in our horizontal relationships with other human creatures and nature. Neither can serve to enlighten us regarding the relationship which God establishes with us as Creator and Re-creator.

The epistemology of the vertical relationship relies on the voice of authority which comes from the Author of life. The Word of the Creator is a creative and re-creative Word: "if the gospel had to do with matters which were independent of it, plainly its veracity could be established." But, "a word which creates and which poses the reality of which it speaks cannot be verified. Such a word calls for faith."[64] The unique event which constitutes God's decisive saving intervention in human history, His Word of re-creation in the cross and the empty tomb, lies beyond human dominance, also in the form of testing. If I could test, and thus prove, the truth of the incarnation, then it would not be unique, from a natural scientific point of view. The resurrection of Jesus, for instance, is significant not just because someone came back from the dead, remarkable though that is. Others have come back from the dead according to the biblical writers: the son of the widow of Zarephath (1 Kings 17:21), Lazarus (John 11:1–45), the son of the widow of Nain (Luke 7:11–17). Christ's resurrection is of ultimate significance because it has ultimate effects in the farthest corners of God's creation, for the furthest people among His human creatures, to the end of time and beyond. It is an event of unique significance and cannot be subject to the empirical proofs which give the human investigator dominance over whatever is being investigated. The event itself has historical witnesses, equal to that of many events, superior to that of many events accepted universally as historically verifiable. Yet because there is no comparable series of human experiences, it lacks an important criterion which modern investigators insist it must have to be accepted as verified, specifically, repeatability of its essential characteristics. Even with that verification, its truth and validity for me lie in the impact of Christian proclamation, interpretation, and application to me. That proclamation can only be heard and believed. This knowledge of the resurrection and its significance is not thereby inferior to the knowledge forged under my dominance, but it is different. It is knowledge from the Author of life, and it is certain knowledge because He has spoken it, to my faith. "Faith is dealing with a reality which I cannot prove and yet which exists without me, which enjoys objective givenness and yet which is not accessible to me in an objectifiable way. It is not objectively verifiable, and yet it is an objective truth."[65]

Believers need not be able to conduct a lengthy discourse on epistemology in order to present that objective truth which rests on God's promise rather than on human proof. Neither should they be intimidated by popular claims in behalf of empirically tested truth claims. They should be prepared to use logical argument and cultural common sense to destroy false systems of security and false sources of meaning and identity, and they should be able to make the faith as plausible as possible. At the same time, they must always remember that plausibility and proof without the Holy Spirit cannot effect acceptance of the promise in faith. That is simply the nature of the promise, the form of human communication which God has chosen as the instrument of His re-creating power. The initiation and nurture of faith is the task of the re-creating Holy Spirit alone as God comes in His re-creating Word.

2

Against You, O Lord, Have I Sinned

SOMETHING IS WRONG

"Suddenly we awoke from our pleasant dreams with a fearful realization that *something was wrong*."[1] Karl Menninger made that comment on the American dawn of a consciousness of evil two decades ago. Vietnam, Watergate, and the Arab oil embargo were beginning to impress upon the North American consciousness that perhaps the existence of evil could not be so lightly dismissed as Americans had always hoped. The dissolution of the family, epidemics of AIDS and addictions, violence in homes and on the streets, have only strengthened this conviction in the intervening years. Biblical Christians presuppose that the Creator God has fashioned His human creatures in and for a series of harmonious relationships, and they also presuppose that the disruption of these relationships has blemished and even destroyed true human life. These presuppositions have not been shared by many people in our society, including some who talk about sins. Some do not understand that the withering and warping power of evil is so great that it reduces the individual human creature to helplessness in its face. Others do not take the perversion of human sin seriously enough to perceive that it destroys what life ought to be for God's human creatures.

Indeed, it is increasingly less possible, even in the cozy corners of Western culture, to avoid confronting evil and to skip merrily along life's pathway in the fashion of a Pollyanna, denying that anything is really all that wrong. However, even if we perceive that something is wrong in this world, we often find it easy to deny our personal responsibility for any of that wrong. As a matter of fact, apart from trust in God, a certain degree of self-deception regard-

71

ing that responsibility seems to be necessary if we are to cope with life. To be liberated from a life entrapped in deception and personal evil, people must die to the shaky systems of security and the wobbly explanations which give meaning to their lives, constructed because God has been banished from their thinking.

The first task of Christian conversation involves leading unbelievers to see that they are as spiritually dead as are the objects of their trust. Then we must lead them to die as devotees of their self-constructed gods. These idols, in whatever form they provide identity, security, or meaning, must die as gods and be transformed once again into instruments of service. The spouse who has been an idol will be better cared for if no longer viewed as a source of security but rather as a partner in God's design for human living. The job which has served to give meaning to my life will be better performed if I recognize that meaning comes from God, who also gives me opportunities to care for others through my work.

We often make several critical mistakes in trying to define what sin and evil really are. One of those mistakes involves the attempt to escape from personal responsibility, identifying what is wrong with this world as something outside ourselves and beyond our control. "In all of the laments and reproaches made by our seers and prophets," Karl Menninger comments concerning modern America, "one misses any mention of 'sin,'.... It was a word on everyone's mind, but now rarely if ever heard. Does that mean that no sin is involved in all our troubles—sin with an 'I' in the middle? Is no one any longer guilty of anything. ... Is it only that someone may be stupid or sick or criminal—or asleep?"[2]

Menninger attributes much of what has gone wrong with life in North America in the past quarter century to the disappearance of a sense of guilt and the ability to deal with it. Deprivation, caused by environment rather than my own depravity, seems a good explanation, and at the same time a good excuse, for what is wrong with my life. Or it may be convenient to believe that evil lies deeply rooted within my genes, where I can do little or nothing to change it. In either case evil lies outside my responsibility. This kind of self-deception may comfort me for a while, but as we have seen in Chapter 1, accepting personal responsibility is a vital part of preserving the integrity of one's personality. As I rest quietly in the

American Middle West toward the end of the 20th century, it may be hard to imagine that I could ever commit atrocities such as those of my cousins on another continent half a century ago. I deceive myself if I do not recognize that under the temptations and pressures of another societal setting, I, too, would be liable to preserve my own skin at the expense of others', and very possibly to receive from that a fiendish delight which seems so foreign to me now.

Not only a glimpse of the evils for which I am responsible, but also an honest confrontation with the depth of evil to which I could potentially drive myself, reveal that evil is not just out there. Evil dwells within me. Confronted with evils outside ourselves, we may resist or run, but we cannot escape sins which gang up on us and threaten our lives from within us or from outside ourselves. As believers intervene in the lives of others, they must recognize both the sinner's responsibility for evil and the sinner's being a victim of evil.

Believers, secondly, may fail to understand that the evil which the human creature has loosed in the world has indeed gotten beyond our control. Much of what goes wrong in our lives does indeed lie beyond our individual ability to stop or change it. Human sinfulness has bent nature out of shape, and it takes vengeance on our homes through fire and flood and on our bodies through stress and carcinogens. Human insecurity has perverted our sense of neighborliness and twisted love into hatred, viciousness, and barbarism. Raging evil on a massive scale defies the best human efforts to control it, and at times threatens to consume us.

A third mistake which Christians often make in dealing with sin and evil is to define evil in terms of the last nine commandments while ignoring or reducing the significance of the First Commandment. This reduces sin to a series of wrong actions, and these wrong actions presumably should lie within the power of an autonomous individual to correct or at least deal with, manage, or control. Such a short-sighted, nonbiblical view of sin can cripple Christian witness. We must take seriously the depth and the power of the grip which the perversion of our nature has made on ourselves and others.

The strength of that grip reasserts itself whether we try to deny it or not. Many people in our culture exercise autonomous decision-making power as they declare actions which their grandparents thought sinful to be sins no longer. "Lots of sins have disappeared," Menninger notes, and yet he finds that the disappearance of individual sins has left behind "a general sentiment that sin is still with us, by us, and in us—somewhere."[3] Douglas John Hall calls this process the "domestication of sin." In our culture sin has become merely immorality, no more than a matter of disjunction in our horizontal relationships, especially our relationships with other human creatures.[4]

Separated into discrete moral components, individual sins seem on the one hand less threatening, and on the other hand easier to explain away, excuse, or justify. If we limit sin to the *actions of individuals,* and if we define the individual as an integral unit, autonomous and self-contained, then there is no reason why this individual may not act without thought for the welfare of others. There is no reason why individual actions need ever be defined as sins. Absurd as that conclusion is when pressed into practice, in theory it holds; in fact, it illustrates the bankruptcy of a philosophy of "rugged individualism," or "narcissism" in our society.[5]

Sin is more than those actions which disrupt our personal relationships with our neighbors. Sin is more than the evils which cloud the horizon of life on every side (if we look closely enough). Both sinful actions against other human creatures and evils beyond individual or human control are symptoms of sin at its root; they grow out of the original sin.

Psalm 32 begins with three synonyms for what is wrong with the human creature. The first, *pesha'*, means "transgression, rebellion, revolt." It is the act of defying one's Lord. The second, *khata'ah*, is often translated "missing the mark" or "missing the right point." Sin is being off-target, not being where one is supposed to be, being outside the proper relationship. The third word for sin in Psalm 32, *'awon*, means "iniquity," the negative form of righteousness. David confessed to being trapped in iniquity, bound to miss the mark, always ready to rebel against his Creator and God, from the very beginning of his life: "in sin did my mother conceive me" (Ps. 51:5).

North Americans like to stand on their own two feet. They like to believe that a new person should have a clean slate, whether the person is new in political office, on the job, or at life. Gustaf Wingren observes that the Bible has a different point of view. "It says that we are all 'in Adam.' I am more than myself. In me all past generations are at work; I take over the stored-up destructiveness of the race before I make any decision with regard to my own activity. I cannot break that chain through any measure that I may devise."[6] Offensive as that judgment is to the individual who thinks himself autonomous and independent, experience confirms that from the beginning of life the human creature in our world is caught in a web of iniquity, sin, and rebellion, whatever names we may give to the evil which besets us from within.

Clinical psychologist John E. Keller points out that the tiniest infant exhibits characteristics which mark the sinful appropriation of the focal point of life away from God to self: a sense of omnipotence, sitting on the throne of life, expecting all else to spin around his or her needs; an expectation that all one's needs must be met, a low frustration tolerance; and a sense of hurry, a demand for immediate satisfaction.[7] From Genesis 3 we see what has gone wrong with us from birth on and what continues to go wrong with us. There we view in Adam and Eve what the church has called the original sin, the root of all human sinfulness.

"HAS GOD REALLY SAID?" GENESIS 3 ON SIN

The human creature is by design dependent upon the Creator and takes direction for life from Him. That we do not acknowledge this accounts for all that is wrong with our world and our life within it. The Scriptures follow the report of human origin from the Word of the Creator with a record of our desertion of God, our defection from the stance in which God placed us initially as the product of His Word.

Doubt

"Has God really said?" the serpent asked, and with the deception implicit in that question the spiral of human desertion from the haven of the Creator's hand began. The question fostered doubt. The devil deceived, and Eve became confused. She knew better, and yet she failed to answer the serpent with what she knew. She could tell the serpent what God had said, "You shall not eat of the fruit of the tree which is in the midst of the garden" (Gen. 3:3; cf. 2:16–17), but she was not certain she could rely simply on that Word. She added something of her own: "neither shall you touch it." She was going to make good and sure that the Word could defend her as she was defending it, so she spliced on an extra bit to it.

She had already begun to doubt whether God had really given her and Adam the truth about the structure for human life which He had shaped. She was uncertain whether ultimate goodness lay in that Word of the Lord. She began to doubt whether she needed to trust and love and fear God above all else. The deceiver had "sowed two poisonous seeds in Eve's heart. First, he persuaded her that one must not take God too seriously, because what He says is by no means a matter of life and death; and second, he made her distrustful of the goodness of God."[8] Therein lies the origin of sin. That doubt was the root of every human failure to be on target and not miss the mark as a creature of God. Every human creature since has been born sharing Eve's refusal to recognize God as God, to depend upon His direction, to rely upon His supporting love and sustaining power, to rest in confidence in His continuing presence. Faith in the Creator places human life on the mark, on target. Doubt destroys that, for us all.

The heart of sin—evil, and its mastery over man—is seen according to biblical teaching "not so much in a corruption of his physical, psychological, or rational substance, and therefore in a morbid weakness and unfitness for the good as such, but rather in the perversion of will, in apostasy, in the usurpative 'no' of him who wants to be like God."[9] The attitude which biblical writers often summarize with the word "flesh" is not "the body with its lower desires"; it is "the free exercise of man's highest powers of mind, heart, and will in antagonism against the Creator he is commanded to trust and love."[10] That antagonism began where the human creature began: at the Word of the Lord. When Jesus advanced into the garden turned desert to engage the deceiver once again, the script had already been written. He was "tempted in his flesh, in his faith, and in his allegiance to God. All three are the one temptation—to separate Jesus from the Word of God."[11] Jesus defeated the devil's deceit with the only effective weapon, the Word of God (Matt. 4:1–11).

Original sin is not a popular concept, even among many Christians. It seems unfair. But it is a diagnosis, above all. The crushing power of the diagnosis remains the determining factor in our lives, even when we deny it and protest against it. In Christian witness we are not there to defend the vocables "original sin." We are there to make clear how God's demands crush us when we live apart from Him, when our lives are governed by our sinful defiance of God at their very root. The root of sin is inextricably linked with the primary relationship of the human creature, the vertical relationship with the Lord of creation. Sin ultimately stems not from the disruption of horizontal relationships; in fact, the opposite is the case. Sin is originally and ultimately a matter between us and God (Gen. 39:9).

Bonhoeffer explains Satan's attack on the Word of God in this way: the decisive point is that [the serpent's] question

> suggests to man that he should go behind the Word of God and establish what it is by himself, out of his understanding of the being of God. Should it contradict this understanding, then man has clearly made a mistake. Surely it can only serve God's cause if such false words of God, such misunderstood commands are swept aside before it is too late. The misleading thing about this question is therefore that it obviously wants to be thought to come from God. For the sake of the true God it seems to want to sweep aside the given Word of God. … The serpent claims to know more about God than man, who depends on God's Word alone. … And from this position of power the serpent fights against the Word of God. It knows that it only has power where it claims to come from God, to be pleading his cause.[12]

God had revealed Himself to Adam and Eve by walking and talking with them in the garden. They thought there might be more to God than His Word. They doubted that Word and sought a hidden god. They found instead a void in which they had to create gods. Every human creature since has inevitably repeated their experience. The statistics are clear. The potential of every sinful heir of Adam and Eve has been fulfilled in the actual sins of daily life. Doubt is in our genes, as one says today.

Some people like to boast about their doubts and praise them. It is true that in a fallen world faith grows in the same way a muscle grows, with exercise. A person whose faith has not been tested by doubt may well have a shallow level of trust. There are times for most of us when we are not so certain we will not slip from His hand—or are uncertain that His hand is there at all—and we doubt. Such doubt may have salutary results in the Christian life, but this does not alter the fact that doubt is evil. We were created to trust, not to doubt.

Doubts also can be expressed as uncertainty, and sometimes we confuse certainty with arrogance and boast of our uncertainty. It reveals a healthy kind of humbleness, we assert. However, "uncertainty is not humility but cleverly masked pride. Uncertainty becomes a place of refuge" in which a person refuses to listen to God and "seeks to be protected from the flames of the most terrifying issues of life. The twin sister of doubt is not humility but pride. He who seeks to prove that all human experience is basically uncertain and that doubt is the only true approach to reality is actually defending his right to retain the positions and formulations which he has chosen as his starting point."[13]

The Christian witness should recognize that uncertainty can indeed be a symptom of disintegrating security systems. It can also be a means by which unbelievers entrench themselves behind their own security devices, including that uncertainty itself, which removes responsibility from themselves for decisions regarding their vertical relationship. That kind of bid for freedom in uncertainty springs from the original doubt that added to and undercut the Word of the Lord in the Garden.

Denial and Defiance

This doubt then led to the denial that God had the right to say what should determine proper human living, which in turn led to a defiance of the God who had spoken the Word of life when He said, "let there be." Eve indeed knew better. She was able to explain to the deceiver what God had said, even though she added a codicil of her own. But she was also able to listen to the devil's proposition: "You will be like God."

78

When doubt gives birth to the denial that God has the right to say what human life is all about, we have denied that God can function as *our* God. We have denied that He is our Creator and Lord, the source of our security, our meaning in life, our identity. When doubt gives birth to the defiance of God's structure for human life, it has created the more fundamental defiance of His person. It has broken the relationship of mutual love and favor, of peace and joy and harmony, which Creator and creature enjoyed at the beginning. Eden has broken into blight; the garden withers. The denial of God and the defiance of His lordship produces a deadly deafness in Adam and Eve. A deathly silence descends upon the garden. The human creature no longer listens to the Word of God. The Word indeed may be heard, but now it judges and accuses. Human doubt and defiance wrongly refract the Word of the Lord.

This was no "friendly" divorce. What is true of sin in our horizontal relationships is above all true in the vertical relationship: "the wrongness of the sinful act lies not merely in its ... departure from the accepted, appropriate way of behavior, but in an implicitly aggressive quality—a ruthlessness, a hurting, a breaking away from God and from the rest of humanity, ... alienation or act of rebellion."[14]

Having deserted God, having lashed out against Him, Eve felt immediately the impossibility of her situation. She needed a god. She could not get along without identity, security, and meaning in her life. She needed something which would make sense of her existence and give her protection against a threat which she had never felt before. Her fear was not unallayed. She discovered delight in a newfound autonomy. She naturally wanted to share the delight with Adam, and she must also have sought support against that threat. Together, with God dethroned, they sought a new god. For as creatures they felt a sense of dependence, and they needed to establish the object of their dependence upon which they could rest, the object of dependence which alone could give them an explanation for life which would not be shaken, a haven and a harmony for life which would not disappear.

Desiring to Be Like God

So Adam and Eve fashioned a god in their own image: themselves. God's creation was so finely tuned that any diversion from His score meant dissonance and destruction. In accepting the invitation to be like God, Adam and Eve thought they were aiming to be something higher than those perfect stewards of God's creation, who were good and who commanded all goodness as the specially placed and specially formed human creatures of God. In trying to be like God, they did not become more than human but less than human. They did not add to their well-being but rather destroyed it. They emptied themselves of the heart of their humanity, their love for God, their trust in their Father. They tried to be like God by fashioning themselves in God's image. All they accomplished was losing the image of God in which the Creator had shaped them. The result was that they had to fashion gods in their own image. Worse yet, they took delight in what they had wrought. They became downright proud.

John Milton defined pride as the root of Satan's sin, as the original sin of the human creature,[15] in accord with much of Western Christian tradition. Pride certainly is a most important symptom and result of our doubt of God's Word, an inevitable product of our defiance of Him. When we dethrone God, we must transfer our worship and confidence to ourselves, at least for that moment at which we decide what in all God's creation will give us security, meaning, and identity. The pride which exalts me above God and above other creatures is born of an inferiority complex which must be masked if I am to preserve the charade I play with myself as I play God. Pride serves as self-defense against the fear and enmity I feel against God—and anyone or anything else who or which might challenge my claimed prerogative of deciding what makes my life secure and worthwhile. Pride places me on a ladder; I must scramble to its top to be on top of life. I must throw anyone above me off the ladder, and I must kick down those who scramble up behind me and threaten my position. Harmony has vanished. My adversaries are all about me. The fullness of life in community with God and other creatures has opened up, or closed up, into a void. Humanity had not been crafted to be like this. But I have fallen victim to my pride. False gods always control their worshipers.

The void which our denial and defiance of God imposed upon us must be filled. The desire for meaning and security grasps us and consumes us until we forge some kind of stopgap to fill this void. We must have a god, or two or three if one is not sufficient. Our desire will be calmed only so long as our new god delights us with a measure of meaning and security. We like to think our desires are means of pursuing and mastering what we want and need. Our desires actually chase us, pursue us relentlessly, from one crisis to another, from one makeshift god to another. These desires master us. We are always restless, for we find true rest only in the Creator. Our ultimate desire is not to die but rather to be like God. Our ultimate desire is to achieve the independence which immortality promises. But desire hounds us to death. It delivers us out of the hand of the Author of life and into our own hands, where life can neither begin nor be sustained.

Dread and Defensiveness Produce Disobedience and Division

Self-worship works only for a time. Inevitably, sinners recognize that their self-crafted false gods do not function well. The demise of the identity, security, and meaning they provide fills us with dread. Dread leads us inevitably to defensiveness. To defend themselves sinners try to use other people. The defensiveness of our idolatries divides us from others. Instead of mutual support, we experience mutual exploitation. The deafness of our defensiveness causes us to listen no longer to the Lord or to others. This defensiveness then gives birth to disobedience. Eve took the fruit and ate. Her disobedience was not the root of her sin. Her disobedience was not the original sin. Her disobedience was but the symptom of the root of her original diversion from the mark which God had set for life. Doubt had given birth to disobedience. The inner defiance of God had achieved its outward expression. Reaching for mastery, Adam and Eve desired to devise their own rules for living. They thought they could improve on God's structure for life. Instead, they began butting their heads against the walls of that structure.

Their doubt and defiance had turned their world upside down. When they thought that they were rising above the limits of God's structure for daily life, they were actually sinking under them; they were descending to sub-human status. They did as they pleased, not realizing that doing whatever we please cannot ultimately please us.

Their desire to be like God was a desire for independence from the Creator, and therefore a desire for independence from the claims of other human creatures and from a feeling of dependence upon them. When we attempt to forge our own security and meaning for life, we must do so at the expense of other human creatures and nature. Because we no longer approach our interpersonal relationships in the image of God but rather in search of a god, we generate and experience hostility in these horizontal relationships. In Eden the desire to be like God sought isolation and transformed individuality into individualism. "To live in a false relationship of independence of God who gives is likewise to be in a false relationship of one's neighbor who receives."[16] Desire and defensiveness created division and disobedience. The resulting assault on the structure of God's creation produced division among God's human creatures.

"The woman you gave me," Adam snarled defensively at God, simultaneously assaulting God and Eve. "So instead of surrendering Adam falls back on one art learned from the serpent, that of correcting the idea of God, of appealing from God the Creator to a better, a different God."[17] Denial that God is my God brings with it a denial that my wife can exercise the claims of wife upon me, that my brother is really my brother and my responsibility, that my neighbors live out their lives *that* close to mine. Cain made the point succinctly (Gen. 4:9). The collapse of the vertical relationship between me and my God has damaged the horizontal relationship between me and those with whom God has joined me.

The destruction of life in relationship to God has twisted, perverted, and weakened my ability to live with other creatures. I must now try to dominate the nature under which I had been given dominion. But it dominates me. By clinging to the things of creation without being able to abandon them for fear of losing them, the door through which fallen human creatures ought to pass in order that they might give to their neighbors becomes barred even more tightly, and their unkindness to their fellow beings grows stronger. By bowing down to what is created, as though we are subordinate to it, and by making ourselves slaves to it, we lose the possibility of proper exercise of dominion.[18] The ground is cursed under our feet; it has been bent out of shape by our falling upon it. We can no longer get a foothold or feel secure upon it. The destruction of our vertical relationship with the Father has removed the basis of that ground, and the safety net which He had provided in the warp and woof of human interdependence.

Now I think that I must also lean on and dominate my human neighbor in order to secure my own life. Karl Menninger quotes a poem by his colleague, Dr. William R. Boniface, which expresses this dilemma well:

> You came near as I was falling
> And I—threw you down to right
> Myself. I threw too hard. Now,
> I have you on my conscience
> As a counterweight.[19]

Such disobedience and division cannot be separated from our doubt of God's Word and our defiance of His lordship. Gustaf Wingren links love of God, love of the neighbor, and human dominion under nature.

> By man's act of sin in the Fall all three aspects are lost. The sinner who separates himself from God the Giver, to stand in false isolation from Him, also separates himself from his neighbor, the one who receives, to stand in false isolation from him. Fear of "losing one's life" is a part of unbelief (in relationship to God), and suppresses any willingness I may have to give of myself (to my neighbor), and forces me to bow down and cleave to some part of God's good Creation (in idolatry). These are not three separate sins but one sin seen from three aspects—my relation to God, to my neighbor, and to the world.[20]

Disobedience against God's plan for human life makes its impact not just as we abuse His holy name or ignore His call to proper worship. Disobedience against God takes form in every kind of division by which we destroy or abandon or exploit our proper relationships with those around us, through hatred, lust, and envy, through murder, fornication, and theft. Through every means whereby we try to exact meaning from life at our neighbor's expense or seek security for life using other people at our convenience or abusing nature for our pleasure, we disobey God. For instance, people use money less to love their neighbors than they use their neighbors to obtain and secure the money they love.

The evil of our disobedience and division does not parade itself in spectacular form for the most part. Evil can be big, as in the holocaust, but at its heart, as Hannah Arendt observed precisely in that situation,[21] evil is as banal as the adolescent next door, as my own desire to feel secure or worthwhile as I drive to the shopping center or scramble for the boss's favor. At its insidious worst evil is not awesome, but it is rather a matter of small compromises with wrong, small bargains in the black market purchase of security and meaning at the neighbor's expense.

This never really helps, for meaning and security for life come only from God and His design for life. Damaging other people as we trample on them to secure our own fortunes damages us more severely than it damages them.

Damned

We have become curved in upon ourselves. We focus on ourselves. We worship ourselves or at least determine what we will worship by our own decision. We have contracted a terminal case of ingrown self-centeredness. We avoid acknowledging this fatal disease. Some may finally face the fact that there is nothing inside this shell of our humanity worth seeking, but most human creatures have learned well from the devil the art of deception. Contemporary psychologists suggest that "*the* great cause of much psychological illness is the fear of knowledge of oneself—of one's emotions, impulses, memories, capacities, potentialities, of one's destiny."[22]

God created us with eyes directed at Him and hands outstretched to His creation. Human life is cruciform. When we turn our eyes from God to ourselves, we become self-conscious rather than God-conscious, and our hands withdraw from the neighbor to protect and warm ourselves. Adam and Eve discovered they were naked when they looked from God to themselves. They had never noticed their nakedness before. That they had nothing with which to cover themselves was not really the point. Now for the first time they needed something to cover themselves, for they no longer permitted God to cover for them. Now they also became defensive in relationship to each other. Self-consciousness must have held out some promise of mastery for them, but they discovered, as has contemporary culture, that self-consciousness is a harsh master, a form of enslavement.[23]

Such enslavement twists our relationship with ourselves into despair, or at least some less serious symptom of despair if we refuse to take our situation seriously or face it honestly. The brokenness of the harmonious relationship with oneself which God initially gave the human creature may express itself in several ways. Believers often encounter the symptoms of gnawing despair in others. They often do not need to convince unbelievers that despair lurks in the back of their minds:

> the alternatives are not faith versus experience, but different kinds of experience of God … dismay or comfort in C. S. Lewis, terror or grace in Elert, negation or affirmation in Tillich. All three point to certain experiences which bear witness to the fact that human existence is threatened not only with finitude but also with judgment. And we bear witness to the judgment not only when we acknowledge it (e.g., Albert Camus, *The Fall*) but also—and perhaps more generally—as we try to erect and maintain defenses against it.[24]

The brokenness of our relationship with ourself appears in what we call mental illness. Ernest Becker observes that sin and neurosis are two ways of talking about the same thing: the complete isolation of the individual, his or her disharmony with the rest of nature, "hyperindividualism," and the corresponding attempt to create one's own world from within himself. Sin and neurosis both represent individuals' blowing themselves up to larger than their true size, their refusal to recognize their "cosmic dependence."[25]

All the harmony which God had created within us and in the network of our other relationships fell into dissonance when God's human creatures refused to play their parts and rejected God's score for life. Dissonance may sound great for a time as a defiant exercise of human independence and individualism. But ultimately the dissonance produces despair, on one side of the grave and/or the other, and eventually this dissonance convinces us that life is not being conducted properly. Despair will only result in finding some new source for identity, security, and meaning when the old one wears thin.

Each of us can go through any number of cycles of despairing of old gods and then forming new ones for new needs. We may struggle mightily to keep the old gods in good repair, bailing water ever faster in a losing battle to be able to patch a ship which will not keep us afloat. Or we flit from a false meaning and a phony security system of one kind to a phony philosophy and a false safety net of another kind with increasing frequency, always barely satisfied with the new gods which we have fashioned. But, as Saint Augustine observed, we are restless until we rest in God.

We may be so good at creating means of coping or at fooling ourselves that we never despair of our false gods and never encounter the despair which those gods have repressed for us until death. Whatever the individual pattern for this kind of existence may be, the end of the life which errs from the mark of devotion to the Creator is death. This is not just its reward (Rom. 6:23), but its inevitable end. Life was meant to be lived in communion with the Author of life. Our first doubt of His Word created death. Our first defiant denial of His lordship invited death. Our first disobedience embraced death. Our first desire to produce dissonance and our first delight in it set in inexorable progress the march of death.

Adam cast off the image of God to seek a new god in his own image, and in so doing he threw life away![26] The god which issues from his own miscreating hand has no source of life itself, and it therefore certainly cannot give life. The rebellion of human defiance against God has won death as its reward. When we miss the mark which God has set for life, beginning with a relationship of mutual love and favor with Him, we have missed life itself. "There is thus a double interconnection between sin and death: the power of death depends on sin, but the power of sin also depends on death. The necessity of self-preservation which forces man to seek idols springs from the threat of death, and from man's fear of the threat of death"[27] (1 Cor. 15:56). Death grows out of our rejection of the Author of life.

Death leads to damnation. Death confirms forever our decision to separate ourselves from the Author of life.[28] In defying God we seek to become the light of the world and end up in outer darkness, in weeping and gnashing of teeth (Matt. 22:13). The judgment of condemnation for our breaking out of the relationship which God established between Himself and us haunts our existence because we recognize our responsibility for the breach. God's final judgment of death and damnation only confirms our own decision to live apart from Him.

In Christian witness, we work with victims of doubt, perpetrators of defiance, experts at denial. They have had to lie to themselves about the realities of their lives, and they will not know how to speak the truth with us either. Sensitive listening and sympathetic conversation are the only approaches which we can expect to bear fruit—even though the Holy Spirit can even work sometimes through our insensitive reactions. This sympathy and sensitivity is born of our own honest assessment of our own sinfulness, for we recognize that we, too, have engaged in such doubt and denial. We recognize that we continue to lie to ourselves and deny God's loving lordship—even though we know better.

HUMAN RESPONSIBILITY, GOD'S WRATH, AND THE LAW

Recognition of our own responsibility is called guilt. We usually use the term to denote our sense of regret over the things we have done wrong in our horizontal relationships: our sins against commandments four through 10. We may also see ourselves as guilty of transgressing the Second Commandment with abuse of God's name, and recognize our failure to worship God properly with a feeling of guilt over against the Third Commandment. Still, the guilt of the First Commandment is as unique as that commandment is. This particular guilt recognizes that the evil of the world stems from my failure to be truly human: to function as God created and intended me to function at the very heart of my life—to fear, love, and trust in Him above all.

Our Fall and Our Guilt

Dietrich Bonhoeffer looked at the fall in Eden, then looked at himself and us, and observed three things:

> First, the inconceivability of the act and hence its lack of excuse. The reason for this event cannot be uncovered either in the nature of man, or in that of the creation, or in the nature of the serpent. ... Secondly, this act, from man's point of view, is conclusive. Man cannot go back upon it. ... Thirdly, this act of man whom God created as man and woman is a deed of mankind from which no man can absolve himself. The guilt of the act becomes boundless because no man commits it [only] for himself but each man is guilty of the deed of the other. ... Adam falls because of Eve, Eve because of Adam.[29]

All three points are important for Christian witness. First, no explanation for the Fall is possible. How sin could invade the creation of a good and all-powerful God will not be explained within the context of the Fall. Second, there is no other help than death to the life of sin and rebirth as a child of God. No compromises with the necessity of this death are possible. Third, no one sins as an individual even though we individually bear the weight of our sin. But just as all fell in Adam's fall, so we are still falling all over each other in sinful defensiveness. The defensiveness of our self-centeredness invites and provokes defensiveness in others.

Our sense of responsibility, which had been a good feeling of freedom for service to Creator and creation, has turned upon us. It has become a feeling of guilt which bedevils us, even when we suppress and ignore it. At its root guilt is more than being forced to acknowledge responsibility for the sins of the day: guilt acknowledges responsibility for exercising "freedom" against God, for evil itself. My guilt recognizes that my sin is

> revolt, ... the creature's departure from ... the only possible attitude for him; ... the creature's becoming creator, ... the destruction of creatureliness, ... defection, ... a fall from being held in creatureliness, ... a continual falling, a plunging into bottomless depths, a being relinquished, a withdrawal ever farther and deeper. And in all this it is not simply a moral lapse but the destruction of creation by the creature.[30]

That guilt overwhelms; it pronounces the death sentence upon us. This is why we usually become shortsighted when it comes to seeing our guilt and look only at commandments two through 10.

Guilt over against the First Commandment recognizes the justice of the wrath of God. God's wrath can be perceived as chunks of the structure of life falling upon us in the course of trouble and tragedy in daily life (Rom. 1:18; 4:15). The human fall pulls parts of God's world and the structure which He created for it in on top of us, and we suffer the natural consequences of this.

Behind these consequences stands God's wrath, clearly visible when we look squarely at His command that we have no other gods before Him and there discern that God can have but one reaction to the destruction of His prized creature, the human me: "Toward the creature-sinner, the Creator has neither benign indifference nor abstracted regulations. He has a zeal for righteousness. He has wrath. The creature cannot escape by blaming another (Adam, Eve, parents, society). Neither will the Manichaean escape work: God hates the sin but not the sinner."[31] Guilt engulfs my whole person, me as well as my actions, for I recognize that my actions arise from my being, now a broken being in the midst of the relationships which I have broken.

Coming from a knowledge of God in the Scriptures, the believer will not find this entire concept of sin and guilt surprising or new. As we address the unbelievers around us, we must recognize that they do not have the biblical insight into what lies at the root and heart of evil. On the North American continent people are seeing mounting evidence that something has gone wrong, and some feel fearful, and perhaps even guilty, about some wrong or another. The sharply-focused biblical analysis of what is wrong "is not accessible to human wit, reason, or science. Such knowledge is by the revelation of God." Biblical insight into the origin of sin, the root of personal sinfulness, is indeed a diagnostic tool. But much more than that, "it is a confessional presupposition, in response to revelation."[32]

God's Structures for Human Life

The Christian witness has God's plan for life as a diagnostic tool for what is wrong with human life. The structure which He created for its harmonious functioning is revealed in the Scriptures, for instance, in the Ten Commandments. It is also perceivable in the responsibilities of the situations in which God has placed His human creatures: in home, occupation, society, and congregation. It is perceivable from within us, through conscience and reason. God's structure for living forces us to perceive it at times even when we do not wish to see it, because it can be stretched only so far before it bounces back and sends us reeling under the impact of disease, dismay, degradation, or death.

This structure acts as God's Law. God created structure for human life in order to ensure that it would work well for us. Because we have defied God and His plan for human living, His Law has become an expression of His wrath. It restricts what we would like to do with our existence in order to feel secure and thus fabricate some meaning of our own and a new identity for ourselves. It constricts our own plans for existence. Its hostile judgment now pronounces us dead because it shows our responsibility for evil. Sin has even turned our relationship with God's Law or structure upside down. In Eden we stood upon the structure of the Law, looking only to God, with life planted securely upon God's good structure. In turning our world upside down, so that we might stand over God, we thereby fell under the Law. It crowds us now; it crushes us.

God's Law Curbs

The Law functions first to keep us in line, to curb us from going too far in breaking out of God's structure. It limits the destructive urge of our rebellion against God. It preserves some semblance of the original order which God designed to protect and nourish His creation; it must now try to protect the creation from the human creature. What was designed to function as an instrument of human freedom has been forced to serve as an instrument to compel human responsibility.

This function of the Law serves us only in our horizontal relationships. The Law cannot force any semblance of love and trust in our vertical relationship with our Father. It can only compel or entice us, with its threats of punishment or offers of reward, to conform externally, to one degree or another, with God's plan for our horizontal relationships with other human creatures and with nature. Thus, God's plan still works for good in the horizontal plane, even if it works only external compliance. The compliance it enforces is not necessarily begrudging, even if it always does arise from other motives than pure fear, love, and trust of the Creator.

External conformity to God's plan for human living does make sense to people who analyze the working of human interaction well. It makes sense for the sake of the world and for its people, both of whom may command our high regard as we seek to construct security and meaning for ourselves. In addition, for those who are less than altruistic in constructing plans for existence, enlightened self-interest spurs more people to deeds of what theologians call "civil righteousness," externally correct actions in the horizontal plane of existence, than does the fear of getting caught by the police. Some may defy the Law with glee to assert their own autonomy, but others feel comfortable with its blandishments and enticements, which hold out the promise of the good life to those who keep it. Still others respond to the Law in a fear that wrings obedience out of them.

Whatever the motivation for striving to keep the Law, the outward actions produced by the curbing, or societal, force of the Law are to be evaluated, as outward actions, as good. They are certainly better than the alternatives, in actions against God's plan for living, and they also build a human society in a positive form and keep the worst of external evils from that society. However, this societal function of the Law cannot do anything about the worst of all evils, the brokenness of the vertical relationship which has separated the human creature from God.

The societal function of the Law is easily misunderstood as a device which can contribute to restoring the creature's relationship with the Creator. Here is the root of the lie common to false religion, that we can earn the favor of God by doing good to others. God created His structure; the structure itself is a creature. In relation to the fallen human creature this structure, codified as Law, functions as an instrument of enforcement and evaluation. It cannot motivate true service to God, and it certainly cannot exercise the function of giving and preserving true life with Him, a function reserved by the Creator for Himself alone. When we believe that the Law can give life to those who conform to it, then we have misrepresented the Law and created an idol. Even if we kept it perfectly, we would enjoy the good life only because of the gracious will of our merciful and gracious God.

Life comes from God Himself alone, in our vertical relationship of His favor toward us and our trust in Him. The Law has different functions than the giving of life. Thus, even though the deeds of human creatures which comply externally with His plan for living are useful and good on the horizontal plane, they are risky if they are viewed as contributions to the restoration of the vertical relationship which is basic to genuine life.[33]

> The Decalog does not tell us positively what might bring about membership in the covenant, for this is in force already through the decree of Yahweh. It tells us what this membership excludes. … The moral commandments which He lays down for Christians are not designed to produce a status which will dispose them for the grace of justification. Grace has already been imparted in Christ, just as institution of the covenant preceded the Law.[34]

In dealing with the functions of the Law it is absolutely necessary to keep straight on which plane, in which set of relationships, the Law was designed to perform what it now performs.

God's Law Crushes

The Law does perform a second function in regard to our vertical relationship; namely, it accuses and condemns. It crushes. It crushes the life out of sinners. It holds a mirror before us and displays both the symptoms of our broken horizontal relationships and their cause in our broken vertical relationship. Adam's fall transformed his relationship with the structure which had placed his life within the bounds of God's goodness.

> Now that he has transgressed the limit, he knows for the first time that he was limited. At the same time he no longer accepts the

limit as the grace of God the Creator but hates it, looking upon it as the envy of God the Creator. In the same act he has transgressed the limit the other person had embodied for him. Now he no longer sees the limit of the other person as grace but as the wrath, the hatred, the envy of God.[35]

The Law has become our adversary. It never ceases to perform that function of evaluation, and thus of condemnation, so long as sin clings to the human creature. Whatever else it may do, it always accuses; it always crushes.[36] It cannot do anything but condemn us sinners.

While we still rely on other gods, the Law cannot but encourage and fuel in us a negative response, a resentment against God's wrath. The Law provokes the sinner, who envies God and who at the same time strives to be like Him, to hate God. Helmut Thielicke observes,

> Paul especially perceives the more negative character of the law. When sin is in a state of incubation, the law makes it virulent. It thus has the function of a starting impulse (*aphorme,* Romans 7:5, 8). For Luther the true and proper use of the law, its real office, is that by the law sin should grow and become great, and that man should thus be shown his sins, weakness, blindness, death, hell, the thunder and lightning of God's wrath.[37]

Just as Christian conversation can seldom begin with the believer's discourse on doubt as the fundamental cause of the human break from the good life, so also we cannot begin to talk about an unbeliever's problems by placing them directly in the context of his or her hatred for God. This biblical perspective on what is wrong with the world and with us as individual human creatures lies first of all in the realm of presupposition, and later in the realm of Christian instruction. The liberation from sin's grip must come to terms finally with my hatred for God, my doubt of His Word, my defiance of His lordship. As long as I have to hang onto my own gods for security and meaning, I cannot be so honest with myself that I admit hating God. I cannot blame myself for the fundamental fault and flaw of my existence if I still must count on my own powers or my own decisions to insure my identity. Thus, Christian conversation often begins with the symptoms, the actual sins of daily disobedience and the tangible, perceptible evils of daily life in the midst of tragedy and trouble. In many instances, original sin can be addressed only later, when the sinner has once again begun to listen to the Word of the Lord. When the symptoms of sin have made their mark on our hearers, they may be ready to move quickly to the diagnosis of the root of their problem in the vertical relationship of their lives.

Christian Witness to the Law

Must Christian conversation begin with the negative, with the judgment of the Law's evaluation of the fallen creature? Why do you want to know? If the question is asked regarding the very first words which a believer speaks in a relationship with an unbeliever, then the answer is "no." The believer can only begin to develop the unbeliever's perception of what is wrong with life, and why, when some modicum of personal trust exists between the two. Plunging into the negative at once is not likely to encourage that relationship which is basic for Christian conversation. If, however, the question is theological and not just a question of personal dynamics and evangelistic tactics, then the answer must be "yes." The sick person must become convinced that he or she is ill before seeking treatment. The goodness of God in Jesus Christ, in His death and resurrection, cannot make sense to people who have enough goodness at hand in their self-formed gods, or in their self-constructed systems for security and meaning, to cope with life and to feel comfortable with their existence. Law must precede Gospel. The burden must be felt before our hearers will want to have Jesus lift it from them.

This is a theological order and not necessarily in every case a chronological schedule. The unbeliever may feel no need to replace an old security system and to seek a new identity in Jesus Christ but may nonetheless be intrigued enough by the story of Christ to pursue conversation with a believer. The Gospel narrative may open the door to a conversation regarding sin and evil, in which the Law begins to crack the old security system and sufficiently question the former explanation for the way things are, so that these old gods begin to give way. But as long as the old gods continue to function as sources of identity, security, and meaning, God has no place in a person's life, and there is no need to hear His life-giving Word.

However, in many cases the despairing unbeliever cannot face honestly the full significance of the fallen creature's defiance of the Creator. Only from the perspective of Christ's cross, and conscious of the protection against our own doubt and denial of God's lordship which the Crucified One provides, can we confront the depth and breadth of the evil within us. The Gospel will open the human heart and mind to be able to recognize and confess more fully the devastating effects and destructive source of personal sinfulness.

Some Christians suggest that life has so worsened on this continent that we do not need to point out the judgment of God's structure for human life because condemnation and judgment are so plain in our world. Indeed, many more people are openly hurting from family strife, broken dreams, criminal activities, and the senselessness of what existence amounts to than ever before. Yet the North American corner of the world still offers a great deal of security. Its way of life has a way of explaining itself quite cogently. Identities can still be forged with relative ease for many of us. It is not at all obvious in many people's lives that life is broken at its heart. The symptoms of our sin can be suppressed and glossed over for shorter or longer periods without great difficulty for many comfortable Americans. Christian witnesses must often spend time patiently diagnosing the fatal flaws of their hearers' old gods.

Other Christians suggest that the believer ought to leave judgment to God (Matt. 7:1) and simply put on a happy face. But God has commissioned His reborn people to retain sin, that is, to pronounce judgment in His place (Matt. 16:19; 18:18; John 20:23). We would hold someone criminally culpable who failed to warn a blind person at a street corner of an oncoming vehicle as he was about to step in front of it. We must hold ourselves spiritually culpable if we let an acquaintance flirt with eternal death without giving warning. Alan Paton's novel *Too Late the Phalarope* is entitled *I Never Spoke the Word* in its German translation. This tale of the ruin of a man and his family through his moral and social shipwreck begins with the words of his aunt, "Perhaps I could have saved him, with only a word, two words, out of my mouth. Perhaps I could have saved us all. But I never spoke them. ... I *held,* in the strange words of the English, *I held my peace.*[38] Her refusal to call her nephew to turn from evil destroyed their peace, or rather prevented its reconstruction. Beyond warning, believers are also commissioned to preach the Law to the sinner, to pronounce the threat of God's punishment, and finally to retain sins, to pronounce the fact of God's retribution upon specific sinners.

In some instances the believer who succeeds in breaking the sinner's old gods may have had to speak so sharply that another believer must take his or her place in continuing Christian witness. Ideally, the broken sinner should be grateful for the destruction of old, unworkable gods, but the clash of personalities in some instances of witness to the Law may make it impossible for the same believer—who effectively brought death to a sinner's old idols—to speak the Word of life with effective power. This is why Christian witness is an enterprise of the people of God, not only of the individual person in the congregation of His people.

Responsible Christian witness includes witness to the condemning judgment of God's structure for human living. Our Lord has commissioned us for this task, and the unbelieving neighbor needs to have this task performed.

WHY?

Before focusing more precisely on how the believer assists the unbeliever in recognizing the meaning of evil's assaults from within and without, we turn to another problem involved in many discussions of sin and evil, the problem of theodicy. Theodicy is defined as the attempt to vindicate the justice of God in ordaining or permitting natural and moral evil. The term comes from the 18th-century philosopher Gotthold Ephraim Lessing. The effort itself is much older. *But it is an effort in which the biblical writers did not indulge.* As often as they recognized and posed the question of God's justice, they refused to forge an answer, for they did not believe that God must justify Himself to His creatures. His fallen creatures continue to wonder, however, why evil assaults them. Nonetheless, people caught in the crushing use of evil vices want to know "how come?"— "how does it come to this if there really is a good and almighty God?"

For the hints of the destruction which we have visited upon our once-harmonious relationships tease at us in the course of daily living. We try to drown out the dissonance of disobedient living, and we may succeed for a time. Yet crises do arise, and troubles do appear. Rumors shake the solid facade of the plans constructed successfully for a time, and cracks creep across those facades. We ask, "Why?" "Why did it have to happen to me?" "Why did my baby die?" "What did he do to deserve that?" "Why should she be the victim?" "Why?"

We ask, with Jesus' contemporaries (Luke 13:1–5), "Why did the Galileans whose blood Pilate had mingled with their sacrifices have to die? Did they sin more grievously than others?" "Why did the 18 upon whom the tower of Siloam fell have to die? Was it because they were worse offenders than all the others who dwelt in Jerusalem?" "Why did the neighbor boy fall from the top of the local grain elevator and now is doomed to the life of a paraplegic? Did he sin, or did his parents?" "Why does my sister have to live with the scars of both mind and body which resulted when she fell asleep at the wheel, strayed across the median, and killed the mother, father, and two small children in the other car? Certainly she did not bring that upon herself by being worse than—well, say, (the sinking feeling drives us to the brink of despair) I am?" "No," Jesus replies. He then directs our gaze away from the victim of evil to ourselves. He refuses the explanation for which we are begging. He says simply, "Unless you repent, you will perish."

The struggle with such questions is at least as intense when it concerns my own life. When the question returns to me and to the evil with which I am wrestling, "Why me? Why should I be the victim?" He has the same response. He focuses the attention at first more determinedly than ever upon the evil and upon ourselves, locked as one in the struggle for life. He repeats, "Unless this changes, you will perish." We shout our response, "I realize that. But why?" And He will not answer.

This is, of course, not completely true. The eyes of faith see that ultimately God does work out evils in our lives for His good and ours (Rom. 8:28). The muscles of the Christian life are repeatedly strengthened by engagements with various kinds of evil, from doubt to multiple forms of disaster. Furthermore, there can be no doubt about God's strict and steadfast opposition to and abhorrence of evil. Habakkuk pounded on God's door with the question, "O Lord, how long shall I cry for help and thou wilt not hear?" (1:2). In his struggle against evil, he heard the Lord pronounce His "woe" upon those who perpetrate every form of evil (ch. 2). Francis Schaeffer summarizes God's reaction to the invasion of death into His humanity. Commenting on Jesus' reaction to Lazarus' death (John 11:33), he writes, "The one who claims to be God stood before the tomb, and the Greek language makes it very plain that he had two emotions. The first was tears for Lazarus; but the second emotion was blinding anger. He was furious; and He could be furious at the evil of death without being furious with Himself as God."[39] God is not responsible for evil, nor does He find it in any way attractive or good. We confess that, but we still wonder why there has to be— how there can be—evil in the first place in a world created by a good and almighty Father.

Attempts at Answers

Theologians and philosophers have devised all sorts of answers, some in defiance of God and some in an attempt to help Him out and save His reputation. "Today the God-remodelers are a dime a dozen. Everyone, it seems, wants to do God the favor of making Him less objectionable."[40]

The ancient Manichaeans said that evil exists because there are two eternal principles, one good and one evil, and they are locked in eternal combat. There really is not much help for us who suffer evil according to this viewpoint, for evil is as strong as good under the Manichaean explanation of life.[41] The ancient Gnostics suggested that evil exists in the material creation per se, but that not only contradicts God's insistence that His material creation is good; it also seems to indicate that deliverance lies only in the complete obliteration of life as we know it, in which, whatever we are, we are unable to separate the material and non-material elements of which we are composed.

Some would tell us today that evil is simply the way it is and there is no way out. Still, however, from the back of our minds comes a faint memory of what it must have been like when we trusted God and knew that life was good. Others would suggest that evil simply does not exist, that it is only an illusion or a delusion. We are able to laugh at evil only until it really hurts. Laughter's anesthetic effects have their limits.

Over the past two centuries our society has tried to dismiss evil as largely overrated. Based upon the ideology of the Enlightenment, which placed supreme confidence in the human capacity to forge the good, this point of view expects that the blessing of modern technology and contemporary investigation and mastery of nature will combine with the exercise of human autonomy to create the good life for the continent and the world.

Even Christians in North America have been captivated by the American dream of continuing human progress. "The basic thrust of [Norman Vincent] Peale's 'modernism' is the same as [Billy] Graham's 'Biblicism.' It is to alleviate and remove the experience of negation." North American Christianity has largely been "unable to entertain an *unresolved* negative."[42] Some Christians struggle to promise only the positive to their hearers, and they thus make Christian faith some magic amulet for warding off whatever seems unpleasant in the world. When a Christian makes that kind of offer to the unbeliever, he can take himself off the hook when the goods are not delivered by blaming the hearer's failure "to *really* believe" (whatever that means) for the absence of the expected blessing. The result is that "in that zeal for identification with the expectations of the most expectant epoch in the history of mankind, the dominant Christianity of the West—especially highlighted in North America— became a stranger to the age-old experiences of mankind: the experiences of guilt and judgment; of tragedy, chaos, failure; of despair and death; of the whole range of negation."[43] This evades the charge of our Lord that we lift the crosses of others, that we bring His presence in the form of the love, care, and concern He has taught us to those who confront evil. It evades His call to suffer with those who suffer just as *He* has suffered for them and us. It may be safer to attempt to testify of our faith from a distance, from a secure spot insulated from the sufferings of our neighbors, in our own self-devised capsule protected against the bone-grinding, soul-wrenching dilemmas of lives not anchored in Jesus Christ. That is not God's design for our lives, however, nor does it match His appraisal of the way evil must be confronted in a fallen world.

Christians have also often talked about the permissive will of God. With this term we seek to excuse God for evil, a proper exercise indeed, but the term can also divert us from looking squarely at evil and taking it as seriously as we must. "God does not want evil; He does not will evil," we correctly affirm, and then we decide, "He only permits it." This does not make God look any better to me as I suffer. Whether the Almighty inflicted this upon me in person or simply gave another license to put me to the test, I still suffer, as Job did. We still want to know, even of God's permissive will, "Why?"

Manifesting the Presence of God

The answer of the biblical writers was paraphrased by Philip Melanchthon nearly a half millennium ago: "It is taught among us that although almighty God has created and still preserves nature, yet sin is caused in all wicked men and despisers of God by the perverted will. This is the will of the devil and of all ungodly men; as soon as God withdraws his support, the will turns away from God to evil."[44] Evil comes upon us because we are evil. We suffer evil because we have doubted and defied God.

It may be said that this answer begs the real question. Further questions remain. Why did the almighty God not use His power to fashion a creature who would not be susceptible to evil? How could a good God not fashion a creature who would be immune to evil? The 19th-century art historian Charles Pierre Baudelaire observed that "if there is a God, He is the Devil," and Francis Schaeffer finds that Baudelaire's judgment makes sense if "there is an unbroken line between what man is now and what he has always intrinsically been."[45] There is not, of course, for all the lines about us were broken by our doubt and defiance of God.

Even when we ascribe the presence of evil in human life to human defiance of the goodness of the Creator, we have not solved the logical problem involved in affirming that God is both good and almighty at the same time we acknowledge the existence of evil.

100

Archibald MacLeish, in his play *J.B.*, drove the question of the origin of evil to its logical conclusion. His character Nickles sings:

> I heard upon his dry dung heap
> That man cry out who could not sleep:
> "If God is God, he is not good;
> If God is good, he is not God."[46]

Human logic and human experience drive people to that point.

We may argue, as suggested above in the discussion of human freedom in the context of a Creator-centered theology, that God had to give us enough freedom "to fulfill our humanity." The fact remains that human freedom is freedom in relationship; it is freedom created, and thus conditioned, by God. It must be "freedom from evil" and "freedom for service." It cannot be "freedom against" the Creator if it is to be genuine human freedom. Freedom exercised in defiance of God does not fulfill our humanity. It pulls the plug; it drains us of our humanity and destroys us as human creatures. In rescuing us from evil, the ultimate evil of alienation from Himself, God does not just make us a good offer and hope that we will exercise (an actually non-existent) "freedom of choice" which will turn us back to Himself "of our own free will." He re-creates us. He transforms us, through functioning psyches, to be sure, but exclusively by the power of His gracious and merciful hand. The only solution, the only cure, for freedom exercised against the Creator is a new creation. The Word of life must be spoken anew, as the Word made flesh, in order to remedy our rejection of God and to restore us to truly human life. It makes utterly no sense to argue that evil exists so that we might have had the opportunity to fulfill our humanity, for that "opportunity" could have only one result, to ruin us and deprive us of true life. To argue so is to assert that God made a miscalculation here which finally cost Him His life on the cross.

We can—indeed, we must—attempt to place evil in a larger context of meaning for people entrapped by it. Yet, however we explain it, if one is able, or is forced, to be brutally honest with himself, he will see that behind our explanations the void still lurks and chaos still churns. Then he may catch a glimpse of the fact that explanation is not the point. Christian conversation about the origin of evil functions only to confirm for us that evil exists and that we feel in some measure or other responsible for it, at the same time we feel caught as its victim. "Unless things change, unless you change, you will perish."

Jesus faced the question in another form when He and His disciples encountered the blind man (John 9:1–5): "Who sinned, this man or his parents?" Jesus again avoided the question of the origin of evil. He assured His disciples that the man's blindness was not due to his own sin or that of his parents, but rather "that the works of God might be made manifest in him." We might debate whether Jesus intended to say that the purpose or plan of God was to blind this man for His own glorification, an idea more horrific to us than to God's Old Testament people. We would prefer to say that the Lord's words simply affirm that the result of the blindness is that an occasion is given in this man to see the saving work of God at close hand. The underlying premise which He advanced in either case is that God is indeed at work in the midst of this evil. He will not leave His people alone but will sustain them when evil attacks, whether that evil can be traced to human sin or Satanic initiative.

People ask about the origin of evil for various reasons. Some may wonder about the reason for evil simply because they want to know; they are curious about questions which defy the philosophers. One of life's ultimate and most important questions certainly is, "why is there evil in the world?" Some find the question a good one to use to bedevil pious people of any religion. But most people ask because they are curious not so much about the origin of evil but rather about its outcome. We ask "why?" because we are trapped under the impact of evil in some specific form. We ask "why?" because if we can prove that we do not deserve it, we should be able to escape it—if there is any justice in the world. We ask "why?" because if we know where evil comes from, we figure we ought to be able to calculate where evil is going, or how we can get it going out of our lives. Or, if even that lies beyond our beleaguered ability to hope, we at least want to know how to cope with evil, how to endure it, how to bear it with sufficient courage, grace, and grit to survive.

This puts the nagging question "why?" in a different context as we consider its significance for Christian witness. When those whose lives we touch demand from us an answer to their question, "why me?" or " why her?" we will begin the process of witness by putting the question and the problem in which it is framed in better focus, finding out precisely why they want to know. Then we will be able to focus the answer we have to give into the framework in which Christ placed it as He said, "Things have to change; you have to change." "Why?" invites us once again to focus on ourselves and our problems. All our problems originate from that first "successful" attempt to refocus our lives upon ourselves. "Why?" only intensifies the introspection which curves us again in upon ourselves, even when we struggle to make it curve outward against God and others, whom we want to blame for our evil. "Why?" begs the ultimate question, "who?" "Who is in charge here?" "Who is really trustworthy?" Thus, God's only reply can be to beg the question "why?"

When the believer trusts that God has intervened in His own flesh to transform our lives and now is present to provide on the basis of His goodness and power, then he "believes against the law, against destiny, against fate, against contradiction. Even more: he trusts against God, against the hidden God, against the God of law and destiny because he trusts in Him who is revealed in His Son and calls us to reconciliation with Him."[47] Such trust in the midst of and in spite of evil can be cultivated by Christian witnesses only when we turn our hearers from the "why?" to the "who?" of their dilemmas. This can be accomplished only through the combined demonstration of God's love in the care and concern of the witnessing believer, and through the articulation of the biblical answer to evil's ultimate power in Jesus Christ.

For instance, in comforting a grief-stricken fellow believer, there are two things which a Christian must remember. The first is that nothing we can say is going to stop the flood of tears and the torture of grief immediately; our presence may be all we can offer at certain moments of grief. But our presence provides great comfort; it provides the presence of God. The second thing to remember in such a situation is that we must speak the Gospel, for even though the Gospel may at first elicit anger or a more intense expression of grief, the repeated articulation of God's love in Jesus Christ does alter the framework in which our hearers view life. But this goodness must never be a generic, superficial, "put on a happy face" kind of Gospel. It must be the Gospel of a God who grieves over evil, who joins us in the flesh under its tyranny, but who has promised and already procured the final triumph over evil. Thus, when we are beginning the process of witnessing, we will remember that both our unspeaking presence and our unexplained demonstration of love, on the one hand, and our clear expression of God's Word on the other are extremely important, each at the appropriate times. In such situations we project the model of God's intervention against evil in our own presence which assists the other person in the struggle against evil. We project the model of human trust in the God who provides through our faith as we turn to God in prayer.

Finally, we must also explain—and for people who have no experience with the Gospel explain repeatedly—why we are able to love and trust as we do. "That faith that God provides, which lives on the basis of the gospel, does not refer to what happened to others, not to paradigms for what happens, nor, least of all, theories about what ought to happen. That faith is the 'here' of the human creature,"[48] who intervenes and makes the presence of God felt in the midst of evil, under the cross of whatever kind of tribulation, trauma, or tragedy afflicts our neighbor. That presence is to be felt in specific situations and in specific ways in the lives of those who have found their own gods wanting and whose despair has prepared them for the intervention of Jesus Christ. Believers must learn how to deal with and speak to those situations so that they may bring the Deliverer and Re-creator of life into clear focus in the midst of the blinding force of evil.

APPROACHING SIN AND EVIL IN THE UNBELIEVER'S LIFE[49]

Relatively few conversations with unbelievers begin with ultimate questions, although hurting people may move on to them fairly quickly. In front of questions regarding the origin of our problems with respect to false sources of identity, security, and meaning, lie a number of *categories* into which people sort their problems. The list we shall discuss here is not exhaustive; no single one of these categories occurs alone in most people's lives. But such a review serves as a reminder that we dare not limit our view of what goes wrong with human living merely to sins such as murder, adultery, stealing, and lying. More importantly, as witnesses to the Gospel we must be sensitive and responsive to the much wider range of evils which befall us after the Fall, and to the depth of this Gospel which brings the good news of Christ's conquering evil to bear on evil's every form.

Unbelievers very often encounter evil without defining it, or its impact in their lives, in terms of what they do wrong. As believers begin Christian conversations, they must be aware that their hearers conceptualize what is wrong in the world in a variety of ways, all of which can provide the starting point for an examination and evaluation of the false gods of the hearer's life. Believers must be able to analyze not only those problems which lie heavily on the consciousness of their hearers who are faced with broken or breaking gods; they must also analyze the defenses of unbelievers who are secure with their old gods. These people may not always be as comfortable as they would like. Their gods may not be functioning as adequately as they ideally should to provide a totally secure sense of identity. Nonetheless, they are not yet ready to give up on these sources of security and meaning because they know no better alternatives. Thus, the believer must analyze their thought to ascertain how best to bring them to the conscious realization that these gods offer no security or comfort in the midst of life. In this chapter we shall only point toward specific approaches to use in the process of restoring broken sinners through the Gospel.

As we discuss the following categories of the impact of evil (see the chart on page 122) we shall note that sinners react to them in two basic ways, either from a stance of security, as long as old gods provide security, or from a stance of brokenness moving toward despair, when the old gods no longer work. Christian witness involves both assisting the secure sinner to perceive that the old gods provide false security and aiding the broken sinner in perceiving that God provides true security and genuine meaning for life.

The Evil from Outside Us

Many people attribute what is wrong in their lives fundamentally to evils outside themselves. They do so with good reason. First, that excuses them from having to deal with responsibility for evil in addition to the evil itself, and that is no small advantage. Second, evil beyond the control of the individual exists, and holds tremendous potential for driving us to despair. Evils assault us from two directions outside ourselves, from nature and from other human creatures. The nature which groans under the weight of sin (Rom. 8:22) lets us know about its discomfort, and fires, floods, and disease have from earliest times afflicted us (Ps. 46:1–3; 69:1–3). The animals which were placed in our dominion evade and attack us.

Even when we try to do our best by nature and to use our technology or knowledge to solve problems, nature still turns on us. For example, the use of pesticides and chemical fertilizers has contributed to the battle against starvation for many and has markedly improved the quality of life for many more, but those chemical aids have also placed carcinogens into the food chain, and these cancer-causing elements have taken their toll in our bodies. Even with the technology which aids us in limiting the effects of fire, flood, drought, excessive wind, and nature's other evils, we still become victims of its aggressive power from time to time.

People assault us as well, sometimes intentionally, as they seek their own security at our expense; and sometimes unintentionally, so absorbed by their own needs that they notice neither us nor our needs. Human assaults on other human creatures may come in organized form, as in war, genocide, massive political detention and torture, or in a more individualized form, such as street mugging, arson, prejudice, blacklisting, or innuendo. We may blunder into some evils by playing with matches or taking a walk down an alley at 2 A.M. We may set ourselves up for other evils because our expectations from life exceed what human experience should tell us is reasonable to expect.[50] Or we may be at the receiving end of these evils simply because tornadoes move across our landscape, or we are born Jewish or black or poor or female.

The secure sinner has the luxury of raging against those evils and plotting redress or revenge. It is sometimes difficult to get revenge on the people who have attacked us, and there is never much we can do to show the inanimate forces of hurricane or drought that injustice has been done us. The inner rage which must assert our identity as master and lord turns against whoever is within reach and weaker than we are. Pride and self-concern take shape in personal tyranny and cruelty against a weaker sibling or neighbor. When evil is perpetrated by a person whom we can attack, perhaps a boss who has us fired, the plotting of the revenge which will prove who really is the better man consumes the plotter. The revenge is designed to assert my mastery over him, but most often the plotting possesses me and leads me about as if I had a ring through my nose. The compulsion to right the evils against me becomes my lord. For the secure sinner it is mandatory that the compulsion exert that kind of influence, because one's security, meaning for life, and very identity depend upon the assertion of one's own ability to defend and to care for him or herself.

Human rage may try to defy the assaults of evil with self-assertions which are not outward-directed in revenge but inward-directed toward self-satisfaction, a reward given to ourselves to compensate for all that we imagine we have suffered, or that we might suffer in the future. Ernest Becker labels this "defiant self-creation" and calls it demonic. He gives examples:

> We are witness to the new cult of sensuality that seems to be repeating the sexual naturalism of the ancient world. It is a living for the day alone, with a defiance of tomorrow; an immersion in the body and its immediate experiences and sensations, in the intensity of touch, swelling flesh, taste and smell. Its aim is to deny one's lack of control over events, his powerlessness, his vagueness as a person in a mechanical world spinning into decay and death. ... Socially, too, we have seen a defiant Promethianism that is basically innocuous; the confident power that can catapult man to the moon and free him somewhat of his complete dependence and confinement on earth—at least in his imagination. The ugly side of this Promethianism is that it, too, is thoughtless, an empty-headed immersion in the delights of technics with no thought to goal or meaning. ... On more ominous levels ... modern man's defiance of accident, evil, and death takes the form of sky-rocketing production of consumer and military goods. Carried to its demonic extreme this defiance gave us Hitler and Vietnam; a rage against our impotence, a defiance of our animal condition, our

pathetic creature limitations. If we don't have the omnipotence
of gods, we at least can destroy like gods.[51]

The believer will be able to point out to the sinner whose security rests in raging defiance against a sense of impotence that its cause lies not in an "animal condition" or "creaturely limitation" but rather in the curse of sin. Becker's analysis demonstrates how interrelated are the categories into which we place the impacts of evil. Evil outside myself generates a sense of meaninglessness and acts of disobedience, two other ways in which sin makes its impact upon me, in its very process of generating rage against the evil beyond my control. The structure of God's world or the power of evil may force the raging resister of evil outside himself to confront the powerlessness of the sinful human creature. God's shape for life, or evil's transgression of it, may finally awaken the person who held off evil with studied apathetic indifference to the fact that this very evil *has* the power to triumph. The believer may hasten the necessary realization of evil's might and human impotence through a conversation which focuses on the threat of the former and the dilemma of the latter. The believer may have to wait, cultivating a friendship which seeks to befriend without pushing the Christian faith down the throat of that friend, awaiting the evil day on which the death of a loved one, the burning of a home, the loss of a job, or the effects of war force the friend to take a glimpse, however fleeting, of naked impotence. Then the process of the destruction of old gods can begin, perhaps moving quickly, perhaps much more slowly.

In either case, coming to an honest confrontation with my own impotence deprives me of my sense of security and of life's meaning. Even my identity becomes problematic under the shadow of impotence. I have but two alternatives: finding another way to establish identity, security, and meaning in the face of the evils outside me, or dying. The Christian can come to the impotent person with a message of God's power, of His personal presence in Jesus Christ, who confronted all sin and evil in His death and resurrection and who continues to confront it in our lives through the power of His Word and His people.

Alienation or Estrangement

A second category into which people place the result of human sinfulness is alienation or estrangement. As we have previously observed, many in our culture exult in their individualistic prerogatives and freedom from responsibility. Youth flock to Fort Lauderdale in the early spring, Alvin Toffler notes, not just out of an irrepressible passion for sunshine or even for sex but rather because, as one said, "You're not worried about what you do or say here because, frankly, you'll never see these people again."[52] The opposite of a carefree and careless putting of distance between ourselves and others is the pain and agony which loneliness, separation, and divorces of all kinds bring to human creatures who were created for community.

Some alienation arises out of our rejection of the simplest conventions of polite interpersonal behavior. We reject this part of God's structure in an attempt to make ourselves into something bigger than we are, or to protect ourselves against the threat of another personality, whether that threat comes from that person's being too kind or too much of a rival. Such calculated slights or assaults against other people, and against the assignments which the Creator has given us to serve them in the situations of home, occupation, society, or congregation, hurt us as much or more than we manage to hurt those against whom we act.

So often we blindly pursue the alienation that tears us apart as it rends relationships because of fears of obligations, anger over slights, desires to prove we do not need to be dependent—even though that is the way we were made. Solutions abound, of course, in the American marketplace. A host of methods of cultivating happiness have been invented in recent decades, and many of them provide prescriptions for coming to peace with self in the midst of a world of alienation through more intense preoccupation with and consciousness of the self. But

> the trouble with the consciousness movement is not that it addresses trivial or unreal issues but that it provides self-defeating solutions. Arising out of a pervasive dissatisfaction with the quality of personal relationships, it advises people not to make too large an investment in love and friendship, to avoid excessive dependence on others, and to live for the moment—the very con-

ditions that created the crisis of personal relations in the first place.[53]

According to God's plan, however, we reach our full purpose in life only when we make a total investment of ourselves in love and friendship, in serving our Creator by serving the needs of those for whom He has given us responsibilities in home, job, neighborhood and state, and in the congregation of His people.

Others do little to perpetrate alienation, at least as far as they can tell, but simply suffer as its victims. In their suffering they are sorely tempted to lash out in vengeance against those who have taken themselves away. Alienation creates a spiral of savagery against God's structure for human life, against our relationships with other human creatures, and this cannot be separated finally from savagery against ourselves. Estrangement generates and feeds upon itself, creating a loneliness which consumes the individual in his or her isolation. The distrust which characterizes such broken relationships has a built-in stimulus for uncontrolled growth. For example,

> distrustful parents sometimes have reason to be concerned about their children. Untrusted youth often act in ways that cause their parents to trust them even less. ... It is difficult to tell whether parents sense an inclination toward unacceptable behavior and become distrustful or whether the youth, sensing distrust, make deliberate decisions to justify their parents' suspicions. Whether parental distrust or rebellious behavior come first, it is reasonable to say that distrust is a snowball rolling downhill, getting bigger and dirtier as it goes.[54]

Christian conversation with acquaintances who are securely situated in the practice of alienation may begin by exploring the implications of that practice in its drive toward being alone. Believers may point out to the "alienating alienated" that the blows aimed at others somehow also seem to land back on themselves. Sometimes believers must just make themselves available to the neighbor who is accelerating the plunge into alienation. Such a person is usually difficult to befriend and even to maintain contact with. This is the challenge of being a witnessing and caring Christian neighbor.

110

When the alienation becomes so intense that we no longer can strike out against those with whom we should be linked in mutual respect, responsibility, and love, when our calculated aggressive responses to estrangement no longer provide security or make life seem worthwhile, the broken sinner faces the despair of loneliness which engulfs those who have lost their natural ties to another or others. For that kind of person the believer has a message and a model of reconciliation: Jesus Christ, who came to rescue God's prodigal children (Luke 15:11–32) from estrangement and to end all alienation by reconciling us to our Father and to the life which He designed for us in relationship to Himself and to others. We come to build bridges of escape from the bitterness and loneliness of alienation. The building material for such bridges is the body of Christ, the reconciler.

Meaninglessness

A third category of common experience of evil in our time is a sense of meaninglessness. Hans Küng describes the "typical neurosis" of the late 20th century as the "lack of orientation, absence of norms, meaninglessness, futility, and consequently the repression of morality and religious feeling."[55] Europeans in two world wars saw the order and meaning which the positivistic civilization of the 19th century had forged for them disappear, not just in bombs falling from the skies but in vicious hostilities against their neighbors released from their own souls. They concluded with the existentialists that the 20th century human being neither can nor needs to search for meaning anymore; "he accepts the darkness as darkness and maintains an attitude of resignation,"[56] at least so long as this acceptance and resignation provide the modicum of security which is required when one's only meaning in life is that life just will not have meaning. As the century moves toward its close, a number of factors are bringing many North Americans to share this European perception, usually without its sophisticated philosophical trimmings.

This occurs, George Forell argues, because we have lost confidence in ourselves.

But our problem today is the death of man. Since the sixteenth century man has constantly lost significance. First Copernicus removed him from the center of the cosmic stage to some minor planet circling a minor star. Then Darwin took man and brought him into such close proximity to the animals that "man as the measure of all things" has become a statement increasingly obsolete, and the "ape as the measure of all things" would seem more accurate. Then Freud proceeded to show that the former "master of his soul and captain of his fate" is actually determined by a vast subconscious over which he has no control. It is not surprising, but significant, that one of the most popular books with teenagers was at one time *Robinson Crusoe;* it is now *Lord of the Flies.* ... Defoe believed that man could conquer the wilderness and make the desert bloom. Golding tells us that a civilization is a strange interlude and the beast will conquer.[57]

Gustaf Wingren analyzes our refusal to perceive meaning in the world as a reaction, perhaps unconscious, to our failure to provide life with meaning by living out our relationship of trust toward God and love for the neighbor properly. He labels that reaction guilt, which

arises from the fact that none of us lives without having received and benefited from the self-denial of others. We cannot look into our own life without realizing that each of us is called to be a person from whom someone else draws the courage to live. Meaninglessness results when we fail to answer this call and instead burden and spoil other lives. This sense of meaninglessness is the experience of guilt in an unarticulated form. It is the claim made by those natural expressions of life which belong to one's health but which have been lost.[58]

Those who find meaning absent from their lives cannot blame themselves consciously even when they are conscious of their own shortcomings, and therefore they cannot perceive that the world's failure to make sense stems from *their own* lack of understanding.

The world does not make sense to some modern people because they feel frustrated with their own powerlessness to accomplish what they think important. The excuse for my failure may be ascribed to the massiveness of the forces against me, or to my own inability to make anything worthwhile of my potential. The secure sinner may release this frustration in a narcissistic storm of self-indulgence since nothing makes much difference anyway.[59] The secure sinner may enjoy his or her own defiant dedication to specific courses of action in spite of their lack of meaning and take pride in doing what is to be done even though there is no value or significance perceivable. The secure sinner may lapse into a kind of indolent apathy. Mounting pressure rises from a world which lacks the basic ingredient of life: *meaning,* the fundamental characteristic of life's foundation. Pressure may move the secure sinner rather quickly toward brokenness and despair. Believers may play a role in accelerating that process by advertising the meaning and worth which Christ gives to life. This kind of living can serve not only as a proclamation of God's Good News for us in Christ, but also as a mirror which reflects the failure of a life content to ferment in frustration and rage or to dissolve in apathy and indifference.

Meaninglessness is inextricably linked with the failure and demise of self-confidence and positive regard for oneself. These feelings of worthlessness can immobilize:

> It is living with the nagging fear, "I'm going to blow it. [I will fail,] and everyone will laugh at me." Unchecked, the fear goes a step further and actually inhibits the flow of ideas. ...

> According to [Dr. Morris] Rosenberg, an adolescent suffering from pangs of self-contempt may: (1) retreat into the world of imagination where he can dream of himself as worthy, or (2) put up a false front to others to convince them that he is worthy. Both responses tend to separate the person from others.[60]

Thus, a sense of meaninglessness which grows out of a sense of alienation from self grows into estrangement from others, and it also is a symptom of an anxiety about one's faith in God.[61] To that emptiness and distress coming from being unable to put the pieces of life's puzzle together, the believer comes with an affirmation that human life is meaningful because God created it and was willing to invest Himself in it through His incarnation and cross, in order that He might restore its meaning by restoring both its vertical and its horizontal relationships to their proper form.

Weakness and Failure

A fourth category in which we find sin and evil making an impact upon our lives is our own weakness, our failure to do the good we really intend and want to do, and instead falling into the evil that we try to avoid (Rom. 7:19). We make mistakes, not because we enjoy making mistakes but because we cannot seem to help ourselves.

> I am not in charge of my own life and am only partially able to achieve the goals that I set for myself. I experience that I myself am not under my own control. The problem is not that I set out to do the wrong thing … but that I set out to do the right things. I want to be the kind of person that God and the community want me to be. And I do my best. However, my best turns out differently than I expected.[62]

If I am secure enough to tolerate even my own more serious failures and mistakes, I may project a kind of false pride in them, or I may with some bravado ride right over them and try to deny them by boasting of them or by obliterating them as far as possible from the memories of myself and those around me. All this is, of course, pretty hollow, but I may be able to put up a good front to myself and my friends, who are often the victims of my mistakes and failures.

A Christian friend can hasten my honest appraisal of those mistakes by pointing out that, however inadvertent they may be, they still hurt. They break my relationship with those who become victims of my failure, and they break my self-respect as well. When I break and can no longer fool myself about my own reaction to these weaknesses or about the reactions of others, I feel ashamed. I recognize that I am "inadequate to the situation or role in which I find myself, … unable to achieve the good goals which I have set for myself."[63] I was so clumsy with life that I could not hit the mark; my aim at living was so poor that I could not hit the target. What a fool I am. To such fools the believer comes with the message of a God who clothed Himself in what appears to the wise of this world to be foolishness (1 Cor. 1:17, 23, 25). This God, and His people, accept us in our flawed and faulted foolishness. God's acceptance of what is flawed and faulted always transforms at the same time it accepts. He accepts us as we are and simultaneously transforms us into His righteous children. The Christian witness accepts the neighbor with failures and mistakes and applies the Word of acceptance to combat the foolishness and its devastating effect on the neighbor's life.

Bondage

Related to the mistakes and failures of everyday life, but more debilitating, are those habits which hold us in bondage, habits which we cannot escape, it seems, even when we turn our best efforts against them. Evil's impact of bondage is difficult to grasp for those not tied in knots by some enchaining habit. Generally, we think of others' bad habits as disobedience which they could cure quite easily if they would just throw off the habit. When the habit is ours, however, we find it less easy to dismiss kleptomania, or alcoholism, or masturbation, or smoking, as something over which we can exercise effective control with our own willpower. They seem at times to defy our strongest efforts.

Habits to which we are bound may provide life with some meaning, if not with much security, and there can be a kind of defiant delight which marks the addict's practice of the habit in pursuit of meaning. We can enjoy making bricks for the devil, even when he takes away the straw. The Christian friend can serve to reflect the glint of the chains back into eyes studiously trying to avoid looking at them, although the person in bondage can often effectively conceal the enslaving bondage from even the closest friends for long periods of time. A spiritual claustrophobia lurks ever near such habits, for bondage is bondage even to those who have convinced themselves that the sound of the chain gives some comfort and the feel of the bars provides something to hold onto. Christian witness cannot simply proclaim liberty for the captives of such habits but must intervene with a forceful presence to assist in doing the captor to death, in coping with the rattle of the chains, and, finally, in leading the captive into the pathways of genuine freedom.

Disobedience

Intertwined in some of these other categories has been the usual way we think of evil's impact on our lives, as we succumb to temptation to disobey specific commands of God and demands of His structure for human life. These conscious, planned acts of defiance of what we know to be right occur in the lives of most of us less frequently than mistakes and failures do, but more frequently than we care to admit to ourselves. We disobey common standards for human conduct for a variety of reasons. We feel the world is out to get us, and to right that wrong in our favor we disobey. We disobey, and the world, the structure of God's universe, *is* out to get us; for that structure cannot tolerate a thief or someone who hates or envies. We feel alienated, and we disobey; we disobey and exacerbate our alienation. The world's lack of coherent meaning provokes us to disobey, and our disobedience in turn renders the world a less meaningful place for us to make our home. Bondage may incite disobedience, or disobedience may open the door to the imprisonment of addiction. Whatever the case, disobedience haunts us all, and our defiance of God's plan for specific situations disrupts relationships in every direction.

The secure sinner may disobey and transfer the blame. Caught in the organization and service of huge corporations, of a political, economic, military, or social brand, I may surrender my moral responsibility to the group. "The corporation never suffers from a sense of guilt. It can kill and it can be killed; it can do evil and it can do good; it can be sick, and it can die. But, on the other hand, it has no pity and, no matter what suffering or damage it causes, it suffers no remorse."[64] If I have transferred my responsibility to my duty to the corporation, my disobedience is no more than its disobedience, and I let myself go, leaving blame at the office or command post. Or I may shift blame to another individual whose actions can plausibly pass as the occasion which lured or provoked me into disobedience for one good reason or another. Or I may try to justify my disobedience, arguing that it was necessary for my own preservation, or for some nobler good. While it may often be true that the sinful complex of this world's living conditions imposes a choice between evils rather than between the good and the evil upon us, this does not excuse our acts of disobedience. There is no justification for those who break the structure of the good life.

In some cases I may also try to make disobedience less serious by defining it as a venial sin, a medieval Christian term for sins other than those "mortal" sins which deprived the person of grace. This is grounded initially in our failure to distinguish the root sin of our doubt of God's Word and defiant denial of His lordship in our vertical relationship with Him, from the resulting sins by which we confirm that doubt and defiance, acting it out in sins against commandments two through 10. It is certainly true that in our horizontal relationships some sins have more serious consequences than others. Even God, who cares for all aspects of human life, recognizes that some sins are worse than others within the horizontal plane of our lives. But little sins grow up altogether too often and too quickly. "Christian experience teaches that no sin is in itself venial … also venial sin is an evil, a fire that can flare up and lead to damnation. *Little sins become big sins when we think little of them.*"[65] Furthermore, every act of disobedience, however minimal its effects or casual its motivation from our perspective, offends God equally, for all disobedience is but a symptom of the deeper flaw and fault which is our original sin, our failure to fear, love, and trust God above all things.

The secure sinner often disregards the results which disobedience wreaks upon relationships all around. In so doing he ignores the fact that disobedience which visits harm upon a neighbor not only harms the neighbor in a variety of ways but also brings judgment upon himself for providing the occasion for the neighbor to sin. In puzzling over the imprecatory psalms, C. S. Lewis came to believe that they reveal that "the natural result of injuring a human being, … of cheating a man, or 'keeping him down' or neglecting him is to arouse resentment," to tempt him to become vindictive and hateful.

> He may succeed in resisting the temptation; or he may not. If he fails, if he dies spiritually because of his hatred for me, how do I, who provoked that hatred, stand? For in addition to the original injury I have done him a far worse one. I have introduced into his inner life, at best a new temptation, at worst a new besetting sin. If that sin utterly corrupts him, I have in a sense debauched or seduced him. I was the tempter.[66]

117

Security in disobedience may be broken by alerting the sinner to the larger context, and enormity, of such acts of disobedience. Or the structure of God's gift of life may snap back at those who try to break it and knock some sense into them as it pronounces and works judgment upon them. That judgment may arise externally or internally in the voice of conscience. Conscience speaks negatively to the secure sinner if it is not silent. It condemns.[67] It secretes guilt into the human system. Guilt acknowledges that no justification of disobedience can maintain its own validity. Guilt acknowledges that there can be no security in excuses. Guilt recognizes that blame rests upon me because of my conscious disobedience of what I knew to be right. Guilt also tears apart the heart of the functioning human creature; it is "the sense of burden which inhibits the organizational function of the personality."[68]

Guilt may fester beneath the surface in a sinner who is fighting hard to maintain the facade of security with internal gods which would be destroyed if guilt were admitted. In some people genuine guilt cannot be remembered, and in others guilt for nonexistent sins is manufactured, at times as a means of achieving a false brand of piety. Sometimes guilt manifests itself as an expression of a latent self-hatred. Witnessing believers should be aware of the distinction between genuine guilt and such guilt feelings. The latter must be taken seriously, for they torture and torment the guilty as much as does the guilt of those who accurately assess their rebellion against God's structure for human living. Both cry out for forgiveness. But in addressing the guilt feelings which do not grow out of disobedience against specific commandments, our witness must clarify the hearer's perception of God's will at the same time it deals with the offense against God involved in a belief that the hearer has offended the Creator. Actually, guilt is also an honest recognition of my own responsibility for specific evils and thus serves as the diagnosis which can prepare the way for the cure, if the antidote is offered. The Christian witness is a physician licensed to treat the broken vertical relationship, commissioned to diagnose and analyze the guilty person's condition. With this diagnosis the believer can then proceed to bring an end to guilt and to the sinner as sinner. The believer then can extend the gift of new life through the forgiveness of the disobedient, through the gift of pardon for sin and the removal of guilt through absolution.

Death

The last category to be explored as a framework for identifying the effects of evil in the sinner's life is the final impact which touches all who exist under sin's curse, namely, death. Death lies beyond our control. We may occasionally stave it off, from our perspective, through careful planning or judicious use of vitamins or chemotherapy, but "the one place where the law of averages is suspended is death. Half of us do not, on the average, survive. We are in the grip of that over which we have neither control nor the possibility of chance."[69]

Death is inextricably linked with meaninglessness. Acts of disobedience may so damage the structure of our bodies that they expire, humanly speaking, more quickly than necessary, and bondage can wrap its chains so tightly that they squeeze or grind the breath right out of us. Death alienates. We naturally shy away from the dying. Alienation hastens death, for in many cases it cuts off proper care for psyche and physical system alike.

Death's tentacles reach into our personal calendars at great distances from the date of demise. They force us to try to grab all the gusto we can. Because we think we are only going around once in life, death keeps us spinning in a dance which chases the wind and reaps the whirlwind. Aging writes lines of judgment on our bodies, and particularly in contemporary North American culture we strive to avoid the wrinkles and the graying which remind us of death's inevitability by expending money and energy to hide them from our view—hoping they may hide us from death's searching gaze.[70]

> The prospect of death, Dr. Johnson said, wonderfully concentrates the mind. ... The idea of death, the fear of it, haunts the human animal like nothing else; it is a mainspring of human activity—activity designed largely to avoid the fatality of death, to overcome it by denying in some way that it is the final destiny of man.[71]

Believers and unbelievers alike fear death because they dislike the physical pain that so often accompanies it and because they nat-

119

urally resist the tearing of horizontal relationships which death imposes upon its victims. People dread death above all because it is the final judgment on their lives. Viewed solely from the perspective of the coping systems of this life, the cessation of existence means the cessation of all security, of our own ability to preserve the meaning of our lives, and of our identities. Until death threatens, some people can believe that they are the masters of their own fate, but death ends such illusions if we look no further than our own experience.

Death strikes terror into the human heart. The terror may be put off by racing the engines of failing life full speed ahead. Or the dying person may follow Dylan Thomas' rather empty advice to rage against the dying of the light.[72]

Some simply refuse to admit that death is stalking them, and some invest the greatest amount of energy, time, money, and faith which they have ever been able to scrape together in deceivers and quacks of one kind or another, who will help them fool themselves in the face of death. Facing death honestly means confessing my total impotence, and I cannot confront that without terror in view of all that I can imagine might rightfully or wrongfully assault me.

Only by being brought to recognize my own impotence and guilt, however, will I be able to recognize the power of life in the resurrection of Jesus of Nazareth. Only out of the terror which arises when I cannot imagine how my life can be secure and meaningful, or how I might be able to hang onto my identity, can I be prepared for receiving peace and calm, harmony with myself, my neighbor, my world, and my God. The believer must often simply wait as the increasing pressure of contemplating death itself explodes the security of the friend who is raging against dying or perhaps is trying to purchase escape through a quack. We may begin to call the friend to turn from the old gods to God Himself by insisting on the inevitability of death and holding out the promise of new life and everlasting life, a promise which will enable the breaking, dying person to feel honest terror and thus let go of old gods, so that the one true God can incorporate this dying person into His gift of life.

The spiral which begins in our doubt of God's Word and in defiance of His lordship, and which leads ultimately to our death and damnation, has been broken. It is broken by God's forgiving and re-creating Word, the means which He gives us to convey forgiveness and new life from His incarnation to those whom He has placed around us. Defiant sinners listen to this Word of new life only when they no longer find security, meaning, and identity in the idols which they have fashioned for themselves. Thus, Christian witness involves bringing the Law, the expression of God's plan for human living which has now turned into an expression of His wrath against human rebellion, to bear on secure sinners. God's re-creative Word of new life can be heard only after this proclamation of God's wrath—in connection with an honest confrontation of what has gone wrong with creation through our doubt and defiance—leads to the death of the sinner to old gods and to self. Only when the sinner dies can new life come forth in that individual.

Law and Gospel in Christian Witness

THE IMPACTS OF EVIL produce	THE IMPACTS OF THE LAW		to be met by EXPRESSIONS OF THE GOSPEL
	Reactions of the Secure	**Reactions of the Broken**	
Evil outside self from natural or human sources	Rage Revenge (often displaced)	Impotence	Redemption and liberation Resetting of priorities God's power and goodness
Estrangement or Alienation	Savagery against vocation	Withdrawal from vocation	Reconciliation
Meaninglessness	Apathy	Emptiness	Incarnation Service in vocation
Weakness or failure of self	False pride, bravado	Shame	Acceptance—and transformation
Bondage	Delight	Spiritual claustrophobia	Liberation
Disobedience	Defiance Indifference to criticism	Guilt	Acquittal Forgiveness
Death	Refusal to admit Rage Flight to quack cures	Terror	Resurrection

3

I Have Come That They May Have Life in All Its Fullness

WHO DO YOU SAY THAT HE IS?

The man who claims all authority in heaven and on earth had earlier asked His disciples, "Who do you say that I am?" Peter answered, and His disciples have been answering that question ever since, trying to convey in their own cultural situations who Jesus of Nazareth is and what He has done for His human creatures by joining them in the flesh. Peter's answer, that Jesus is the Messiah, the Son of the living God, did not arise out of his own rational investigation. Instead, Jesus said, the Father had revealed it to this disciple (Matt. 16:15–17). Sin-twisted rational investigation cannot discover the significance of this Galilean rabbi who lived in the reigns of the Roman emperors Augustus and Tiberius. Only the voice of God, through His prophets, apostles, and disciples, can reveal who Jesus of Nazareth is and what He means for fallen human creatures (Eph. 2:20). Nevertheless, rational study of the biblical text and careful formulation of its testimony regarding Jesus is necessary for effective Christian witness.

Believers encounter people with various bits of knowledge about our Lord and varying impressions of what He has done for us. As we formulate our confession of faith, it is very important that we convey the biblical teaching regarding Jesus Christ accurately and clearly to these hearers. In this chapter we review the biblical writers' approach to conveying Jesus and His benefits to others, and we suggest ways in which we may bring our contemporaries to trust that Jesus is God incarnate, the enfleshment of God's saving will and action for us. Each witnessing believer must first have a clear understanding of the biblical message concerning Jesus and then must always be striving to present that message plausibly and imaginatively, in ways which are understandable to people in our day.

THE HISTORICAL CONFESSION OF THE CHURCH

Twentieth-century Christians continue to use the formulations of our fathers in the faith to convey the biblical testimony regarding this man from Nazareth who is God. These formulations are challenged by cult members, such as Jehovah's Witnesses or Mormons, by agnostics and atheists, by members of Christian denominations who cannot bring themselves to believe that God could actually come in the flesh. Thus, the witnessing believer can profit from a brief historical review of the development of the church's testimony that God has indeed become human for our sakes. We usually begin a discussion of who Jesus is with the formulations of the fourth and fifth centuries, the period of the great ecumenical councils. The church at this time composed confessions of the biblical faith which made the Scriptural identification of Jesus as God and man intelligible and plausible to the people of that day. These formulations still guide our exposition of the biblical message and our application of it to the lives of our contemporaries.

The official dogmatic statement on the Holy Trinity was composed during the course of disputes in the fourth century. Although we usually think of the subject of this dogma as the doctrine of God, the disputes which led to this expression of the biblical teaching regarding God concerned the question of Jesus Christ being God. A few earlier Christians had questioned whether Jesus was truly God, but the disagreement within the church grew in importance at this time, and thus the Christian community came to resolve the difficulties regarding its understanding of God and Jesus through a long discussion, resulting in the affirmation of the biblical teaching that Jesus of Nazareth is truly God, Creator and Lord, and that He and the Holy Spirit, with the Father, though distinct in person, are one being, God.

This was attested already in the Old Roman Creed, the original form of the Apostles' Creed, composed in the second century. This teaching was expressed in a trinitarian framework, and trinitarian terminology was developed in the accompanying dogmatic definitions of the Councils of Nicea (A.D. 325) and Constantinople (381), in the confession which we know as the Nicene Creed. A later formula, named after the great defender of the biblical teaching of God, Athanasius, the Athanasian Creed, sums up the terminology and teaching of these councils and two others, Ephesus (431) and Chalcedon (451) regarding God's revelation of Himself in Jesus of Nazareth.[1]

We shall review the biblical teaching regarding Jesus of Nazareth, as it was then expressed largely in titles or labels intelligible in their culture, which His disciples used to describe Him. These descriptions were misunderstood or rejected already within the Palestinian religious culture of the second century, and also among converts in the Gentile world at the same time. These false views of the person of Jesus were linked inextricably with false views of His work, His accomplishment of salvation for fallen human creatures. Two categories of false teaching regarding Jesus' person arose: one denied that He is truly God, the other that He is truly human.

Jesus Is True God

In the second century a group of Jewish adherents of the Palestinian church rejected its proclamation that Jesus of Nazareth is God in the flesh. Concerned for the absolute distinction of the Creator from His creatures and for the unity of God, these Ebionites, as they were called, refused to believe that God could reveal Himself in a man from Nazareth. Instead, they taught that God had adopted Jesus at His baptism to be a special Son of God, thoroughly but merely human, exalted to this special sonship because of His superior obedience to the Law. By removing God from the person of Jesus, the Ebionites also removed the scandal of the cross, and its significance for human salvation. God's uniqueness and holy separation from His creation were protected; the human creature remained no more than a human creature. Yet at the same time the creature was cast back upon inner resources for the solution or dis-solution of the problem of sin.

In the wider Mediterranean world a similar doctrine arose in the third century, taught above all by Paul of Samosata, which we label dynamic monarchianism because it taught the unity of God (monarch/one ruler) and the adoption of the human Jesus through the power *(dynamis)* of an impersonal holy spirit of God.

Adoptionists abound in our own religious culture. Christian wit-nesses often encounter people who believe that Jesus was a great man and a special instrument or example of God's plan for humankind. We bring to such people the biblical testimony that God became a human creature as Jesus of Nazareth in the language of the Scriptures and also in the language of the creeds of the church.

Alongside the adoptionists in the classification of ancient Chris-tological heresies stand the subordinationists, the most important of whom was Arius, a fourth-century Alexandrian priest, who tried to make John's description of Jesus as the Word made flesh intelli-gible through the use of a model from Neoplatonic philosophy. This model taught that the ultimate being was utterly inaccessible to the created world; the world originated from a sub-deity, an intermedi-ate power generated by the ultimate being or soul. Neoplatonists had labeled this sub-deity the *Logos* or "word." Arius seized on the similarity between the terminology of John's gospel and this view, and he taught that Jesus Christ was this Neoplatonic word, a sub-deity who was not eternal, did not share the essence of the ulti-mate being, was capable of evil but also of moral progress—the course which Jesus indeed took. Athanasius, bishop of Alexandria, spent his career (mid-fourth century) defending the scriptural teach-ing that Jesus is God against Arius and his followers. In that process he helped develop the dogma of the Trinity. In recent years, "New Age" proponents of a spiritualized, divinized world may find ways in which to incorporate Jesus of Nazareth into their multilayered universe of divine experience. In such a system Jesus ends up as a sort of sub-deity, which is neither truly God nor truly human—as He truly is.

Another threat to the proper understanding of Jesus as God, or of God as Jesus, appeared in the early third-century teaching of Sabellius. His view, that the one God appears in three different modes, or activities, but is not three distinct persons within the unity of one God, has been labeled modalistic monarchianism (one ruler appearing in various fashions) and patripassianism (the Father suffers).[2]

Jesus Is Truly Human

Equally threatening to the proper understanding of God's revelation of Himself in Jesus of Nazareth is the proposition that Jesus is not truly human but rather has only a human facade, which makes the essence of divinity intelligible to human creatures. Since He only *seems* to be human, according to this view, those who taught that Jesus is only God and not truly human were called Docetists (from the Greek word "to seem"). This deprecation of the material and the individual arose from a Gnostic basis in the second century and recoiled from suggestions that Jesus could have truly died. Escape from evil, some Docetists believed, should come from uniting the soul of the individual with the divine essence, prying it loose from all stain of the material or the created. Just as the Ebionites undercut the New Testament understanding of the saving work of Christ by excluding the possibility of God's appearance in human flesh and His dying, so the Docetists undercut that understanding by setting aside the conviction that in His saving work Christ engages evil by confronting sin and death as a *human being* because evil arises from the perverted, death-bound heart of the human creature, not from the material order of the creation.

Related to this rejection of the true humanness of Jesus Christ was the doctrine of the late fourth-century bishop, Apollinarius of Laodicea. In combating Arianism he insisted that Christ was indeed God while denying that He was completely human. Apollinarius suggested that instead of a human spirit Jesus had the divine *Logos* in Him. Against this view the Council of Constantinople affirmed that Jesus is truly and completely human.[3]

Giving Witness to God Come in Human Flesh

There is in fact nothing new under the sun. Believers in North American culture today recognize that the rejection of Jesus Christ as Lord and Savior, as God and man, takes forms similar to those of the first four centuries. In some cases modern misunderstandings of who Jesus is mix elements of these ancient doctrines. Adoptionists and subordinationists are still trying to avoid recognizing Jesus as God by defining Him as a superhuman or sub-divine person. Docetists are still trying to abstract God from His intervention into human history and save Him from the foolishness and weakness of the cross.

To testify of God's coming into human flesh as the man from Nazareth, Jesus, believers should have a good command of the scriptural descriptions and formulations which authoritatively give witness to Him. They should also be ready to assist their hearers in confronting forthrightly and honestly those biblical claims which Jesus made for Himself and which His disciples made for Him. Some may try to dismiss the Christian message about Jesus without confronting precisely what that message states. The Christian witness should also be prepared to point out both the significance of Jesus' claims and the significance of rejecting them.

Even when we convince unbelievers that their reasons for rejecting Jesus as God and man are not valid by some logical argumentation, we must recognize two things. First, unbelievers, like all human creatures, are not designed to live solely by any standard of rationality but also as emotional beings, whose fears and loves shape their view of reality. They may not share our view of rationality or may overrule and override it for other reasons. Second, unbelievers will not automatically trust the alternative to their old gods which we present in Jesus just because we have helped them destroy those former sources of security, meaning, and identity. Jesus must be presented to them in a winsome and appealing fashion—as the biblical writers did—and the Holy Spirit must transform their understanding and attitude.

The early church had not completed its tasks by affirming that Jesus of Nazareth, the Second Person of the Trinity, is truly the Creator and is truly a human being. The mystery of God's incarnation also elicited a definition of the relationship of God and the human creature in Jesus, in the Second Person of the one God. A group gathered around the early fifth-century patriarch of Constantinople, Nestorius, taught that the divine and the human natures in Christ were incapable of a genuine union because the divine and the human cannot be mixed. Nestorians feared that the humanity of Christ might vanish if linked too closely to God. They thus rejected any suggestion that the Second Person of the Trinity could be touched by suffering and death, and they refused to apply the term *theotokos*, "mother of God," to the Virgin Mary. The Council of Ephesus (431) affirmed this term and with it that God and the human creature are inseparably united in Jesus Christ, with His divine nature and His human nature definitely distinct from each other.[4]

In reacting against Nestorianism, the Constantinopolitan monk Eutyches fell into another very serious misrepresentation of the biblical view of Jesus Christ. He taught that the human nature of Christ was not the same kind of human nature which human creatures have. He believed that in the incarnation the human nature of Jesus was subsumed by the divine nature, and that Christ consists of but one nature, the divine. Hence, his followers are called monophysites (one nature). His view was condemned by the Council of Chalcedon (451), which affirmed the distinction of the two natures within the personal (hypostatic) union of the single person, Jesus of Nazareth, the Second Person of the Trinity.[5]

As believers present God's love and His action on our behalf in Jesus of Nazareth today, it is of great help to be able to assure our hearers that God has defied the constructs of our logic and appeared among us as one of us. He has so taken on our being and situation that He shares our characteristics[6] as creature, and, although He does not share our sinfulness, He shares the burdens of our evils, even that of death. At the same time our fully human brother, Jesus, now shares the characteristics of God and exercises authority and power with His human experiences in mind. That God has endured our evils and that One of us exercises creative and re-creative power is of great comfort for those who recognize the power and wisdom of God in the foolishness of incarnation and cross.

Categories for Presenting Christ's Person and Work

A traditional distinction in surveying Christ's work, that between His humiliation and His exaltation, reaffirms that we dare not simplistically separate either His two natures or these phases of His saving activity. Particularly as we look at the hymn of His humiliation and exaltation in Philippians 2, humiliation is not the characteristic of the human Jesus, while God enjoys the exaltation. Instead it is this man, the Messiah, Jesus, who did not hang onto the form of God but emptied Himself into servant form, into human likeness, and humbled Himself into obedience which led to death on a cross. This man who did not hang onto His Godness has been exalted by God so that all creatures should bow down and confess that Jesus is Lord (2:6–11). God is humbled in His obedience all the way to death; this particular human creature is exalted in receiving the honor due Him as God from creation. The one person of Jesus of Nazareth, Second Person of the Trinity, rescues and restores His people through His own humiliation and exaltation.

As soon as we begin to look at the biblical descriptions of Jesus, we recognize that, however useful it often may be to distinguish His person as God and man from His work of rescuing and re-creating, the person and work of Jesus cannot be separated. That Christ Jesus is truly and fully God is linked with His reconciliation of all things to Himself through the peace established by the blood of the cross (Col. 1:19–20).

As God spoke, in His own flesh and through the preaching and the writing of His disciples in the first century, He expressed and described Himself not in the categories which Gentile Christians later used in the dogma of the Trinity but rather in the titles which Jewish Christians had grasped from their biblical heritage. At the end of the 20th century in North America the Holy Spirit gives believers both those sets of categories and those titles as useful aids in framing their proclamation and application of God's Word about Himself, which conveys His presence and power into the midst of the lives of His people today. Some of these titles from the Scriptures will remain perfectly clear to modern readers; others will have to be explained in their ancient context as the hearer begins to be interested in the biblical message, and still others must be translated from Palestinian imagery to modern metaphors.

The 16th-century reformer John Calvin used three biblical titles for Christ to summarize His person and His work: prophet, priest, and king. He grouped the Scriptures' descriptions of Jesus around these three themes.[7] The contemporary exegete Oscar Cullmann has classified Christological titles into four categories: those which refer to the earthly work, the future work, and the present work of Jesus, and those which refer to His preexistence.[8] In this volume we shall review some of the biblical descriptions of Jesus within four other categories: those which speak of Him as revealer; as One who has become victim and vicar, or substitute, for us; as the victor over evil; and as our companion and guide. Such classifications and categories are not sacred nor authoritative in themselves, and witnessing believers will form their own systems of classification to assist them in formulating the message of Jesus effectively for individual witnessing situations.

JESUS AS REVEALER

Jesus came to reveal to us who God is and how He regards us. Marshall McLuhan's study of the ways in which contemporary North Americans receive information suggests that form and content merge: the medium is the message.[9] In Jesus of Nazareth God gives His fallen human creatures the supreme and final medium or proclamation of His message of rescue and restoration. He effected the content of the message as He acted and as He proclaimed the significance of His actions. Furthermore, God's release of His ultimate message for those fallen human creatures embraces both a revelation of His own love for them and of His plan for restoring them while it also reiterates His plan for their full and perfect life. Jesus is, to use a pair of terms from Saint Augustine, both gift (or sacrament) and example.[10] He bestows upon us the gift of a renewed, vertical relationship with the Father and the motivation for living His kind of life in our horizontal relationships. He also offers us the example of how human life in these horizontal relationships should work.

There can be no doubt in the mind of even the most casual reader of the New Testament that its chief subject is Jesus Christ. At the center of the proclamation of the earliest Christians was the confession that "Jesus of Nazareth, whose earthly life is known to the first witnesses, is the one who fulfills the whole history of Israel in carrying out the divine plan and is the one who brings salvation to the world." The church's proclamation concerning Jesus "goes to the kerygma [proclamation] of the historical Jesus, His life and His preaching."[11] For there His disciples found the revelation of God and His message, which brings His power into the midst of human life. So, too, as Christian witnesses today, we aim to acquaint the people around us with this Jesus of Nazareth, God in human flesh.

The evangelist John confessed that God was revealing Himself in Jesus of Nazareth simply by identifying this man as God. In the prologue of his gospel John called Jesus not just the Word of God but God (1:1), and ascribed to Him the act of creation. In some manuscripts the conclusion of that prologue reaffirms this mystery of God's appearance in human flesh with the words, "No one has ever seen God; the only-begotten God, who is in the bosom of the Father, has made Him known" (1:18). John moves toward the conclusion of his entire recitation of Jesus' life with Thomas' confession, as he examines the nail holes in Jesus' flesh, "My Lord and my God" (20:28). Paul was agreeing with Thomas' estimation when he wrote to the Colossians that the fullness of deity dwells in bodily form in this Christ (2:9; cf. 1:19), as was Peter when he wrote of the "righteousness of our God and Savior Jesus Christ" (2 Peter 1:1).[12]

Jesus the Lord

Thomas was using synonyms, as a first-century Jew, when he called this man from Nazareth both God and Lord. It is true that the word "lord" was used in the New Testament and its culture for a human being of superior status, but it was also the term which the Jews used in place of the holy name of God, Yahweh. "Lord" embraced all that the Jews understood Yahweh to be: the One who exercises supreme power on the basis of His person, the person for whom it is of His very nature to be and to exercise such power, the person who had claimed Israel as His children.[13] The apostles understood that Jesus was more than simply a human lord as can be seen in their application of this title to Jesus in connection with Old Testament passages which speak of God.[14] In making the confession that Jesus is Lord, the early Christians were not only identifying Him as Yahweh for Jewish hearers, but were also identifying Him with a term which Gentiles used for divine figures and, particularly from Jesus' time on, for the divine emperors.[15]

In both Jewish and Gentile cultures, then, the earliest confession that Jesus is Lord (Acts 2:36; Rom. 10:9; 1 Cor. 12:3; Phil. 2:11) announced to Christians' hearers that this man from Nazareth commands that worship which alone belongs to God. The concept of lord *[kyrios]* expressed God's unconditional claim over the whole universe for the first readers of the New Testament (Col.1:13–20): God exercises lordship over human consciences and especially over the community of believers. They used the title "Lord" as a special confession of faith in and dependence on their Creator. Furthermore, the "Lord" demands an unlimited validity for all His actions. "The lordship of God can tolerate no other lords beside it. Every other lordship is either only derived lordship dependent upon the divine power, or presumptuous lordship, i.e., rebellion. He who is *Kyrios* is absolute Lord."[16]

Believers today reaffirm Christ's lordship over the entire universe which He created and over the church which He has brought into existence through His re-creating Word of absolution and new life. Above all, they acknowledge His lordship in their daily lives, and they give testimony to that lordship in their witness and their works. This lordship of their loving God enables them to live without defensiveness, with joy and peace, even in the midst of a world falling apart.

This testimony aims at convincing unbelievers that Jesus of Nazareth does exercise lordship as the Author of life and that He exercises that lordship not as a despot and dictator, after the usual fashion of human lords, but rather as the Lord of life, who exercises His dominion *under* us, who even died to restore life to His people. Christians present a Lord whose expenditures for defense and for health, education, and welfare, or the human services of His people, mounted into the worth of His very own life on the cross. To unbelievers who bristle at the thought of anyone trying to exercise lordship in a life which they wish to dominate themselves, the

Christian presents a fatherly and loving Lord, who provides security because He framed the universe, and who provides meaning because He reclaimed human life by entering into the midst of it. No common Lord is He. He is *the* Lord.

Jesus the Image of God

The Scriptures use other images, metaphors, and descriptions to show their readers that Jesus is God, to reveal what God is like. Paul calls Jesus the image of God (2 Cor. 4:4; Col. 1:15); Jesus offers a photographic likeness of God and His disposition toward us.[17] He demonstrates God's love for us. The glory of God could take on visible presence, according to the Jews of Jesus' day, in what they called the *Shekinah* (dwelling). John writes that this glory of God dwelt among us in Jesus (1:14), and in Hebrews 1:3 we read that God's Son, Jesus, reflects God's glory. To His disciples of the first century Jesus brought the very presence of God Himself, with all His power and goodness, into the midst of the human situation.[18] In this vein John identifies Jesus with the Old Testament temple, where the *shekinah* rested; no longer does God's glorious presence reside in the temple but rather is now to be found in Jesus of Nazareth (2:21; 4:20–26).[19] In Hebrews 1:3 this idea of Jesus as the representation of God is strengthened by the designation "the very stamp of God's nature," who upholds the universe by His word of power. Such a stamp was the impression made by a seal or die stamp in wax or metal, and thus "an exact replica, copy, or reproduction."[20] Again, the biblical writer affirms that Jesus reveals God to us.

An understanding of these biblical terms assists the Christian witness by providing material with which unbelievers can be confuted when they say that the New Testament provides few if any claims that Jesus is truly God. This material can also spark the believer's imagination to use these or to formulate similar metaphors which express clearly what it means that Jesus is God in the flesh.

For example, although we usually do not use the term "father" for Jesus, it is important to note that He exercises His role as God and Lord with a father's love, with the love of a brood hen for her chicks (Matt. 23:37). In a world in which parental love sometimes seems scarce and many are growing up scarred by the lack of parental concern, such imagery may seem meaningless or provoke a hostile reaction in response to Christian witness. But all human creatures feel the need for parental love, perhaps those who have not experienced much of it even more than those who have. The Holy Spirit works through believers who in their own care and concern articulate and demonstrate God's love for others in Jesus. We thus affirm and display the love of the creating and re-creating Father whose care and concern for His children exceeds the bounds of life itself.

Jesus the Word

The significance of God's appearance as Jesus of Nazareth is focused sharply in the use of the term *"Logos"* or "Word" for Him as well. In the Gentile world the term had more than one connotation: Heraclitus had taught that the *Logos* held the world order together in spite of the constant flux of life; the Neoplatonists believed that the *Logos* was the agent of creation generated by the ultimate being or soul. For the Jews the Word of the Lord was the agent of His creation (Gen. 1) and of His preservation of His creation (Ps. 107:20; 147:18; Is. 55:11).[21] Thus, when John identified Jesus as the Word of God—not just with God but God Himself— Jewish readers were not shocked by the identification of the Word, the instrument of God's power, with God, but rather at the association of that power and person with this man (1:1–3). Jesus as God's Word comes to human hearers not simply to describe God or to offer a dissertation on abstract concepts of identity, security, and meaning. He comes as a Word which commands our attention and puts a claim on us, a claim expressed in the authority of the Author of life and in the love of the dying and rising human creature who is in the process of re-creating creatures who have abandoned and rejected the life which He had originally given them.[22] He is the Word of life (John 1:4).

The life for human flesh comes from the Word made flesh. The prologue to John's gospel affirms that God is born a human creature (1:14), confirming Matthew's citation of the angel's word that Mary's child was "conceived in her of the Holy Spirit ... to fulfill what the Lord had spoken by the prophet, 'Behold, a virgin shall conceive and bear a son' " (Matt. 1:20–23). The angel had assured Mary that her child would be born without a human father because the Holy Spirit would come upon her and the power of the Most High would overshadow her, so that her son would be holy and be called the Son of God—in ways in which no other human creature could ever be labeled holy or a child of God (Luke 1:31–35). We usually think of the biblical teaching of the virgin birth of Jesus as attestation that He is truly God, and it is. But it is also an attestation that this Son of God, Christ Jesus, is truly human as one born of a woman, born under the Law (Gal. 4:4). The second-century theologian Irenaeus compared Jesus to Adam at this point also: both issued from the creative power of God to be truly human, Adam taken from the dust of the earth, Jesus from the womb of Mary, in a normal birth which resulted from a unique conception.[23]

God reveals Himself in human flesh, believers must tell unbelievers. Contradictory or paradoxical as it may seem, the Creator became a human creature. They may resist the idea that the eternal infinite God could become a finite human creature, but God breaks through the limits of our imagination to enter our plane of existence. He did that not to make us divine but rather to restore us to our true and full humanity.[24] He restores the creature to the right relationship, the right kind of existence in the vertical and horizontal dimensions of life, by "speaking" Himself into the middle of those broken relationships, of that twisted existence. In an age in which good communication is both so highly prized and so extensively fostered—even though not so effectively practiced—Christian witnesses have at their command in the title the Word made flesh a superb vehicle for conveying the significance of God's communication of Himself in human form. Word power like none other is present in God's communication, for He communicates with a personal touch. The Holy Spirit makes His Word clear and to the point, for His Word expresses itself in the actions of dying and claiming life again as the Spirit conveys the benefits of Jesus to us. How? By incorporating us into His death and resurrection through our baptisms—and through the repetition of our baptisms as He works daily repentance in us.

Jesus the Prophet

In our culture very important communication is conducted by the sales representatives of firms or press agents of officials or celebrities. Such people are sent by their superiors to make their utmost concerns clear and appealing to those for whom they want their product and message to be meaningful and effective. Jesus, too, was described as the One sent by God with a special assignment or commission (John 4:34; 5:30; 6:38; 9:4; Luke 4:18; Rom. 8:3) and with the task of proclaiming the significance of this assignment (Luke 4:43; John 3:34).[25] The Jews expected the one whom God sent to be a prophet, not a sales representative or a press agent. They were looking for one who would speak to them on God's authority as Moses had, for God has promised to send such a prophet (Deut. 18:15–18) who would usher in the kingdom of God, according to the expectation of Jesus' contemporaries. Jesus came and spoke with that kind of authority, using the formula, "truly, truly, I say to you" (e.g., Luke 11:51; Matt. 5:18; Mark 3:28, among numerous instances) which denoted that He was speaking as the voice of God. His hearers recognized that He addressed them with that authority (Matt. 7:29; John 7:46) and identified Him as the prophet who was to come into the world at the end time to establish God's rule through His Word (Matt. 11:3; John 14:6).[26]

An understanding of the ancient world's respect for prophetic figures who spoke for God (and particularly Jesus' Jewish contemporaries' anticipation of a prophet like Moses) assists the witnessing believer in comprehending why they were attracted to His words. It should also spark our imaginations to use modern images of those who are sent on special assignments to communicate. No metaphor will ever bear the full weight of an idea it is used to convey; if it expressed the concept so precisely, it would not be a metaphor. Thus, much of the popular image of a sales representative or press agent may not convey the task which Jesus performed as prophet. Their assignment and responsibility to communicate clearly, to be forthright, and to disclose fully what they have to communicate provide points of comparison which may clarify Jesus' role as God's revelation of Himself. Jesus is both salesman and product according to a metaphor developed by Martin Luther to explain Jesus' role as revealer in the 16th century. He used a mercantile term

(Ausbund) "for a faultless sample bound to the outside of a package to indicate the quality of the goods within—such as a flawless swatch protruding from a role of cloth."[27] Jesus provides a sample of God's disposition toward us; He reveals the love which God has for us and will show to us, His chosen people, for eternity.

Jesus the Light

John's prologue not only presents God revealing Himself to our ears through the Word made flesh. The Word is also the Author of life, and the life which He is and gives lights up the lives of His human creatures (1:4). He is the Light which opens the eyes of the blind (Matt. 11:5) and which shines on the pathways on which people walk (Matt. 4:15–16; Is. 9:2). He is the Light who attacks the darkness which reduces us to stumbling and bumbling about (John 1:5; 8:12; 12:46). He functions as the source of light for returning us to the right track of our vertical relationship, for He is the Way, the Truth, and the Life (John 14:6) onto which He shines His light. He enlightens us with the knowledge of God's glorious presence (2 Cor. 4:6), probably a reference to the power of God dwelling on earth in the *shekinah,* now moved from the temple to the body of Jesus.[28]

Light provides knowledge. As it shines from Jesus' life, it reveals what is wrong with those lives conducted in the shadows and darkness by our own choice (John 3:19). It also reveals what is now right in our relationship with God through Jesus, and it reveals how we may convey His light into the lives of others (Matt. 5:14–16).

Light provides security. For those who fear the darkness of the world which seems to be falling or closing in upon them, Christ can light up their lives. He can illumine the nature of that darkening hostility, and embrace us with the light and warmth of His loving intervention against the darkness, which seemed to triumph at noon on Good Friday (Luke 23:44–45).

Light provides growth. John's connection of light and life reminds us of the process of photosynthesis. The life-giving properties of light in the plant world provide a model for talking about how His creative and re-creative radiance fosters new life as it shines its light into our dying world.

Specific forms of natural light serve as effective metaphors. "Perhaps the most beautiful title ever given to Jesus, and certainly the title most instinct with poetry, is given to him in Rev. 22:16, where he is called the Bright Morning Star."[29] This image sets forth Jesus in all His godly splendor; the title "Morning Star" was applied to kings in the ancient world. Furthermore, Jesus as the Morning Star of the newly re-created humanity of God's people heralds the dawn of a good new day, in which we live as His people in ever-lasting light.

Finally, in a society in which light is provided to such a large extent by electricity, contemporary Christian witness can employ a metaphor which couples light very clearly with power, with the power to provide enlightenment, safety, and transformation. The universally recognized benefits of light make it an ever-useful vehicle for describing the actions of God in Jesus Christ in our behalf to those broken sinners who cry out for rescue from their despair and impotence, and their guilt and shame.

Christian witness centers around the confession that Jesus of Nazareth, the Second Person of the Trinity, is truly and completely God and truly and completely a human being. He sheds all the light we need on the definition of who God is and the definition of what it means to be human. The process of bringing unbelievers into new life involves bringing them to recognize Jesus as He really is, for in Him they will have that light and that life which God gives as He restores us to know Him and to trust Him in the way in which He designed us to know and trust Him in Eden.

JESUS AS VICAR AND VICTIM

Jesus came as a substitute or vicar for us; He became a victim of the accusing Law of God and all the assaults of evil in every form. Jesus reveals not only that God is kindly disposed toward us. His perfect life as a human creature also reveals the flaws and faults of our life. He reveals in the thunderous voice of prophetic wrath that we have failed to exercise our responsibilities as God's assigned stewards and caretakers of one another, nature, and ourselves. Somehow our sense of responsibility for evil, our guilt, must be dealt with. So must our responsibility for evil and evil itself. Yet we are unable under our own power, on the basis of our own now twisted, perverted, and destroyed capabilities, to address evil, our responsibility for it, or our sense of that responsibility, effectively. Jesus came to take our place, to serve as our vicar, or substitute, in exorcising our guilt, our feeling of responsibility under the wrath of God.

He came freely and obediently (Phil. 2:6–8; Heb. 5:8). He took our place under the Law (Gal. 4:4) and its wrath; He experienced our confrontation with temptation (Matt. 4:1–11).

> Obedience means a return to the pure and undestroyed creation. The power of the Law is not the normal condition which can continue because of Christ's obedience, but the abnormal situation which is removed as a result of His obedience. It is good only for dealing with disobedience. Where obedience supervenes, the law, wrath, and judgment give way, and the Law is fulfilled and put to silence.[30]

In taking our place in obedience to His Father and to the plan which He shaped for human life, Jesus became the victim of that Law and of the Father's wrath.

God's fury against evil, against the human destruction of His good gift of life, is real. It had to be combated. It could not be assaulted in power; it was assaulted in the weakness and foolishness of the cross. There Jesus became sin in our place (2 Cor. 5:21), or, according to another interpretation, an offering for sin. "On the tree" He assumed the full weight of the curse which rests upon defiance against God (Gal. 3:13).

> Within this death which loomed before Him at Gethsemane there lay the wrath of God. It was not simply death in general to which He submitted, but a felon's death. This was the verdict passed against Him by the authorities, the servants of God's justice on earth. ... He has been given for the world. In one sense He surrenders His life to the wrath of God.[31]

We know that God must be wrathful at our denial of His lordship, that death results from our defiance of the Author of life, and that the good Creator cannot but be angry with both death and defiance. He loves His human creatures too much not to be deeply angry at our self-destructive intentions. Thus, God came in human flesh to deal with His own wrath before our eyes, on the cross, so that we can have confidence that He does not hang onto His anger forever, simply because He delights in steadfast love (Micah 7:18). We can be confident that, since Jesus Christ has restored our right-eousness, He delivers us from God's wrath, just as He delivers us from our own hostility against God (Rom. 5:9–10).

The Suffering Servant of God

One of the most dramatic figures in the entire Bible is that fig-ure sketched in the "servant songs" of Isaiah 42, 49, 50, and 52–53. In the person of this Suffering Servant, who is vicar and victim, the mission and accomplishment of Jesus is depicted clearly.

> The most important essential characteristic of the *ebed Yahweh* [servant of Yahweh] in these texts is that his vicarious representa-tion is accomplished in suffering. The *ebed* is the *suffering* Servant of God. Through suffering he takes the place of the many who should suffer instead of him. A second essential characteristic of the *ebed Yahweh* is that his representative work *re-establishes the covenant* which God had made with his people,

a task also assigned by Jews of Jesus' time to the Messiah.[32]

In Isaiah 52:13–53:12 the Suffering Servant is depicted in deep-est degradation, despised, rejected, a man of sorrows and grief, wounded for our transgressions, bruised for our iniquities, cut off from the land of the living, placed in the grave with the wicked. He is an offering for sin. He suffers not for His own sins but as the vicarious victim of the sins of others as He bears the sins of many and intercedes for transgressors. But the song begins by announcing that the Servant shall prosper, be exalted and lifted up, even though His appearance was marred (52:13–14). Even though He dies as an offering for sin, He will see His offspring and prolong His days (53:10). Death is not the last word for the Servant. The purpose of His suffering and death is to give righteousness to many as He bears their iniquity (53:11).

Jesus did not call Himself the Suffering Servant of God, and New Testament writers generally avoided the term, which would have had little meaning for a Gentile audience. Jesus did combine the title "Son of Man," a title for a human figure with Yahweh's characteris-tics of divine glory and power, with a description of Himself which reflects the profile of the Servant in Isaiah, for example in the pre-dictions of His passion (Matt. 16:21; 17:22; 20:17–19 and parallels). He did refer to Isaiah 53 in describing His passion (Luke 22:37), and He summarized His mission as one of service and offering Himself as a sin-offering, or "ransom" for many (Mark 10:45; Is. 53:10–12). Peter did combine the title Servant with the verb "to hand over" or "deliver," used to describe the Servant's death in Isaiah 53:6 and, in the Septuagint, verse 12 as well (Acts 3:13; cf. 3:26; 4:27–30). Paul used this image of the Servant's being handed over into death too, for example, in Romans 4:25.[33]

As individuals wrestle with the burden of the responsibilities which they bear for the evils they have perpetrated, the Suffering Servant calls upon them to place these burdens upon Him, so that they may relax (Matt. 11:28). He takes our place in bearing these responsibilities, and He bears them to the cross. As our vicar in relationship to them He has the power to destroy them through His own suffering. The Servant consumes them in the fire of His own passion.

Even in contemporary situations we find examples of that kind of self-sacrifice in taking the place of others in the face of danger and even death: the soldier who spares his buddies the shrapnel of a grenade thrown into the midst of their unit, or the airplane passenger, who, after the crash of a plane into icy waters, passes the lifeline to others and himself drowns in this act of saving them. The classic literary example of that kind of self-sacrifice is Charles Dickens' figure, Sidney Carton, who in *A Tale of Two Cities,* takes the place of Charles Darnay as he faces execution by the guillotine so that Darnay may go free.[34]

In varying degrees these examples suggest that human beings will die for one another, even for some other than their closest friends, in rare instances, but Jesus took our place and became victim of our sins and evils while we were still hostile to Him (Rom. 5:6–8). In the face of the broken unbeliever's guilt and shame the Christian witness can draw on such analogies and demonstrate Christ's love in His greater sacrifice, which is the sacrifice of one with the power not just to save life but to reverse evil and totally revise our relationship to it.

Jesus the Priest

In many religious systems of the ancient world, sin was taken away through sacrifice. In most of these systems the human beings who brought and performed the sacrifices were believed to have the ability to effect the appeasing of God's wrath through their own actions. The Jewish sacrificial system did not provide the means whereby God's people could obligate Him to forgive them through their own efforts in sacrificing. Instead, they recognized the sacrificial system as a gift from God through which He intervened in their lives to reconcile them to Himself.[35] God provided the expiation, that which takes away His people's sin, by becoming the propitiation, that which sets aside divine wrath, for them (cf. 1 John 2:2; Rom. 3:25).[36] The servant or minister of God who stood at the pivotal position between God and His people in any sacrificial system was called the priest, in Latin, the *pontifex,* or the bridge-builder, who connected human creatures with divine beings.

Particularly the writer to the Hebrews emphasized Jesus' role as high priest for God's people. He served as a human high priest (2:17), but one without sin (4:15), who completed the final, ultimate, and all-sufficient sacrifice for the sins of the people; the sacrifice which He completed on the cross has once and for all won forgiveness of sins for the whole world (9:26–28; 10:10; 1 John 2:2). This high priest fulfills that office of the mysterious priest and king (or Messiah figure) Melchizedek (Hebrews 7:1; cf. Gen. 14:17–20), who encountered Abraham, and who was an important deliverer-figure for intertestamental Judaism. But Jesus the High Priest is a unique bridge-builder, for He builds the bridge with His own blood (Hebrews 9:12–14, 28); He is both sacrificial victim and priest. He combines the role of priest with the Servant's vicarious offering of Himself for the people.[37]

"Behold, the Lamb of God, who takes away the sin of the world!" John the Baptist said as he heralded Jesus. Peter also hailed Him as the sacrificial lamb, without blemish or spot (1 Peter 1:18–19), whose blood rescued His people from the futile ways of their fathers. His blood possesses cleansing properties; it is God's means for washing away all that has fouled and soiled our relationship with Him (1 John 1:7–9). It is His means for purifying consciences (Heb. 9:14) and for liberating His people from our oppressors, thereby gathering us into His own kingdom (Rev. 1:5–6). That perfect lamb which was brought for sacrifice in the Old Testament took into itself the sins of the people, as did the scapegoat which was annually sent into the wilderness, bearing the sins of the people (Lev. 16:8–10).[38]

Yet sheep are described as "dumb and dirty." As our perfect sacrifice Jesus came to be one of us, who like sheep easily go astray. As our perfect sacrifice Jesus resisted the temptations which we encounter to wander into the wilderness on our own, meandering away from God. He consumes our sins into His own innocence, making His body the means whereby our sins are hidden from the sight of the Father and His blood the means whereby our sins are washed away and blotted out. In the biblical descriptions of Jesus as our sacrifice the Holy Spirit gives believers a host of expressions for the results of His love in lifting from us our guilt, our responsibility for rejecting God and His plan for life.

Christ's exercise of His office as priest and victim did not end in His humiliation as the obedient sacrifice. He remains a priest forever (Heb. 6:20). In His exaltation He continues to serve as the bridge between the Father and His people. He plays the role of mediator, or advocate and defense counsel for us before the heavenly throne (1 John 2:1). Helmut Thielicke depicts the scenario of Jesus in action as the defense attorney, a role He plays by virtue of being both our priest and our sacrifice. The accusers, Satan and God's Law, bring before God my past record which, I must admit, condemns me. "But then my advocate and representative steps forth. Christ speaks: 'All that you have said, accuser, is true. And yet it is also false. For what this man has behind him, and it is really behind him, he no longer is. I have cancelled it and taken it as a burden on myself'" (Col. 2:14). The result of our defense counsel's association with us, and His association of our sin with Himself, is that, as He argues before His Father and ours, "I am no longer identical with my past. I live, yet not I (Gal. 2:20). I am the friend of Christ, and thus acquire a new identity. My true nature and essence is to be included in his vicarious work."[39]

This metaphor of defense witness and defense counsel, combined with the work of Christ as the vicarious victim of our responsibility for evil, offers the Christian witness a basis on which to make intelligible Christ's work in behalf of the broken sinner.

The priest served as something of an arbitrator as well. The modern picture of the labor or diplomatic arbitrator has its flaws since that arbitrator serves generally as a neutral go-between who brings together two parties of roughly equal power. The task of the ancient mediator in public disputes extended

> beyond merely establishing communication; he has to establish between the two conflicting parties a new relationship in which suspicion has turned to trust, enmity to friendship, and hatred to love. ... It was the essential task of the mediator to establish, not merely a legal relationship, but a personal relationship in which love is the bond.[40]

Whatever problems there are with the modern analogy, Jesus' role as the One who reconciles us to God may become clearer through its use. This arbitrator settles differences by dying Himself. There could be no white flags in the battle between God and our evil. The middleman reaches from the far side of the gulf of our differences with God to the other to draw us to Himself, as God, yet comes from our side, as a human creature, to effect our reunion with the Father. Like the shepherd willing to risk all to bring the straying sheep back to the flock (Luke 15:3–7; John 10:14–16), this mediator draws the erring children into the arms of the waiting Father (Luke 15:11–32). Jesus is the mediator who brings together two lovers who have drifted apart, and for whom life can never be complete until they are again in fellowship. The human creature, weak and sinful and helpless, needs God. Jesus is the mediator, the middleman, who stands in the midst, and draws us and God together again.[41] Believers can fashion a number of effective descriptions of Jesus' work in our behalf from the biblical teaching that He is priest and sacrifice, victim and vicar for us.

Here we stand before the heart of God's revelation of Himself in the human person of Jesus of Nazareth, and at the heart of the way in which He goes about His redeeming work. God takes our place as sacrifice; God is the victim who turns away His own wrath through this sacrifice in the deepest of all mysteries. This is the scandal of His cross (1 Cor. 1:23). Against all apparent reason God died for us. Against every concept of power we have, God becomes victor over evil by becoming our vicarious victim. On the basis of His saying so, however, Christians recognize the death of God on Golgotha as wisdom and power. They see things differently than the world's kind of reason and its view of power do. To those who feel oppressed by their own sinfulness, separated from the Ultimate Good by the evil in their lives, we give witness of the destruction of our sinfulness at the hand of the priest who sacrificed Himself and consumed our sins in the fire and passion of His own death.

Jesus the King

We claim this priestly victim as the divine king as well (Heb. 7:1), and yet

> the treatment He receives as king runs counter to the accepted idea of what a ruler should be—He is crowned with a crown of thorns and beaten and mocked. Before He dies, the scoffing cry is heard again: "Let the Christ, the King of Israel, come down from the cross that we may see and believe" (Mark 15:32). ... the One on the cross is forsaken and humiliated in a threefold sense. He has none of the attributes of a ruler—He has no dominion over anything. He is, moreover, completely cut off from God, who affords Him no assistance (cf. Matt. 27:43, Luke 23:39). And finally He is totally unable to give anything to anyone. He is unable to arouse faith in any of them, even in His disciples, who flee away. But those who taunt Him are themselves the prisoners of a mistaken view of what it means to rule, and to have faith in God, and to have love for men. They are all in error—only the Crucified knows the truth.[42]

Because the cross claims to be redemptive inasmuch as it is an alternative to repaying evil with evil and to be the revelation of what the power of the universe is really like,

> the confession that Jesus is divine is therefore not in antithesis to His suffering and death, but rather its expression. That is what His divinity meant! His death is the only death of God worthy of the term. He is God taking death into His own history in order to overcome its power to shape our lives. He can be unconditionally committed to us because there is now no condition to His freedom to be for us. He can make unconditioned promises because His promises are not conditioned by death ... He has

death behind Him; and He is God. Only thus can we, too, live as
if we had death behind us.[43]

Recognizing Jesus as our vicarious victim means that we are free to
relax, even about death, because our death is behind Him. He
answered death's destruction with the destruction of death, swal-
lowing up death by turning His suffering and death into the instrument of death's demise. With that death dies our impotence,
despair, guilt, shame, and fear, as well as the alienation and meaninglessness which choke off life.

For sinners broken by the weight of their own guilt and shame
the message of Jesus' substitutionary and atoning death on the cross
brings the comfort of forgiveness. It delivers the gift of death to all
that has trashed our lives. To those who wish they were dead,
believers come with the promise of being joined to Christ's death, so
that life can begin anew in Him.

The past, with all its doubt and defiance, its mistakes and failures, lies beyond our power to alter. It can, however, tyrannize us
and drive us far away from the God whose wrath we feel. Believers will therefore emphasize to the shamed and the guilty that the
Lord of the past, the only one who can do anything about it, has
consumed its doubt and defiance in the passion of His own cross
and death. Through this assurance the Holy Spirit will conquer their
alienation from God.

JESUS AS VICTOR

Jesus has indeed conquered everything that separates us from
His Father. With Pilate we acclaim the suffering and dying Jesus of
Nazareth as the king of the people of God (John 19:14, 19). With
Peter we confess that He is the Messiah, the Son of the living God
(Matt. 16:16). The Jews of Jesus' day expected a king like David,
who would come with royal characteristics familiar to people of
many nations and who would liberate them from Roman oppression.[44] He might have come in that fashion if He had viewed the
political tyranny which His people were suffering under occupation forces as their fundamental problem.

Instead, however, He knew that He must do battle with what
was actually their fundamental problem, their own doubt of His

Word and defiant denial of His lordship. This king came to do battle with every form of evil. He won. He became the kind of victorious king His people really needed. In humiliation He engaged evil in combat in His own way, by submitting to it as our vicarious victim. He won His victory by entering the battle at the doorway of death and by coming out of it through the door of His tomb. Jesus' work on our behalf as victim and as victor cannot be separated.

> The glory of the One who is exalted thus does not erase or cancel humanity, suffering, and lowliness. As it was the basis of His secret majesty in the time of His earthly being and His humility, as crown and cross belonged together here, as He "reigned in weakness" (Luther), so the exalted One is still He whose love impelled Him to become man and to enter into the solidarity of the most profound humiliation. Even as the risen Lord He still bears the nailmarks of the crucifixion (John 20:24ff.). Even as the Lord who returns in glory He will do again what He has done on earth, namely, gird Himself and serve His people. His service is His glory. It is the hallmark of His lordship (Luke 12:37).[45]

Jesus as Savior

As our king, Jesus the Christ first of all rescues or saves us from our enemies, from our own guilt or our responsibility for sin and from those evils which make us their victims. He accomplishes that rescue operation by plunging into the midst of our existence and burdening Himself with the full weight of responsibility for our sin. Our guilt becomes His so that His innocence may destroy it, become ours, and thus save us. Jesus' name itself means "savior" (Matt. 1:21), and so the New Testament writers speak relatively infrequently of Him as Savior, at least as compared with the later very prominent use of the term in the church. For Jesus' Jewish contemporaries the title Messiah embraced the concept of His coming to conquer the enemy and rescue His people from all hostile foes.

As the Christian message was formulated for proclamation to the Gentiles, the apostles, such as Paul, encountered religious cults which had a strong concept of a "savior" figure and/or a rite of salvation, and thus in later New Testament writings, which reflect Christian proclamation in a Gentile world, we find the term more frequently. Paul rejected the claims of the so-called "mystery cult" savior figures of his day when he affirmed that the Lord Jesus Christ is the Savior whom we await from heaven, who has the power to subject all things to Himself (Phil. 3:20). Paul emphasizes against those Gnostic cults that the true Savior is in the business of restoring bodies, the material element of us, as He acts as our Savior (1 Cor. 15:35–57). That, of course, is why He came in the flesh and rose in that flesh from the dead as our victor. Paul again identified the Messiah Jesus as the Savior who abolished death and brought life and immortality to light (2 Tim. 1:10), against those cults which offered other saviors who claimed to do the same. This Savior not only conquers enemies and rescues His people but also insures the peace and harmony of life purified as God designed it (Titus 2:11–14).[46]

While the term *savior* has a rather limited, religious significance in North American culture today, the fundamental human experience of rescue is not foreign to our world. Believers will find any number of examples of rescuers who take risks in behalf of others so that they might conquer a specific threat which is about to consume another's life: the lifeguard, the bodyguard, the fireman, the person who prevents a serious accident by rushing to divert a vehicle or to snatch a child from its path. To those whose gods have collapsed and who feel themselves going down for the third time, believers can bring the presence of Christ the Savior by using such metaphors.

Jesus the Resurrected One

We are able to call the Messianic king Jesus our Savior because He is the Resurrected One. The originator of life, He made life manifest again for His dying creatures by His dying (1 John 1:2; John 1:4; 11:25). He saves us from death, the culmination of all the evils which afflict a creature designed for life in relationship with the Creator. Our doubt and denial have earned us death (Gen. 2:17; Rom. 6:23). He comes to open the door to the safety and protection of life in God's community once again; He even announces that He is that door (John 10:7).[47] He comes to restore us to life, not just by showing us how to live but by laying Himself down as the red carpet on which we find the only reliable way through death into life (John 14:6). Jesus assures His followers that His resurrection is, means, and brings, life for all who trust in Him as the Creator and Re-creator of life (John 11:25–27).[48] He has served as a forerunner, as a pioneer or scout. He who has gone before us into death (Heb. 6:20) has trekked the wasteland of sin-ridden lives to engage our enemies and to clear our paths into true living as God originally designed it. He has met every enemy which could ambush, waylay, and destroy us, and He now brings us through the tomb, with which He is so familiar, into everlasting life. He is the firstborn of the dead (1 Cor. 15:20), and He gives us the courage to stride through death in His track. This is the first element of following Jesus. Since His tomb is open at both ends, we shall not just go around once in life but shall go straight on through this plane of our existence into a life which lasts forever.[49]

For His resurrection made a mockery of death. The sound of His tomb's stone rolling out of the way is the sound of a contemptuous chuckle, a giggle of secure disdain, which echoes across history into our own lives as we now dare to look death and all its results in the eye and smile. Because we can do that to death, we no longer need to get all the gusto we can because we know that we are not just going around once in life. We are going straight on through to the Lord.

We shall rise as the bloodied and beaten Lamb rocks the universe with His laugh of triumph—not like our nervous laugh when we wish we could get out of a tight situation with a little humor. His laugh is rather the last laugh of one who mocks evil and evil people who thought they could triumph by using death as their instrument but who discovered that the Creator of life will not let His own people die, even if He has to die for them to bring them to life. For the Lamb of Calvary's sacrifice fooled death, Satan, and evil people by making the path of surrender and sacrifice, the path of submission and suffering, the path to high ground, the road to peace and life, out of the midst of every terror, turmoil, tribulation, and tragedy.

In Christian witness the fact that God has in His own flesh conquered death gives reassurance to broken sinners against the worst of their enemies, the shadow of deepest darkness which haunts us all, death itself. If He has successfully entered into combat with that result of our sin (1 Cor. 15:56–57), then certainly He can manage all other problems which we face as well and contain and encapsulate every evil which threatens us. Christians are realistic. They do not underestimate the pains of all kinds that death brings. Christ's triumph does not make us callous to fears, regrets, and sorrows which death imposes. Therefore, we come to those encompassed by death with sympathy, in the root meaning of the word, ready to suffer with those who suffer under death's shadow. We stand with the dying and the grieving and hold them in our arms. With our tears flowing, we explain the notes of triumph which underlie the wailing and the dirge which is the ritual accompaniment of death. For the wailing reflects the fact that Jesus, too, wept over this unnatural invasion from our sinfulness, death.

Our lyrics of resurrection need no metaphor, though Christians have found many, from the mythical phoenix bird to a host of natural metaphors, with which to illustrate the regenerative power of God's own resurrection from the dead. In using such metaphors it is important to note that in mythology it is of no consequence whether the deity awakens himself to life again or whether magical powers come to him through the help and influence of the devotees. In contrast, we believe that our Lord's death and resurrection stand outside any natural causation; rather, "it is God's intervention alone which overcomes death and raises Jesus from the dead. The resurrection is here no autonomous natural process, but a sovereign act of God, which has no parallel in mythology."[50]

Believers encounter a fundamental objection to trusting in Jesus as the Resurrected One in the comparatively recent development, largely in the North European-North American religious ghetto of the last quarter millennium, of the idea that Jesus did not actually rise from the dead. This objection arises out of a number of arguments. One is that the historical record of the resurrection is quite flimsy. This argument is difficult to maintain. We have less evidence and attestation for many events in the ancient world which we accept as historically verified, and we have a variety of historical witnesses and arguments to support belief in the resurrection of Jesus. Some people in good conscience may argue that historical proof is much sparser for Christ's return to life than for events in more recent centuries, but that does not set aside the historical

151

records and reasoning which do support the fact of the resurrection.[51]

History here very easily becomes mixed with ideology. As Gustaf Wingren points out, the facticity of the resurrection of Jesus Christ posed no problem until the 18th century, when Christians began feeling intimidated because a shrinking number of epistemological options began to take hold of the Western mind. Our culture became heavily influenced by the presupposition that the superior route to knowledge is through empirical testing, through the eye and the human ability to observe and check, and, finally, to judge.[52] We have misled ourselves into thinking that what is real cannot be unique, as Jesus' resurrection is. Because we cannot repeat it for testing, we tell ourselves, we cannot accept historical witnesses as true in the case of this event. We find it difficult simply to take someone's word for it, even if that someone is God Himself. We would rather retreat into a Docetic, spiritual world in which our own imaginations can mold security and meaning into wispy shapes convenient to our own longing and dreams.

Furthermore, Christianity's historic flirtation with the spiritualism of Platonism has conditioned modern Christians to be less concerned about our Lord's bodily resurrection than we ought to be.

> The difficulty the modern westerner has with the physical aspects of the resurrection is only partly of an intellectual nature. In addition, there is the emotional opposition to combining God and bodily functions. This feeling does not come from our encounter with contemporary science but from our ancient platonic heritage.[53]

Our contemporaries do want to live in a world in which they can set their own feet on solid ground. They would like to persuade themselves that they live in a world of facts, not myths. The physical intervention of God into human history appeals to them once they can recognize that knowledge comes through the ear as well as the eye or the reasoning process, once they realize that the Creator views His creation as good and uses selected elements from it in restoring life to His human creatures.

Walter Künneth summarizes the intersection of history and theology in the cross and the empty tomb:

The meaning of the empty tomb is given as an expression of the concrete, bodily reality of the resurrection of Jesus. It is true that the resurrection of Jesus implies a wholly new corporeality, yet at the same time also a corporeal existence which is inwardly and essentially connected with the historical concreteness of life. This, the resurrection's face toward history, is expressed by the empty tomb. It establishes on the one hand the genuineness of the death in the domination of man by the tomb, and on the other hand correspondingly, the genuineness of the life in the freeing of the body from the tomb. The empty tomb thus becomes the strongest expression of the Easter message's concern with the concrete, bodily resurrection, and at the same time the clear safeguard against every spiritualizing tendency to evaporate the central declarations of the resurrection. To that extent it is by no means a matter of indifference whether theology takes the empty tomb seriously. There is hardly another point at which the Platonizing of theology shows itself more clearly than precisely on this question. For a theologian to take offense at the report of the empty tomb is therefore a mark of the ultimate motives and principles of his basic theological outlook.[54]

The Creator's historical intervention in human flesh into the midst of our histories of sin and death to conquer sin and death is the Gospel. The cross of Golgotha plus the empty tomb "gives rise to a confident migration toward the future and a sovereignty over against outward dangers, which the experiences of visions alone could never give." The key to the earliest church's unbelievable history is in this very combination of Golgotha and Easter.[55] That is also the key to the church's life in our age.

The North American society in which we live tries to deny death. It does not succeed, of course, even when its people manage to sublimate their fears. Recently, one approach to this sublimation has taken the form of affirming death as "natural and good." This approach may allow some to rationalize away fears, and it may cause others to legitimate specific forms of death, such as euthanasia or abortion. Nevertheless, it cannot still that voice which rages against the dying of the light.

Witnessing believers should be sensitive to the many ways death can twist their hearers' perspectives and try to help them probe the fear of death which lies behind various exhibitions of self-centeredness. The Christian witness will point out the inevitability of death to the secure sinner, and, to the broken sinner, he or she will proclaim the end of death in the resurrection of the Author of life. The reality of this message rests on the promise of the Lord's resurrection alone. We gain hearing for it, however, by filling the holes of the absence of loved ones at the same time we repeat the promise.

Jesus the Second Adam

In Romans 5 Paul describes how Jesus' entry into human flesh and then into death, and the reassumption of life again repeats and then reverses the history of the human creature, as seen already in Adam. Paul describes Jesus as a second Adam whom God graciously gives to restore right relationships and to release the abundance of life and righteousness so that His people may become lords of sin and death (5:17). Adam was created human and then led the human race out of humanity into sin and death through a single trespassing of God's structure for life in relationship with Him (5:12, 16). Jesus Christ recapitulated—to use the term of the second century theologian Irenaeus[56]—this course of Adam's life, of the lives of all of us, that entered into death, so that He might draw us in His train into new life, which never ends. That recapitulation, then, has reversed the effects of Adam's fall for God's people.[57] The first Adam found death by poking around at the edges of life. We have been given life again because the second Adam found life by entering into the heart of death and confronting it, smashing it forever, so that it and all evils have no more power over us.

The restoration of our humanity, perfect in our vertical relationship and with renewed capabilities in our horizontal relationships through the Holy Spirit's power, offers a new vision of hope to the broken sinner to whom the witnessing believer addressed the Gospel. We bring the message of the restoration of our humanity to people who do not know the biblical stories, and so we may not use the phrase "second Adam" when we begin the conversation with them. Nonetheless, they dream of more possibilities for their humanity than they have been able to realize. Thus, "second Adam" is not hard to translate into their world. For Christ's promise of new life now, through the power of the Word, bestows upon repentant sinners a kind of hope and purpose in this life. This sometimes-overlooked element of the forgiving and renewing work of Jesus provides a particularly effective point of contact with those who are plagued by the seeming meaninglessness of their current perception of existence.

Jesus the Son of Man

Paul's description of Christ's work through the image of the second Adam affirms His coming as a human creature to become our victor. Another biblical title for Jesus, one which He frequently used to describe Himself, affirms that He exercises the power of the lord and conqueror, the final judge. Strange as it may seem to modern ears, that title is "the Son of Man." In Daniel 7:13–14 the Jews of Jesus' day found the description of "one like a son of man" who received dominion and glory and rule which would last forever. Intertestamental Judaism recognized in this human figure who enjoys divine characteristics a possible form of the Messiah, certainly a redeemer who would come at the end of the age to save God's people.[58] Jesus paradoxically combined this title and image with the image of the Suffering Servant in predictions of His passion (Matt. 16:21; 17:22; 20:17–19), but He also used the title Son of Man as He spoke of His return to bring this age to an end and to complete the rescue of His people from this world's evil, as well as to pronounce final judgment upon that evil (Matt. 24:27–44; 25:31).

The title Son of Man, in keeping with Jewish idiom, emphasizes Jesus' humanity, but the biblical use of the title emphasizes His activities and powers as God. The title does not offer the contemporary Christian witness much basis for analogies. It is a foreign image in this culture. Nonetheless, it does provide important testimony that Jesus, in claiming to be the Son of Man, was clearly witnessing to His right to exercise divine rule and power and to receive the glory which is due to God alone. To those who deny that the New Testament faithful clearly held Jesus to be God, the witnessing believer can explain this term in order to affirm Jesus' divinity. Furthermore, the Holy Spirit uses Jesus' description of Himself as Son of Man to reinforce our confession that He who conquered in His resurrection will complete His gift of life on the Day of the Lord, as He, the Lord and Son of Man, concludes this age with the culmination of His victory over evil in behalf of us and of life.

JESUS AS COMPANION AND GUIDE

Christians, for whom the promise of everlasting life gives an anchor to steady life in this world in the midst of the tremors of every tragedy and tribulation, are often surprised that contemporary Western culture has been able to spawn a generation in which widespread indifference to heaven and life after death flourishes. We believe that people, at least in the history of our own culture, have depended on the hope of everlasting heavenly existence as the mainstay of daily meaning and security. That is, of course, not true. Even in the face of the much more public display of the horrors of death in the Middle Ages, where those horrors were not disguised by our clinically sterile cultural gauze, popular religion concentrated more on offering its adherents the help of pagan magic to solve pressing problems of daily life than it did on insuring release from eternal torment, as strong as that emphasis also was in medieval Christianity. In many primitive religions afterlife is at best a shadowy concept, perhaps permitted to a generation or two but not something that can sustain itself forever. In a society which is falling apart, both immediate and ultimate concerns cause pain and threaten strangulation. Christians address both the immediate and the ultimate concerns. In word and deed we must meet the concerns for today which cry out for the presence of our Savior and God.

God has created us for a life with Him which never ends, and He restores us to that life through Jesus' resurrection, which leads without fail to our resurrection for a heavenly life without limit (1 Cor. 15:13–19). Yet Jesus did not send His disciples forth to bring people to heaven but rather to bring people into that life of discipleship determined by and dependent upon Him (Matt. 28:19). Believers should be sensitive to the fact that many Americans today initially can be best approached through the promise of Jesus to be present and active in their behalf in daily life. Later we lead them to see that His presence in our behalf is most important in its eternal dimension.

Wilhelm Dantine connects Jesus' promise of His presence with His continuing role as our advocate or mediator before the Father:

> What else has Jesus' office among men been but His intercession for widows and orphans, for the crowd of individual sinners or for those destined to be sinners through their vocation, for the God-forsaken world of the poor, the sick, and the desperate, who, according to Pharisaic judgment, justly suffer under divine judgment? Jesus' free association with prostitutes and tax collectors, His meals taken with highly secular figures, His blessing of little children no less than His efficacy at healing, liberating from disease, and indeed overcoming death—this whole picture of the man Jesus of Nazareth, as the gospels draw it, is precisely the picture of the Advocate[59]

Because God and the human creature share their characteristics in Jesus of Nazareth, He who is present with us—because He is omnipresent—appreciates the human dilemma in a world crowded and shrouded by death. He has shared that dilemma, and the many dilemmas which stem from it, except for actually sinning. In taking our place He knows what it is like to feel the weight of our responsibility for sin, our guilt, and to feel the alienation from the Father which that guilt effects (Mark 15:34).

Jesus the Physician

A number of metaphors depict Jesus in ways which can be related to His daily presence in our lives as our companion and guide, although most of these titles can be used to reflect His everlasting presence with us. For instance, as our physician (Matt. 9:9–13) Jesus does not just heal physical ailments, though He may still intervene against illness without scientific explanation apparent to us, as He did during His public ministry, just as He also intervenes to heal through the explainable miracles of modern medicine. Above all, He heals our broken relationships by reconciling us to our Father and to our siblings.[60] He heals our hurts, self-inflicted and inflicted by others. For the alienated and the alienating, that healing is good news.

Jesus the Good Shepherd

Perhaps the most beloved of those pictures of Jesus which Christian art and piety have celebrated is that of Jesus as Good Shepherd. Living as we do in a culture in which not even pet dogs or cats play such a significant role in the lives of people as did sheep in Palestine, we can probably never fully appreciate what it means to live as the sheep of the caring and concerned Shepherd who is willing to give His life to guard and protect His sheep (John 10:11, 15, 17; 1 Peter 2:25), who leads and feeds, guides and sustains those who follow in His footsteps, and rescues them when they stray (Luke 15:4–7). Jesus' Jewish contemporaries knew what His description of Himself as the Good Shepherd meant, for they had recognized God as a shepherd who could gently lead His flock and gather His sheep in His arms (Is. 40:11; cf. Ps. 23; 79:13; 80:1; 95:7). As our shepherd, Jesus functions in our behalf in two ways: "He goes before and does every good for the people, suffers every evil for men's sakes; and His sheep follow Him first by their faith and reliance and then by heeding His example, doing His works, and suffering as He suffered."[61] He protects us as our companion; by letting us lean the weight of our lives upon Him in faith, He gives us the meaning and security which sustain life. At the same time He guards us in this way, He guides us also into the practice of harmony in our horizontal relationships.[62] In a world without sheep and shepherds, this image may require translation in initial conversation with unbelievers unfamiliar with ancient Palestinian culture through their study of the Bible. A number of images, including that of a "good dogcatcher," might be used to convey the searching, seeking, self-sacrificing love which Christians associate with this image.

Jesus the Good Parent

Because we use the term "Father" for the First Person of the Holy Trinity, we almost never think in terms of Jesus as the Good Parent, as we have noted above. Even in a society where, increasingly, the image of parent is tarnished, the image of Jesus as a Father of children (Mark 10: 13–16) can help the lonely and alienated understand that He is their companion and guide. God's love exhibits both paternal and maternal characteristics, as human cultures define these terms. All sorts of scenes from family life suggest approaches for Christian witness, for instance, that of a child just learning to walk tottering along, face filled with joy and delight, in the footsteps of a father, or falling toward the father's arms, in full confidence that the father will be there to catch the falling child.

In the hands of Jesus, our Parent or our Good Shepherd, we can always be confident and safe. Through the Holy Spirit's guidance the witnessing disciple will certainly be able to formulate many such images to help unbelievers, and fellow believers whose feet have been lifted from the ground, to see how secure we really are with Jesus as our companion and guide.

Jesus the Bread of Life

When security seems to have evaporated, as we struggle with forces which seem to choke off life by starving the soul slowly of its meaning and identity, Jesus' calling Himself the Bread of Life provides a way to affirm His life-sustaining power in our lives. Bread is a daily necessity, and it reaches us at the foundation of living. Jesus comes to bestow and sustain life (John 6:32–35, 48–51) on a daily basis, by giving us Himself and His Word of promise.[63] His description of Himself as living water parallels this metaphor of the bread of life (John 4:10–14) and offers the basis of any number of effective metaphors for His life-giving and life-sustaining work. This will aid the witnessing believer in beginning the conversation about Christ with those who hunger and thirst for a better life.

Jesus the Head of the Body

Jesus has become our companion because we were designed by Him for companionship. A series of biblical metaphors point to His presence in the reestablishment of the relationships which our doubt and defiance have smashed or skewed. He is the Head of the body, His church (Col. 1:18; 2:19), a metaphor which reminds us that we cannot be in relationship to Him without being in relationship to other Christians.[64] As our head, Jesus is the source of our direction for life and our coordination with others in His company.

This picture is somewhat similar to that of His being the Vine, of whom we are the branches; we receive life as it flows through Him into us (John 15:1–11).[65] For the alienated who long for family, it is good to know that there is a Father who promises to take us, even when we have no other place to go.

Jesus the Bridegroom

Another longtime Christian favorite among the images which describe the presence of Christ as companion and guide is Paul's naming Christ the Bridegroom of His church (2 Cor. 11:2; Eph. 5:22–23). Jesus Himself had employed that image (Matt. 9:14–15; Mark 2:18–20; Luke 5:33–35), and in Revelation the images of Jesus as Lamb and Bridegroom are combined (19:7; 21:9). God depicted His mercy in the Old Testament through the marriage of Hosea to a prostitute (1:2). These pictures can help the Christian witness make clear the fidelity of Jesus to His chosen people and the intimacy of a relationship built on His love and our trust. Furthermore, the unconditional love of God in Jesus is made clear in the unbreakable, indissoluble nature of marriage as He created it to be.[66]

Jesus Present in Our Love

Christian witness to the presence of Jesus as companion and guide must go beyond developing and articulating modern applications of these biblical metaphors. In spite of the contemporary song's assurance that people will recognize our Christianity by our love,[67] they will not, since many non-Christians love pretty well—if not for the proper reasons (out of love and trust in their Creator)— at least in the external forms prescribed by His plan for human life. It is necessary for us to articulate the love of our Bridegroom and Father as we show His love to others. Our lack of love will deny Him of whom we speak and will confound our message. The presence of Jesus as loving companion and guide must be articulated in our loving. The Lord left us in the hands of the Holy Spirit. However, the Holy Spirit is at one significant disadvantage in comparison to Jesus when it comes to caring for human creatures. He has no human tongue, no human hands, no human shoulder for the sorrowing to cry on. He has to borrow them from us to be that other comforter and counselor whom Jesus promised He would be (John 14:16), in the face of every evil which confronts and threatens us.

ATONEMENT MOTIFS:
HOW CAN HIS DYING AND RISING SAVE?

As the Holy Spirit speaks through us, He addresses questions regarding the way in which God has saved His people through Jesus. Since the early church began to proclaim the person and work of Jesus of Nazareth as the basis of our once again receiving true identity, security, and meaning, Christians have either tried to explain *why* God had to become flesh, suffer, die, and rise again, rather than go through some other process, or *how* His death and resurrection amounts to the basis of our redemption and restoration. These explanations are called atonement theories. Ian D. Kingston Siggins has observed in his study of Luther that the reformer follows the Scriptures in propounding no single, all-explaining theory which purports to give a complete answer to the why and how of God's atoning work, a theory which would pierce and analyze the mystery of God's saving will. Siggins finds in the Scriptures and in Luther a recognition that the accomplishment of Christ in our behalf exceeds our comprehension and that a rich variety of descriptions of His saving work are to be used to call people to faith in Jesus Christ.[68]

One theory used to explain how and why the work of Jesus effects salvation is too atrophied and too misleading to be of use in contemporary Christian witness. It is the theory of the 12th-century theologian Abelard, who especially emphasizes that Christ is the great example and teacher, who arouses responsive love in His disciples. This love is the basis on which reconciliation and forgiveness rest. Abelard's view certainly fails to deal adequately either with the horror of human sin and God's wrath or with the death and resurrection of Jesus Christ. As Abelard taught his theory, it also emphasized the human creature's contribution to salvation and viewed Christ's merit as that which "makes complete the merit of man by virtue of His intercession for them."[69]

So understood, this theory obviously undercuts the biblical view of the relationship between Creator and creature, between

Redeemer and redeemed. It has had parallels during the past three centuries in the doctrines of Protestant theologians under the influence of the Enlightenment and in the schools of Albrecht Ritschl and Adolf von Harnack. Ritschl taught that the "atonement" takes place as "man gives up his mistrust of God, which had been based on a misunderstanding of God's character and is dissipated by the sight of Christ's faithfulness to His vocation even unto death; this human faithfulness is a revelation of the Divine Love."[70] Christian witness which sets forth only such a view defeats itself. It is not faithful to the biblical witness, fails to take seriously the power of evil and personal sin or guilt, and ignores the power of God in the flesh.

Christ the Victor

The early church had a much different view of the atonement; the chief strands of its proclamation of the work of Christ are summarized in the atonement motif labeled "Christ as victor" *(Christus Victor)*. It emphasizes Jesus' engagement with evil, above all with death, in His own self-sacrifice, which led to the triumph of His resurrection. This resurrection victory He shares with His people through their Baptism. The liberation of the people of God by means of Christ's movement through the waters of death into His resurrection was frequently paralleled with the exodus, by which God redeemed His ancient people from bondage and captivity in Egypt. This motif of the atonement focuses more on God's love and His power than on His wrath. In his study of one of the leading proponents of the *Christus Victor* motif, the second-century theologian Irenaeus, Gustaf Wingren notes that here Jesus is described as

> entering to the darkness where man is held prisoner. As Jesus was tempted in order to destroy sin, so He was put to death in order to destroy death. In both temptation and Crucifixion Christ breaks right through the opposition of His adversary without being held back by the snares in which Adam was caught—in fact, these bonds of the enemy are torn aside by Christ's power and are rendered ineffective as shackles to hold man in bondage. The Incarnate One *is* man—in and through His survival and freedom man survives, is free. Man has been created to live and not to die, and he reaches this goal of his humanity in the Resurrection of Jesus.

> The resurrection life is not an unnatural addition to what is truly human, but is the uncorrupted life of Creation, and as such it breaks through into an unnatural world in which death holds dominion. Jesus's way forward to the victory of the life of Creation passed through the Crucifixion. Christ had to descend into human life as it was, and then—with man alive within himself—break out of the barriers and shatter all that was pressing man's life out of him.[71]

God's powerful intervention into the midst of human life as the crucified and risen Lord means that He has become the Re-creator, the "giver of life, who pours out His Spirit over the arid and dead world of men." Against Him still stands Satan, with His instruments of chaos and void, sin and death, the evil human will, and physical decay. "But against Satan there stands likewise a single power—God, the Lord of all physical life and the source of all life, but who also declares His will in the commandments which enjoin righteousness and love, and who is Himself what He commands in His Word, that is, in Christ."[72]

From this gift of life in Jesus' resurrection a witnessing believer may develop an effective means of testifying to the re-creative power of the Risen Lord, for example. This motif may also describe Jesus' work in metaphors taken from battlefield combat, as the king who defends His people and rescues them from oppression. It may also rely on the psalmists' device of describing God's victorious intervention in behalf of His people with a courtroom metaphor. C. S. Lewis points out that the ancient Jews thought of God's judgment in terms of the court of justice and viewed the action there as a civil case in which the human creature comes as plaintiff against an enemy and "hopes for a resounding triumph with heavy damages."[73]

Wilhelm Dantine develops this picture further in discussing the pronouncement of pardon for Christ's people. The despotic enemies of His people,

> deities, demons, angelic powers, death—lose their rights through this verdict. … they lose their claim on man and thus also their power over him. … Instead, they are deprived of their power by the innocence of the righteous man, who has been withdrawn from them. This has lasting significance: the deities are not denied, they just become uninteresting to him whom God Himself has

163

made righteous. The demons are not ridiculed, but they are clearly characterized in themselves in their horrible power. But the righteous man need no longer fear them. Suffering and death remain what they are ... but they cannot impair the joy and life of the righteous man. ... The lawsuit [of Jesus in our behalf] aims at the restoration of creation: the new man, the new creature, the renewed creation, is the victory given to the justified man.[74]

Thus, the Holy Spirit liberates us to live a life redeemed from the power of evil to bend our lives out of shape, to rob us of the identity, security, and meaning which God gives us once again in Jesus. We live our lives now through the victory of His death and resurrection over the ultimate evil, death; over its cause in us, sin; and over its originator, the devil. Christian witness delivers this message of genuine freedom to all who feel threatened or oppressed by any and every evil.

Christ the Vicarious Victim

The other great atonement motif in the history of Christian teaching has been labeled vicarious satisfaction, and although elements of it or variations on it had been present earlier in the proclamation of the church, it is most often associated with the 11th-century theologian Anselm of Canterbury. The *Christus Victor* atonement theory had emphasized the Christian's sharing in Christ's victory through Baptism; Anselm placed atonement theory in the context of the Lord's Supper and penance, since these sacraments had gained greater prominence than Baptism in the medieval church. He used the imagery and presuppositions of the feudal system of his society as he conveyed the biblical message of the significance of Jesus' death in our behalf to his hearers and readers.[75]

R. W. Southern has summarized Anselm's description of how the atonement came to be and why it had to involve the incarnation in the medieval theologian's work on the subject, *Cur Deus Homo? (Why God Became Man)*. The human creature, created by God for eternal blessedness, must submit his will perfectly and voluntarily to God. The deviation of the human will from God must either be punished by deprivation of blessedness or rectified (or satisfied) by an offering greater than the act of disobedience; "there can be no free

164

remission." Since no human creature can offer anything to God beyond his due obedience, but since a failure to redeem fallen human creatures would frustrate God's plan for creation, God Himself must take the place of the creature, as a vicar or substitute, and make the offering which will satisfy His wrath. Thus, the incarnation was necessary.[76]

The *Christus Victor* atonement theory focuses upon Christ's victory against the evil forces which threaten the human creature from outside us; "vicarious satisfaction" atonement theory focuses upon Christ's sacrifice in our place to deal with God's wrath against the evil within us, and thus it comes to terms with our guilt and shame and self-hatred. If we press Anselm's theory in the wrong direction, we may undercut the sense of sovereign grace which moves God to look upon us with favor apart from any condition whatsoever. However, we do need to address seriously our own enmity against God and our feelings of hostility against our own failed and flawed selves. The vicarious satisfaction motif offers the most elaborately fabricated digest of the biblical materials to bring us the means God gives us in Jesus to face the brokenness of our vertical relationship, and of our inner relationship as well, and to be delivered from this brokenness.

Life cannot come together in one whole piece for us unless we face squarely what has shattered it. We cannot appreciate fully the seriousness of the collapse of the good human life without perceiving God's wrath at sin. Yet even as we use the vicarious satisfaction motif which the Scriptures provide in Christian witness, we must recognize that the price of Jesus' blood (1 Peter 1:18, 19; cf. 1 Cor. 6:20) has redeemed us from our own futile ways and the just judgment of God as well, in a manner far more profound than mere commercial calculations can reflect. "If Jesus' death had been merely a payment to God he would not have done enough. Wrath and law would not have been *satisfied* in actuality. They are not satisfied actually until they end, until we don't feel or hear them anymore, i.e., until God acts to put the old Adam to death and to raise up a new one."[77]

Helmut Thielicke calls upon Martin Luther's metaphor of the "magnificent duel" to describe how God came to terms with His wrath as He came to terms with our sin by abolishing it in the per-

165

son of Jesus: God the Judge wrestled with God the Father—and God the Father won. If we only had to address

> the good-naturedness of "the good Lord," Jesus would never have had to die. Then there would have been no need for that sacrificial action and suffering by which he took upon his shoulders the weight of the whole world. No, what is at work here is the miracle through which God conquered the *ira dei* (wrath of God) by means of his love. Here pain and anguish struggle in God himself. And therefore, here again beats the heart that trembles and loves and pities and suffers with me. This is no mere principle of love, this is no God of the philosophers—as Pascal called him— here there is nothing except his loving heart.[78]

This love expressed itself by wrestling with its own counterpart, wrath, and by paying the great price of life itself to put wrath away from God's relationship to us, in a mystery which defies human analysis. This same love expressed itself in forgiveness won by Jesus' death which consumed God's wrath at the same time it consumed our guilt.

> God's vengeance did not strike the sinners, but the one sinless man who stood in the sinner's place, namely God's own Son. Jesus Christ bore the wrath of God. ... He stilled God's wrath toward sin and prayed in the hour of the execution of the divine judgment: "Father, forgive them, for they do not know what they do!" No other than he, who himself bore the wrath of God, could pray in this way. That was the end of all phony thoughts about the love of God which do not take sin seriously. God hates and redirects his enemies to the only righteous One, and this One asks forgiveness for them. Only in the cross of Jesus Christ is the love of God to be found.[79]

In His own death, Jesus did our sin to death. Because He has annihilated our sin, forgiveness comes to us. For Jesus and the Father came to terms with human doubt and defiance and with their own reaction to human sin as Jesus joined us in human flesh under the accusation of His own Law and His own anger against our destruction of our relationship with Him. His death expresses a vital part of His re-creative Word which claims us and seizes us out of our doubt and defiance to return us to Himself. In Romans 5:9 Paul states that Jesus' blood restores us to a right relationship with God and thus obviously saves us from God's wrath. Because He has taken our place under that wrath in His innocence and righteousness, we who are joined with Him become righteous, no longer subject to this wrath.

> Since *orge* (wrath) represents nothing but the judicial and punitive righteousness of God, the being saved, salvation is here evaluated as a rescue from the punishment of the judge ... Salvation and participation in the *doxa* (glory) of Christ is possible only through Him as the Substitute who intercedes for man before the judgment seat of God.[80]

The vicarious satisfaction of Jesus not only deals with God's wrath; it does so through Jesus' becoming a human creature, one of us, and indeed our vicar, our substitute. His coming to die for us, on the cross,

> declares *God* is with you—Emmanuel. *He* is alongside you in your suffering. *He* is in the darkest place of your dark night. You do not have to look for him in the sky, beyond the stars, in infinite light, in glory unimaginable. He is incarnate. That means he has been *crucified*. For to become flesh, to become one of us, means not only to be born but also to die, to fail. But it means that *he* has been crucified; and therefore that the way of the cross, which is in any case our way, need not be regarded any longer as producing only negative results.[81]

His presence in our behalf and in our place in becoming the victim of the Law's condemnation and the wrath of His Father involves more than just His death. His entire assumption of our kind of life expresses His solidarity with us and His intervention between us and God's wrath for our sakes.

> The way of solidarity reaches both its high point and also its low point in the cross. In the light of the cross, the whole of his earthly pilgrimage is seen to be one long way of suffering. Even at his birth there is no room for him in the inn (Luke 2:7). Men reject him. His cradle is among the beasts. Crib and cross are of the same wood. He is also a stranger with neither home nor shelter (Luke 9:58). ... Finally, he is afflicted with an ultimate loneliness which also has a human aspect, for those who had been his companions left him (Mark 14:50),[82]

and He also suffered the greatest pain of hell, the feeling of being forsaken by the Father (Mark 15:34). He did this simply because He loved us. "Loving here is a state of being. It simply means being there for the other, entering into his situation, not keeping anything back. It means transferring oneself. This is how Jesus loved."[83]

The Joyous Exchange

His love did not stop with His joining us in a world of evil. Even more than coming among us as one of us, He came, in the words of Martin Luther, to become, on the cross, in the sight of His Father and our judge,

> the greatest thief, murderer, adulterer, robber, desecrator, blasphemer, etc. there has ever been anywhere in the world. He is not acting in His own Person now. Now He is a sinner, who has and bears the sin of Paul, the former blasphemer, persecutor, and assaulter; of Peter, who denied Christ; of David, who was an adulterer and a murderer, and who caused the Gentiles to blaspheme the name of the Lord (Rom. 2:24). In short, He has and bears all the sins of all men in His body—not in the sense that He has committed them but in the sense that He took these sins, committed by us, upon His own body, in order to make satisfaction for them with His own blood.[84]

As witnessing believers encounter bitter and broken sinners who blame God for the evil in their lives, they can point out that, even though God indeed is not to blame, He has paid the price for that evil and suffered under its impact.

Christian witnesses will recognize in these atonement motifs useful approaches for making plausible the redeeming and re-creating work of Christ. For each contains elements of the other even though they emphasize and approach His saving work with differing concerns. The Christ the Victor motif provides an approach above all for dealing with those who feel themselves the victims of evils outside themselves or outside their control, but it also offers the hope of victory for those who struggle against evil within. The vicarious satisfaction motif not only assists sinners to realize that their guilt is forgiven and their shame is taken away, it also aids them in realizing that life can be meaningful in the face of trauma and tragedy since God Himself has shared our confrontation with such troubles. It aids sinners in recognizing that He is present in the midst of alienation and estrangement. Thus, believers should be ready to employ elements of both motifs, sometimes in tandem, to express God's love in Jesus Christ and to make His saving work familiar and comprehensible to the broken sinner. For the whole of this salvation will not become clear unless finally the significance of both cross and empty tomb are understood, much as Walter Künneth has set forth their conjunction:

> Because Christ was crucified, therefore the world is saved by God. The resurrection is the principle whereby the significance of the cross is made known. ... The death of the Son of God appears as the execution of God's judgment on wrath, as punishment which takes effect in the "curse of the cross." Because Jesus submits to this judgment as the Son, His death becomes a sacrifice, and a specifically vicarious sacrifice at that. Thus the resurrection acquires the character of the "acceptance of the sacrifice of Jesus," which in turn endows Jesus' passion and death with the quality of a work of reconciliation. Further, knowledge of the resurrection lets us see the death of Jesus as a victorious battle with the satanic realm, as the precondition of life and the breaking in of life. The message of reconciling and justifying grace also presupposes the acceptance by God of Jesus' death.[85]

SYNONYMS OF SALVATION

Most frequently contemporary Christians summarize the work of Jesus simply by saying, "Jesus saves." But salvation is not a concept used outside religious circles in our day and thus does not offer as easy an access to the biblical testimony regarding God's saving work as do some synonyms of salvation. Some of these synonyms appear in the chart on page 122.

The Scriptures heap such descriptive synonyms on top of each other, and Christian witness can be more effectively communicated if the believer is familiar with these synonyms for salvation and is conscious of the possibility of finding others in contemporary culture. For instance, Old Testament prophets could sing the praises of God who took away charges lodged against His people, cast out their enemies, was present among them as a warrior who gives victory and as one who rejoices over them with gladness, who renewed them with His love, removed disasters from them, saved the lame and gathered the outcasts, transformed their shame into praise, and would bring them home (Zeph. 3:14–20). Micah could find seven different ways to describe the saving actions of God: the pardoning of iniquity, the passing over of transgression, the setting aside of His anger on the basis of His delight in steadfast love, His compassion, His treading our iniquities underfoot and casting our sins into the sea, His faithfulness which He has sworn to our fathers (7:18–20). Hosea praised our God as a God who heals and loves, who turns away His anger from us, as the freshness of spring which lets us blossom (14:4–7). In differing situations one or another of these synonyms of salvation, combined with formulations of the Gospel shaped by atonement motifs and biblical titles for the Savior, will provide the basis for making Christ's work plausible to the broken sinner at hand.

He Saves Us

Salvation itself denotes deliverance or rescue, a personal intervention by one person on behalf of another. In the Psalms God came as king to wage war against His enemies and the enemies of His people (Ps. 44:7; 74:12; 80:2; cf. Is. 33:22). God's final deliverance could also be described as His work of salvation in the Old Testament (Is. 43:5–7; Jer. 31:7; Zech. 8:7). Jesus' deliverance, aid, and rescue of His people were highlighted already before His birth by Zecharias (Luke 1:69, 71, 77); He described His own mission as seeking and saving the lost (Luke 19:10).[86] Jesus' daring rescue of His people involved braving the dangers of an evil world, submitting to the assaults of the evils which afflict them and which they perpetrate, taking their place even as they continue to resist Him.

A variety of broken sinners, with various afflictions—from the terrors of what lies outside us to the guilt within—can respond to the Gospel of Jesus when it is couched in terms of that kind of rescue, and presented against the background of both Christ's victory over every evil and His coming to terms with these evils and God's wrath, but taking our place under their impact.

He Redeems Us

Closely related to the image of such a rescue is the biblical concept of redemption. The words which we translate "redeem" include the word for salvation or rescue itself. In the Old Testament we find that redemption can denote an action in the sphere of private law, in which another person offers a gift whose value covers someone's fault and accomplishes more than just the cancellation of a debt but actually and above all prevents the taking of a human life. Or it can denote the action of a family member in behalf of the next of kin, to reclaim family lives or goods which have fallen into bondage, to avenge the murder of a kinsman, or to obtain release of relatives from slavery. God acts as redeemer of His people above all in the exodus (Ex. 6:6; 15:13; Ps. 106:10; Is. 51:10). Here the focus is not on the price paid but on the promise of His redemption which remains with them in the midst of present and future evils (Is. 35:9–10; 48:20; 52:9; 63:9; Ps. 103:4).[87]

The biblical use of the word "redeem" to describe God's liberating action in behalf of those whom He regards as family offers the Christian witness a number of avenues for clarifying the significance of the incarnation of our God, His death, and His resurrection to our contemporaries. Liberation from the power of forces outside ourselves means that impotence can be placed aside through the recognition that God has intervened in our behalf. That may not mean that evil will cease nipping at our heels, but it does mean that we will have confidence that it cannot consume us anymore. The icy blasts of other people's hatred or winter's soaring costs in fuel bills and cabin fever will be melted by the presence of Him who exercised power over such evils by confronting them in our place and embracing even death in His own arms. Even though we may have to stand in the puddle for a time, we can be confident that He will not let us freeze to death in those icy blasts.

For those in bondage to alcohol or kleptomania the announcement of liberation or redemption is applied first to the vertical relationship, in which these slave masters are experienced as evil gods which will not go away and which interfere with a healthy and free relationship with our Father. The message of redemption also holds out hope that Christ will conquer the habit of hell which enslaves and tortures as well, but believers should recognize that exchanging the habits of hell for the habits of heaven very often takes longer than the restoration of the vertical relationship. God redeems us for Himself with far greater ease than the implications of that redemption develop in concrete form in our relationships with others, nature, and self. The believer recognizes that it is easier for broken sinners to come to believe the Gospel about God, that He conquers their foes, than it is for them to believe the Gospel about themselves, that their foes can no longer touch them.

In both the case of the sinner broken by natural or human forces and of the enslaved sinner the Christian witness must also remember that the presence of the conquering Jesus becomes real through more than just the articulation of the message of redemption through God's total victory. Jesus becomes present through the presence of the members of His body. They support the broken sinner in the daily battle against the terror and entrapment of forces inside or outside the person whose life they have been choking off.

Believers make their articulation more plausible through the demonstration of that love of God, His care and concern, which is the essence of His mighty destruction of the power of evil. The believer helps the unbelieving neighbor whose house has burned down by providing a bed, a ride to the insurance agent, and a hand of comfort as the neighbor sifts the ashes. On the basis of the demonstration of God's concern and presence the believer can go on to help the broken neighbor rearrange priorities, so that the loss of home, job, or family member, while still taken in all its seriousness, is seen against the background of meaning for life which Jesus gives in His promise of new life which lasts forever. Without the loving and caring presence of the people of Christ, the message of His victory might well remain a message for other people, about other people. They will know Christ by our love—provided we explain that our love is His love.

He Resurrects Us

Jesus' resurrection triumph puts all life into perspective because it renews, regenerates, re-creates: it gives new life. In the face of every kind of loss—the loss of self-respect to guilt and shame, the loss of home or family to natural disaster and human wickedness, the loss of friends and family through alienation, the loss of meaning for life or security in daily living, the loss of one's identity—we all must be newly created, once again, in His image.

> The gospel is the joyful message that in Christ this new creation has already and actually broken in on us, and the promise that it will be carried to its completion. It is the story of one who came down to earth and lived "under the voice" [of the Law] and died under it as we all do, but yet arose triumphant and broke its power and brought it to an end.[88]

This message of new creation through Jesus' resurrection delivers the antidote against death and all the warping terror and rage it generates in human life. Because death ends it all, human creatures living in the darkness of its shadow are blinded to life's true meaning. The frightening thing about death is that it ultimately has no meaning, and it calls into question the meaning of every human attachment and action from which we attempt to force meaning. It is the triumph of meaninglessness, of darkness, of nothing. Death also engulfed Jesus, and it was rebuffed; it was destroyed by trying to gobble down Him who was not on its diet and who thus gave death a terminal case of indigestion.[89]

Therefore, for the person plagued by the meaninglessness of life, a view of life from Golgotha restores a vision of life's meaning in the midst of its seeming senselessness, simply because Golgotha points toward an empty tomb and the corpse of God come back to life.[90] Resurrection and new life in Christ also empower the forgiven sinner to leave behind hellish habits, with all their guilt and shame, for Jesus' resurrection refocuses our gaze on Him as the source of our meaning and identity, our security in life. It thus liberates us from having to seek identity, security, and meaning by taking from others and exalting ourselves at their expense; we are freed to give freely as He originally created us, in His image, to give, love, and show care and concern.

Above all, the Gospel of our Lord's resurrection frees us for living for Him because it frees us from that which is threatening in the certainty of our death within this temporal sphere of existence.

> When I say, "I have to depart," then the values and the things of my life—my house, my garden, my stamp collection, my voca-

tion—are the standard by which I measure the departure. But when I can say, "I am going home," then there is a point in my life where even the greatest things become an insubstantial shadow and I see only the shore of home where I am awaited.[91]

The comfort of knowing not only that I must sometimes wait on God but also that God waits on me does not just give me hope for the future. It transforms my life today because of the promise which the love of my Father and Creator bestows.

Even though Christians will not want to depart from their loved ones and their roles of earthly service, even though they may indeed fear the pain associated with death, even though the deceit of the devil may push the dying believer to flirt with doubt, Christ's people can indeed relax in the face of death. For they know that God protects them through Jesus' resurrection against even the enemy of death. They know that God uses death as the agent of the destruction of sin and of deliverance into new life.[92] Christian witness puts death in all its dimensions—from petty frustrations in a seemingly meaningless world to the pain of terminal cancer—into perspective, thanks to the light shining from the other side of the grave through Jesus' tomb to light up the lives of broken sinners. It does so by testifying to God's gift of new life in the risen Jesus, and by demonstrating this new life in freely given support and concern and assistance with the vexing burdens of the days of boredom, despair, pain, or terror.

He Re-creates Us

Behind our confidence in God's power to regenerate us through the raising of His own Son lies our belief that His original gift of life in Eden was bestowed without condition, apart from any merit or worthiness in us. We believe that human life has worth and value because God spoke and assigned it that worth and value in living out His image in caring for His creatures whom He has placed within our reach. We believe that human life is worthwhile because *God assumed it so that He might re-create it* through His own passion and death, in which He came to terms with all that destroys life, and through His resurrection. As believers confront the sinner broken by despair at the meaninglessness of life, they can testify that life does have meaning on the basis of God's incarnation and also on the basis of His original creation of His human creatures to enjoy their relationship with Him and with other creatures.

"The dilemma of modern man is simple," Francis Schaeffer observes: "he does not know why man has any meaning. He is lost. Man remains a zero. This is the damnation of our generation, the heart of modern man's problems. But if we begin with a personal beginning and this is the origin of all else, then the personal does have meaning, and man and his aspirations are not meaningless."[93] Believers affirm for their hearers the meaning of life as they rehearse the love of God in creating and His mercy in re-creating us as His own, His children, members of His body or family. Within the Christian community the true life is restored and its meaning returns through the presence of God's love in Jesus and His members.

He Adopts Us

A related synonym of salvation is that of adoption. The redeemer God enters into the redemptive process to reclaim a member of His family for Himself. We have left the family. We are runaways and have denied that we are His children. He pursues us as the Good Shepherd pursues the lost sheep. He takes out adoption papers on us in our baptisms. He restores us as His children (Rom. 8:15; Gal. 4:5). He has chosen us to be His own adopted children, again without any merit or worthiness in us, simply because He wanted us to be His own. The broken sinner, the victim of alienation from others or the perpetrator of acts of disobedience, can find in God's free act of adoption the comfort of His love.

He Reconciles Us to the Father

He reconciled us to Himself through the cross, which brought the hostility which separated us from God and estranged us from His family to an end. He did that by creating a new creature, restoring us to the peace and harmony of Eden (Eph. 2:14–16), by now refusing to count our trespasses against us and by speaking anew the re-creative Word which brings us back together with our Father and Creator (2 Cor. 5:18; cf. Rom. 5:10). Jesus entered into human

175

life from His majesty and power as God so that He might end our denial that He is the true source of security, meaning, and identity for His human creatures.[94] Those ultimate evils, our denial and doubt on the one hand and God's wrath which condemns us on the other, are abolished as Jesus our Mediator and Bridge-builder brings us back together with the Father once again.

Particularly for those victimized by alienation and to those who strike back by fostering estrangement, the Gospel as Jesus' reconciling love and power brings a cogent expression of God's merciful will for His people, even though we may sometimes find that it is easier to experience God's reconciliation of us to Himself than reconciliation in our horizontal relationships. Christian witnesses can use the picture of divorce and reconciliation to make clear to broken sinners how God comes without conditions to deal with the sin and evil which drives Him and us away from each other.

In this reconciliation God accepts us once again as His children and moves us to accept Him as our Father. He creates our acceptance of Him simply through His undeserved favor and His striking demonstration of ultimate love in His own self-sacrifice. The God who freely made us acceptable to Himself as His children while we are yet hostile to Him (Rom. 5:10) does not merely accept us as we are; He transforms us. He transforms us in His own sight by His transforming word of forgiveness of our doubt, denial, and disobedience. He transforms us in the sight of other people by freeing us from the captivity to false gods which led us to exact security and meaning from our neighbors rather than giving them love, care, and concern. Thus, our ultimate reconciliation with the Father enables us to work on horizontal reconciliation with a new freedom.

He Forgives Us

Among the synonyms for salvation a fundamental expression is that of forgiveness or absolution. At the beginning of some attempts to witness to the Gospel this expression may not be appropriate. The neighbor broken by a house fire or by the personal assault of a criminal needs to hear of God's liberation of His people from the power, if not always from the effects, of evil. Sinners whose guilt has broken their false gods and who want to put the disobedient practice of the habits of hell behind them will need early on the assurance of God's forgiveness on the basis of Jesus' obedience unto death. As Christian conversation moves from symptoms to substance, forgiveness will also be pronounced upon those who felt broken initially only because they viewed themselves as victims of evils outside themselves or of oppressive habits over which they could, in their bondage, exercise no control. The original sin of doubt, the root sin of our defiance and denial of God's lordship, also cries out for absolution. It too needs to be washed away. That can happen only through the power of the God who was crucified under the weight of sin which caused Him to feel forsaken by His Father.

Forgiveness or absolution takes place because of the incarnate God's own death and resurrection. Forgiveness is conveyed to us from the Word made flesh through the words of God's people. These words from any of His baptized representatives carry His power (Rom. 1:16), the power of the only person who can reverse the human rejection of the Creator in every sin from doubt and defiance to disobedience and division.

> Only God can forgive (for only God has given the Law which we have broken), and when Jesus in fact forgives sinners, He is demonstrably the Verbum, the Word in human form, who has received power from the Father to forgive. He has this power to forgive as God and as man, and in the Savior's enactment of forgiveness God and man are uniquely related when it is declared that as man He has compassion on us, or suffers with us, and that as God He has mercy upon us and forgives us our debts.[95]

As believers move to forgive the sins of those who break under their weight in the course of Christian conversation, or who are found broken already, they must remember that it is difficult to believe that God can forgive and often even more difficult to forgive oneself even after a measure of trust in God's forgiving power has arisen. Many Christians struggle long and hard against and under the curse of a guilt which they say they believe is forgiven already, not present in God's sight anymore. Yet they nurse that guilt inside themselves and keep the fires of hellish misery stoked within. Such memories of specific sins or of a long pattern of sinfulness may indeed be impossible to erase psychologically, but faith should come to view them from the other side of Jesus, through Jesus-colored glasses as it were, and put them in a perspective from which they cannot plague us any longer. The believer will often have to help the growing young Christian in the struggle to believe the Gospel about himself or herself as well as about God.

> Classical Christianity would say two things to the person who is plagued with memories of the irreparable. The first is that guilt before God is blotted out by the gospel. The other is that an individual's guilt toward someone that the individual can no longer get in touch with (one dead, or one living far away) is humanly irreparable—but God is the God of all people, even the dead. We must accept the fact that we cannot heal the irreparable by ourselves. The Creator's possibility of turning evil into good (Gen. 50:20) can never be transmuted into human possibilities. God remains the one who finally conquers destruction, and he does it in a human misdeed which defies all comparison—the crucifixion. The cross is a good example of God's way of creating.[96]

As sinners first die to self-reliance and defiance of God, they may come to trust in His grace but at the same time want to help Him forgive and deliver themselves. Effective Christian witness patiently supports young believers in growing so secure in God's forgiving hand that they no longer need to seek a part of their security in that purgatory of the pew which they create as they enjoy the preacher's whipping them with the Law. Equally tragic is that self-blame and self-deprecation which force them to pay for their own sins with the hellish torture they impose upon themselves. As they also can lay the necessity of such contributions to their salvation behind them, they will realize more fully the blessedness and joy and peace of knowing that God has restored all relationships to their right and proper form. The importance of private, personal confession and absolution in this witness cannot be overestimated. Sinners need other people to take both specks and logs out of their eyes (Matt. 7:3–5). We cannot practice spiritual surgery on ourselves without great risk. Sinners need both their own articulation of guilt, shame, and impotence and another believer's pronouncement of God's love and forgiveness. Both confession and absolution in the midst of the believer's witnessing greatly assist the new believer, for they are integral parts of the process of being turned back to the peace of being God's children.

When we ask those to whom the Holy Spirit sends us if they will accept Jesus Christ and commit their lives to Him, we almost inevitably place the burden for their conversion on them—on their acts of accepting and committing. Confession and absolution, or some parallel acknowledgement of our need and of God's goodness in Christ, provide a much better focus for the "critical" moment in Christian conversion, if such a moment actually must exist. For in the word of Gospel which we pronounce upon our hearers, there is assurance and peace.

He Justifies Us, That Is, He Restores Our Humanity

The biblical and theological term for that restoration of relationships to their right and proper form is justification. Justification—literally "making righteous"—has to do with restoring right relationships, the right harmonies to which God tunes His human creatures as instruments of His love just as He did in Eden. There God made all things good and right through the power of His word. That is what happens when He justifies sinners, when He restores them to the right relationship with Himself and the right relationship with all other creatures.

Justification is also a legal term, and the Scriptures place the justification of the sinner within the courtroom of God. Actually, the term justification is liable to misunderstanding in contemporary North America, for when we justify ourselves, we usually mean that we are proving that a certain action was indeed correct; we present ourselves as righteous. The biblical understanding of our justification is quite the opposite: we must be freed from all that is in fact wrong with us and be restored to right relationships by another.

We can be presented as righteous by the God who forgives and re-creates us only after we have ceased to exist as sinners in His sight. Thus, justification by the re-creative Word made flesh takes our sins seriously as sins; we are ungodly as God comes to justify us. We can prepare ourselves or make ourselves eligible—or more eligible than other ungodly people—in utterly no way. This means that we must lay aside our cultural understanding of justification and return to the biblical roots of the concept of righteousness, that is, the way God made us to be, as we were right with Him and His creation in Eden. He fashioned these right relationships at the beginning as a part of the essence of His human creatures. In our vertical relationship with the Father that righteousness consisted in His unconditional love for us and our unconditional trust in Him. In our horizontal relationships with other human creatures that righteousness consisted in our love, care, and concern for those whom He had placed within the sphere of our exercise of the responsibilities He had given us in the various situations of life. To understand God's restoration of our righteousness, we must keep these two dimensions of righteousness distinct in our thinking, and not confuse the ways in which it is restored through the work of Christ.

The Greek term for justification *(dikaioō)* in the courtroom can mean that sentence is pronounced upon the guilty and punishment is ordered carried out.[97] This happens as God justifies the ungodly, for we are connected as sinners to the death of Christ. We are laid in His tomb, out of the sight of our Creator and Father, as He incorporates us into His death in the execution of Golgotha through our baptisms (Rom. 6:3–11; Col. 2:11–15). Justification spells the death of the sinner who has disrupted God-established relationships by breaking God's pattern for human living and defying His Law. The Law exacts its punishment; the sinner does die, with Christ, in justification. This buried sinner then comes alive as a new creature, in Christ, through God's justifying, re-creating Word.

Justification also means rendering a verdict of acquittal, receiving pardon, even though undeserved, from the judge. Wilhelm Dantine points out that the biblical description of our justification casts the Father and Jesus in various roles, including those of witness (Rev. 1:5; 3:14), defense counsel (John 14:16; Rom. 8:34), judge, the condemned person, and the substitute for the condemned (Rom. 5:6; 1 Peter 3:18). The verdict is based upon the judge's acceptance of the substitution of Jesus for the condemned person and of the arguments of the defense counsel and witness in behalf of the guilty.[98]

Luther's concept of the "joyous exchange" expresses this concept well.[99] On the basis of Romans 6:3–11 and Colossians 2:11–15, he taught that we become righteous because as sinners we are placed in Jesus' tomb, dead in the sight of the Father and dead to sin. We are then raised through the baptismal Word which pronounces us newly righteous in Jesus. He took our sinfulness, our sinful selves, into Himself as He died. As He arose from the dead, we received His righteousness and innocence. He completes our incorporation into Himself through Baptism and through its renewal as He daily turns us from our idols back to Himself.

This exchange affects first of all and most completely the vertical relationship of our lives, at three levels described by Dantine in the legal language of justification:

> The first is the level of God's own time and thus of His eternity. Here Christ Himself is the faithful witness who intercedes for the innocent man, testifies to his righteousness, and frees him from the charge of the evil one. The second deals with the contemporary historical level of the conflict between religions, ideologies, nations, and powers, with their own self-understanding and their struggle against the lordship of Christ. Here the congregation, the church of God, appears as the faithful witness and with the Gospel wins men away from Satan. ... Finally there is the level of the personal day of judgment, toward which everybody is headed. Along the way a faithful witness of the Gospel is aroused who in preaching, pastoral care, and absolution [and, we must add, in Christian witness] promises the sojourner Christ's righteousness, thus awakening and strengthening faith in him.[100]

Righteous and renewed (Titus 3:3–8), we are once again God's own people. From His perspective God restores us completely to His family. We are His children without qualification when His re-creative Word recalls and recasts us in the image of our dead and risen Deliverer. We respond to that kind of love in faith. While yet in this earthly sphere of existence, our trust in God never grows to that degree of psychologically measurable strength which it had in Eden. Nonetheless, we can rest assured that God will remain faithful to the promise of everlasting righteousness, harmony, peace in our relationship with Him. But, as Paul points out, particularly in Romans 6, death to damning sin in our relationship gives us the sense of security necessary to seek the good of the neighbor rather than to seek in the neighbor support and security for ourselves. Our resurrection with Jesus to new life in the sight of the Father means that we are empowered to leave behind the habits of hell and to begin to practice the habits of heaven, secure in His hand.

It is important to recognize that this new righteousness in God's sight has no basis in us. It is what the church has called a forensic righteousness, that is, the righteousness of pronounced pardon, of judgment carried by the Word of the Lord, of a new creation which issues from His incarnate and baptismal "Let there be new life." Our vertical righteousness is simply the Word made flesh and conveyed in human words and in sacramental form. That kind of righteousness may be regarded by those who have no strong doctrine of the Creator as an insufficient kind of righteousness. Biblical Christians recognize that God's Word brought all reality into being as He said, "Let there be ... ," and thus nothing could be more fundamentally real than re-creation simply by the Word of the Lord. Human signs and proofs, in our feelings or our works, are ephemeral. They are ours. God's Word of pardon and restoration is sure. It is God's, His instrument by which He accomplishes His good will. Our righteousness in the vertical relationship has therefore also been labeled an "alien" righteousness, from the Latin word for that which belongs to another, since our righteousness before God is really Christ's—is really Jesus Himself. Thus, God's justifying Word is not an "as if" word—a nice description which regards us who are really sinners "as if" we were righteous when in fact we are not. God's justifying Word is a Word which re-creates; it gives us new life as the children of God. It establishes us as His righteous people, and that has become the fundamental reality of our lives.

In our horizontal relationships we practice the righteousness of love, and that is our own, as creatures fashioned by God to love, according to the term "proper" (belonging to oneself) righteousness. Externally, this proper righteousness of the believer appears to be the same as the external righteous deeds (civil righteousness) of the unbeliever, for both live in the form of their horizontal relationships according to God's original plan for His human creatures. In the believer this horizontal righteousness, living according to the Creator's original design for human life, is empowered by the presence of the re-creating Spirit in the Gospel of Jesus Christ. The believer's ethical righteousness is derived from the forensic righteousness that is Jesus; our trust in Him frees us and moves us to love our neighbor.

The believer experiences some conflict in the perception of his or her own righteousness. We hear the voice of God which pronounces us totally righteous, yet we experience our own lives, in which Isaiah's judgment rings true: even our righteous deeds are a filthy, stinking mess (Is. 64:6). Luther noted that the believer who lives on this plane is both righteous and sinful at the same time, and, indeed, is totally righteous in the vertical relationship established by the Father's re-creative Word from *God's* perspective. At the same time, from *our* perspective, all our attempts at horizontal righteousness, and the psychological aspects of our faith, are flawed and faulted in some way. The infection of our doubt and defiance permeates our whole being even after, in God's plan for our restoration, He has pronounced us righteous in His own sight. Thus, we are really righteous where it counts, and this enables us to contend with, and set aside from our own minds, the burdens of guilt which Satan wants to lay upon us on the basis of our daily slipping and falling into failures and faults. We are confident in the justifying Word of the Creator.

This image of the courtroom and the explanation of God's saving work as the restoration of the relationships which He designed for us through His overcoming God's wrath and Law, our sin and guilt, Satan's deceit and death, through His own death and resurrection sums up the synonyms of salvation. God's rescue and deliverance of His people, our salvation, brings us to these restored relationships, as does the gift of regeneration or new life, which He accomplished through His own resurrection and the re-creation it wrought. Justification restores us to our original state in Eden through God's own incarnation. Adoption, reconciliation, and acceptance all express the result of God's justifying act in Jesus. Our new righteousness in the vertical relationship has become reality through His forgiveness, even though the infection of sin continues to mar the activities of our horizontal relationships (Is. 64:6).

Believers will recognize in the doctrine of justification a multitude of approaches to specific sinners who are suffering the impacts of evil. Although we often restrict our use of this concept to proclaiming pardon for guilt which arises out of specific acts of disobedience and division, we should also be ready to use the biblical teaching of the restoration of our righteousness in relationship to Him as the basis for approaching broken sinners with the re-creative Word of Jesus' death and resurrection. To those who wish they were dead, we come with the gift of death in Jesus Christ—and we throw in new life to boot.

THE ONLY NAME BY WHICH WE MAY BE SAVED

As witnessing believers speak of salvation, they confront the problem of why some are saved and others are not. The argument that God's grace saves all people, apart from faith in the case of those who do not hear the Word, has been raised at several points in the history of the church. The climate of Western civilization since the Enlightenment has driven some Christians to revive the argument in various forms today. Particularly vexing is the problem, insoluble from a logical point of view, of reconciling human responsibility with the kind of responsibility and power which the Bible ascribes to the Creator. Furthermore, a sense of human justice continues to pose the question why some are saved and others are not, an unanswerable question since the Scriptures do not address it. Encounters with converts or potential converts who ask whether friends or relatives who have died without faith in Jesus Christ had any hope of heaven cannot help but torment witnessing believers who have concern and empathy for hearers whose loved ones lie heavy on their minds. Finally, God's express desire that all people be saved and come to a knowledge of His truth (1 Tim. 2:4) and Old Testament prophecies of the gathering of all nations to Jerusalem (Is. 2:2–4; Jer. 3:17; Micah 4:1–3) suggest a universal salvation if not read in their broader biblical context.

The biblical witness is quite clear, however: there is no other name given among God's creatures which provides salvation than the name of Jesus of Nazareth, the Messiah who was crucified and raised from the dead (Acts 4:10–12). It is not just that salvation lies in Him alone, Peter says; if that were so, one might argue that He bestows life apart from faith in His name. Salvation lies in His name, which, like the name Yahweh for the people of Israel, establishes that vital link of trust in Him, which returns us to Eden, to *shalom*, to the vertical relationship as He designed it.

Paul also points out that salvation comes to those who call upon the name of the Lord (Rom. 10:13). He stresses the need for preachers to proclaim the Word of the Lord to establish that faith which throughout the Letter to the Romans is identified as the link, from the human side of our relationship with God, which saves (Rom. 10:14).

The whole New Testament, if read from the standpoint of the Jews who wrote it, affirms that we must come to recognize Jesus as Lord and Savior if we are to receive life from Him. The early Christians recognized that in Jesus God had opened membership in His people to all nations (e.g., Matt. 28:19) and that He desires to incorporate all, Jew and Gentile alike, into His family (1 Tim. 2:4; Eph. 2:14–19). Nonetheless, the apostles' thought patterns had been determined by the Old Testament's insistence on a personal relationship in trust and worship with the Creator and by its perception that the people of God were a remnant gathered by God out of the peoples of the earth and indeed out of Israel itself. The poor in the land, those who kept the ancient faith during the times of Hellenistic acculturation in the intertestamental period, believed that God would judge even Jews who had abandoned their worship and service of Yahweh. The earliest Christians, therefore, many of whom came from this kind of Jewish religious culture, had no trouble believing that those who do not recognize and trust in God's revelation of Himself in Jesus of Nazareth will suffer never-ending judgment, in weeping and wailing and gnashing of teeth (Matt. 8:12, 22:13, 25:30). They will continue in that death which is the rejection of the Author of life because they have chosen the way of death and do not hold the Way, the Truth, and the Life.

If Christian witnesses do not maintain the biblical judgment against doubt, defiance, and denial, and all their symptoms in division and disobedience, then the Law will not be properly and fully proclaimed in all its condemning horror. The proper distinction between and the proper usage of God's message of wrath and God's message of mercy depend on both messages being proclaimed unconditionally in the clearest fashion and in the situation for which each is designed. So long as sinners find identity, security, and meaning in some other god, they cannot be led to think that finally God's wrath against idolatry will cease.

Why some are saved as chosen recipients of God's gift of His favor, and others are not because they refuse to recognize the Creator's revelation of Himself and His grace in Jesus Christ, is a question which cannot be answered in a way which satisfies logical, rational inquiry. The marvel is not that people who choose to center their lives in something other than the Author of life end up in eternal death in hell; rather, the marvel is that the offended Creator has chosen to show mercy to any. This does not diminish the anguish which we feel when we realize that because the church did not proclaim the Word as ardently as it should have, some have perished without hope. We can only rededicate ourselves to the task of making disciples and thus serving as God's instruments for bestowing life which never ends.

JESUS' SAVING WORK AND THE FATHER AND THE HOLY SPIRIT

The saving work of the Second Person of the Holy Trinity, incarnate as Jesus of Nazareth, is inextricably linked with the Father's plan for our salvation and the Holy Spirit's delivery of that salvation for us.

Paul wrote to the Ephesians that God had chosen His people before the foundation of the world to be holy and blameless in His sight and destined us to be His children through Jesus Christ (1:4). Those whom God has called to be justified were predestined to be conformed to that image of His Son which bestows righteousness upon us (Rom. 8:29–30). This doctrine of election often causes great confusion among those who do not properly understand that the assurance that we are God's chosen children can only be correctly used to express the Gospel. When we use it to perform any other function, we abuse it and confuse ourselves.

The Protestant reformers regarded this biblical teaching regarding God's "ordaining" us to eternal life (Acts 13:48) as a vital and integral part of their understanding of the conditionless nature of God's grace, mercy, and favor toward His people. Luther, for instance, insisted that this teaching could never be used as an excuse for exploring the hidden will of God but must always be understood in the context of God's actual approach to broken sinners through His means of grace, through His Word.

Thus, when the question is posed concerning one's election, the believer must ask why the hearer wants to know: if an answer is sought which will permit sinning because of the surety of election, the question obviously comes from an arrogant and secure sinner, to whom we dare not offer the Gospel in any form lest it simply confirm him in his arrogance and false security. If the question is asked in desperation, in the belief that it is hopeless to believe since there seems to be no evidence that I am elect, the assurance of God's choice of those whom He has brought to Himself through His Word and incorporated into the body of Christ through Baptism must be given. Though God's judgment upon sin and those who perpetrate and practice it cannot be abrogated, God desires to save all people (John 3:16; 1 Tim. 2:3–4) and has made provisions for the salvation of each individual to whom we witness (1 John 2:2; 2 Cor. 5:19). Thus, His conditionless assurance of salvation can be given to every broken sinner. For God's unalterable plan works itself out through the use of the means of grace, as believers share the Word with those whom God calls into His family.[101]

The Christian witness will most often paraphrase the doctrine of election in other forms of offering the absolute assurance of God's favor and His faithfulness to His own people. He or she will point to the sureness of the promise which the Holy Spirit conveys in the means of grace, and will point to the investment God has made in the reclamation of His people through His own incarnation and obedience, death and resurrection.

God's plan for our reclamation was executed in Christ Jesus and is delivered through the presence and power of the Holy Spirit, the bearer of the Word. We call His work sanctification. It is the subject of the next chapter.

4

Rebirth and Renewal in the Holy Spirit

THE LORD AND GIVER OF LIFE

When Jesus was preparing His disciples for His bodily departure from them in His ascension, He promised them another person to stand by them, the Holy Spirit (John 14:16), who would come to teach them all things and to preserve for them the peace which Jesus had given them (26–27). The Holy Spirit's task, to bring to remembrance all that Christ had told His disciples, sustains and builds His body, the church.

The Scriptures offer much more information regarding the work of the Holy Spirit than regarding His person. Against the teachings of one Macedonius, who denied the divinity of the Holy Spirit, the Council of Constantinople (381) reaffirmed the church's belief that the Holy Spirit is person and God.[1] This dogmatic decree conformed to Jesus' statement that a person could commit blasphemy, the sin of insulting God or defaming Him, against the Holy Spirit (Matt. 12:31) and that the Holy Spirit is equal with Himself and the Father (Matt. 28:19). Paul too could make the three equal (2 Cor. 13:14). The Holy Spirit's work includes re-creation (Titus 3:5), the work of God. The Holy Spirit comes to continue the work of Jesus as "another counselor" or comforter (John 14:16). While a different kind of being could perhaps continue the work of God in serving as the defense and support of His people, the broader biblical con-

189

text indicates that the Holy Spirit comes as God to continue the work of Christ.

With His re-creative Word the Holy Spirit comes to reenact Eden, to renew the fallen human creature so that we may live again in righteous relationships and inherit the life He gave us in Eden (Titus 3:5–8). The Holy Spirit accomplishes re-creation through Baptism (Titus 3) and through the hearing of the Gospel (Gal. 3:2, 5), for through His "means of grace," the various forms of the re-creative Word, the Holy Spirit empowers the believer to confess Jesus as Lord (1 Cor. 12:3). The faith or trust which the Holy Spirit works returns His people to the sense of *shalom* which enabled both vertical and horizontal relationships to function properly at the beginning: the evidence of *shalom* is to be found in love, joy, peace, patience, kindness, goodness, faithfulness, gentleness, self-control (Gal. 5:22–25).

This return to Edenic trust restores the human creature to a life of worship of God. Paul calls the people of God "temples of the Holy Spirit," where the praise and service of God goes on (Rom. 8:9–11; 1 Cor. 3:16; 6:19; 2 Tim. 1:14). We do not have or get the Holy Spirit. *He comes* to take possession and control (Acts 10:45; 11:17). He is present in our lives as the first installment, or guarantee, of God's pledge to have us as His people forever (2 Cor. 1:22; 5:5, Eph. 1:14). Jesus called this process of re-creation "making disciples" as He commissioned His first disciples to bring others from all nations into His household in Matthew 28:18–20.

It is important for Christian witnesses to note that Jesus did not state as the goal of their testimony regarding Him that they should simply focus sinners' eyes on the rewards or joys of heaven.

> For the truth seems to me to be that happiness or misery beyond death, simply in themselves, are not even religious subjects at all. A man who believes in them will of course be prudent to seek the one and avoid the other. But that seems to have no more to do with religion than looking after one's health or saving money for one's old age. The only difference here is that the stakes are so very much higher. And this means that, granted a real and steady conviction, the hopes and anxieties aroused are overwhelming. But they are not on that account the more religious. They are hopes for oneself, anxieties for oneself. God is not in the centre.

190

> He is still important only for the sake of something else. Indeed,
> such a belief [in heaven] can exist without a belief in God at all.[2]

Instead of merely a heavenly goal, the goal of Jesus' design for Christian witness is the restored relationship with the Author of life, a relationship of dependence upon Him, discipleship. Believers today will insist, against many in our culture, that the eternal life which God gives as He re-creates us as His disciples extends beyond earthly life into heavenly life. They will also take care that the lure of heavenly bliss not become more important than the love of God in the faith of the new disciple, for that is a self-centered idolatry of the worst kind.

Jesus issued a command in the imperative form, "make disciples," and explained the process with two participles, "baptizing" and "teaching." The order of these two actions is not necessarily chronological, though the church has usually begun the process with Baptism. Only in the Anglo-American religious ghetto of the past 250 years has there been extensive uneasiness with this chronological order. There is, however, a theological priority: God's intervention into our lives with His re-creative power through Baptism, when understood biblically, emphasizes that the Lord of life and death is at work in making us His disciples once again (Rom. 6:3–11; Col. 2:11–15). Baptism is to be followed by teaching (Matt. 28:19–20), the teaching of repentance and the forgiveness of sins, which repeats God's death- and life-giving action (Luke 24:47). Theology and witness strategies are formulated by people like you and me, but only God can make a disciple. Nonetheless, He does it through us, through our delivery of the Word which He places in our mouths and hands, in its written, oral, and sacramental forms.

BURIED AND RISEN WITH CHRIST

Throughout the history of the church the term "sacrament" has been defined in various ways; the term is not used in Scripture in the way in which Christians understand it today. The Scriptures do not link Baptism and the Lord's Supper under one category; the church is certainly justified in linking the two, however, since both combine at Jesus' command God's Word of promise with physical elements from the creation, elements which He has specially selected to be the chosen vehicles for His Word of power. Jesus instituted both sacraments to accomplish specific tasks in His church and placed His promise of new life in each. We will note parallels between these two sacraments, but we should not press the concept of sacrament so far as to equate the two in terms of usage at every point.

God approaches His fallen creatures not only though their ears. He comes also in the forms of water, which conveys His Spirit, and of bread and wine which bear His body and blood. God has ordained these elements, widely used throughout human cultures, to convey His presence and His power. "The Word in the sacrament is an embodied Word. It is not a representation of the Word. Only something which is not present can be represented." There is no real absence of God, His Word, or the power which God exercises through His Word in Baptism or the Lord's Supper. "Through the address of the Word of God they [the elements of water, bread, and wine] become the corporeal form of the sacrament just as the creature only becomes creature when God addresses it by name."[3]

God's Word takes sacramental form for the same purpose that it takes verbal form: to work salvation through faith in Christ Jesus. The sacraments bear the promise that God is re-creating us through the forgiveness and new life won by Christ; "the content of the promise of both Baptism and the Lord's Supper is therefore Christ Himself. The sacraments are by this connection with the universal promise of God placed in the center of the story of salvation,"[4] and the unfolding of salvation takes place as God moves through the sacramental Word, along with the oral and written Word, to redeem His people. Thus, our understanding and use of the sacraments must always center on them as actions of God through His disciples. The sacraments are never human actions which approach God but always God's expressions of His gracious disposition and intent toward us and the means whereby He gives us His grace and favor.

We should not confuse God's original creative goodness with His re-creative goodness in the Word made flesh. "The creation is not a sacrament. There is only a sacrament where in the midst of the creaturely world God addresses, names, and hallows an element with His special Word ... Jesus Christ."[5] In Christian witness it is important to distinguish God's general goodness to all creation from

His specific saving and restoring goodness in Jesus of Nazareth and in the means of grace.

Baptism Saves

Jesus Christ encounters us in the Word of Baptism, the Word which takes water as its vehicle to bring the power of God to re-create His chosen creatures. Peter can flatly state that Baptism saves (1 Peter 3:21), and that it does so not in some merely external or symbolic fashion, as though it were washing dirt off the body. It saves because the baptized conscience can appeal to God without hesitation or fear since its appeal is based upon the resurrection of Jesus. Baptism unites us with Jesus in His death and resurrection (Rom. 6:3–11).

Peter compares Baptism to the salvation of Noah from the destruction of the flood. The basis of that comparison undoubtedly rests on both the saving and destructive nature of water. Our old world, gods, and sources for identity, security, and meaning are buried in Baptism. As Paul insists, we are buried with Christ in our baptisms (Rom. 6:4, 8; Col. 2:12). That burial canceled the legal charges against us by nailing them to Christ's cross (Col. 2:14).

> Baptismal death means *justification from sin*. The sinner must die that he may delivered from his sin. ... Sin has no further claim on him, for death's demand has been met, and its account settled. Justification from *(apo)* sin can only happen through death. Forgiveness of sin does not mean that sin is overlooked and forgotten, it means a real death on the part of the sinner and his separation from *(apo)* sin. But the only reason why the sinner's death can bring justification and not condemnation is that this death is a sharing of the death of Christ. It is baptism into the death of Christ which effects the forgiveness of sin and justification and completes separation from sin.[6]

Once we are buried with Christ as sinners, God no longer views us as sinners. The human creature is then raised in union with Christ to new life, to a new relationship with the Creator, which enables the new disciple to live in new relationships with others. Actually, those new relationships are Eden-old, but for the individual born with the terminal infection of original sin, an act of re-creation is necessary for restoration to the original relationships which God had designed for His human creatures. Baptism restores us in our vertical relationship to true humanity,[7] and in our horizontal relationships God's re-creative intervention into our lives makes possible a growth in the practice of heavenly habits as we discard the habits of hell, which had served as devices in our sinful search for identity, meaning, and security apart from our Creator.

In our spiritualized religious culture, in which all that has something of ritual or ceremony about it is regarded as second-class or merely symbolic or both, it is of utmost importance for the Christian witness to emphasize that God works through selected elements of His created order to accomplish His saving and restoring task. It is also vital to note that, contrary to the misimpression held by many contemporary North American Christians, the Scriptures always speak of Baptism as God's action toward us, not our pledge or commitment toward Him—though certainly His gracious approach to us elicits such a commitment as the Holy Spirit transforms our minds and emotions to trust, love, and fear Him above all things. God incorporates us into the body of Jesus in our baptisms:

> Being assigned to Jesus Christ, the Lord, as His property, this being placed under the present rule of the Crucified, comes to the baptized as something done to him. Just as Christian Baptism is not self-Baptism but a being baptized, so the baptized does not become Christ's property by placing *himself* under Christ, but rather he *becomes* Christ's property through Baptism. This is God's deed; this is acceptance by the Lord.[8]

Jesus occupies His newly purchased property through the Holy Spirit. God saved us not on the basis of our righteous deeds, including any self-generated agreement to become Christian which might be sealed through our submission to Baptism. Instead, His goodness, loving-kindness, and mercy have washed us clean and in the process have regenerated and renewed us in the Holy Spirit, through Jesus Christ, our Savior. The result is that His grace has fashioned righteous relationships for us once again, and we are now heirs of eternal life (Titus 3:5–7; cf. 1 Cor. 6:11).[9] God opens His kingdom, His household, through the door of Baptism (John 3:5); through it He opens up new life (John 3:3–6). For those on the dead-end street of materialism, or alienation, or despair, the promise of new life has a deep appeal.

Baptismal Living

Baptism does bestow life in both vertical and horizontal relationships. But, for some inexplicable reason which God does not reveal in the Scriptures, Baptism does not completely eradicate the forces of doubt and defiance from our lives. Therefore, while we remain on this plane of existence, we continue to battle against the temptation to revive our denial that God is our security, meaning, and only source of identity. In Baptism, God has given us a program and a pattern for new life in Christ. God comes to repeat His baptismal action through daily repentance, in which He turns us from sin to Himself. Baptism lays down the pattern for the entire Christian life of repentance and rebirth. It is a pattern of daily dying to a fondness for sin by confessing to God all our troubled and traitorous attitudes and acts. It is a pattern of daily rising to new confidence before God because we know that He loves and forgives us, and of daily rising to new love for those around us since we want to reflect God's love toward us in their lives.[10]

Baptismal life means that the newly fashioned disciple not only lives anew in God's sight but also is alive in the sight of those within his or her reach.

> Although for the candidate baptism is a passive event, it is never a mechanical process. This is made abundantly clear by the connection of baptism with the Spirit (Matt. 3:11; Acts 10:47; John 3:5; 1 Cor. 12:11–13). The gift of baptism is the Holy Spirit. But the Holy Spirit is Christ himself dwelling in the hearts of the faithful (2 Cor. 3:17; Rom. 8:9–11, 14ff; Eph. 3:16f). The baptized are the house where the Holy Spirit has made his dwelling. ... He imparts true knowledge of his being (1 Cor. 2:10) and of his will. He teaches us and reminds us of all that Christ said on earth (John 14:26). He guides us into all truth (John 16:13), so that we are not without knowledge of Christ and of the gifts which God has given us in him (1 Cor. 2:12; Eph. 1:9). The gift which the Holy Spirit creates in us is not uncertainty but assurance and discernment. Thus we are enabled to walk in the Spirit (Gal. 5:16, 18, 25; Rom. 8:2, 4), and to walk in assurance.[11]

As noted in Chapter 1, the piety which flows from God's baptismal re-creation is first of all a matter of faith, or discernment and assurance, which the Holy Spirit works, and, second, of the love which flows through us from the Spirit to our neighbors. God's justifying Word, enfleshed in Jesus Christ and spoken on us through the means of grace, has fashioned a new creature out of, and has bestowed a new identity upon, the believer. Having died and been raised with Christ, believers love because their Lord first loved them (1 John 4:19). God works repentance in us, so that we may love others instead of taking from them to give ourselves security and meaning. When God recalls us to find our meaning and security in Him, through Baptism, He turns us around—He turns our world upside down, which is then right side up—so that we can reflect His image in our care and concern for others.

We do that in relationship to all people but above all to those of the household of faith, the church (Gal. 6:10). We have not only been baptized into the body of Christ's cross and tomb (2 Cor. 4:10); we have also been baptized into His body, the church (1 Cor. 12:12–13). This means that Baptism brings us to a sharing of new life with a group of people not of our own choosing but of God's.

> To allow a baptized brother to take part in the worship of the Church, but to refuse to have anything to do with him in everyday life, is to subject him to abuse and contempt. If we do that, we are guilty of the very Body of Christ. And if we grant the baptized brother the right to the gifts of salvation, but refuse him the gifts necessary to earthly life or knowingly leave him in material need and distress, we are holding up the gifts of salvation to ridicule and behaving as liars. If the Holy Ghost has spoken and we listen instead to the call of blood and nature, or to our personal sympathies or antipathies we are profaning the sacrament. When a man is baptized into the Body of Christ, not only is his personal status as regards salvation changed, but also the relationships of daily life.[12]

From the perspective of the New Testament, then, Baptism is God's way of preenacting Judgment Day for His people, for in Baptism He pronounces judgment on us as sinners, tucks us away in Christ's tomb, out of His sight forever as doubting and defiant people, dead as far as He is concerned. Baptism is also God's way of reenacting the sixth day, the day of creation, for He speaks again a "Let there be ..." as He moves with water and human language, elements which He has selected from His good creation to be the instruments whereby He re-creates His human creatures, just as once He spoke, took dust, and breathed. In Baptism, as in creation, the operation lies in God's hands, not ours. He calls us into our new existence with no more help from us, independent of Himself, than He had when He took dust and made us living creatures through the breath of His mouth.

Baptism of Infants

From this background we can understand why the New Testament writers took it for granted that their readers understood that God intervenes to re-create infants as well as adults through Baptism. Many in our culture, in contrast to most of those who adhered to the faith in the past two millennia, find it difficult to believe in infant baptism. That is due to several factors. One is the failure of some Christians today to believe that the human condition is so wracked and ruined by our defiance of God that even as infants we need God's saving intervention in our lives and that even as adults we cannot on the basis of our own reason or strength of will turn our lives around. Some contemporary Christians suggest that infant baptism arose in the church because of the advent of a doctrine of original sin. In fact, infant baptism has come into question in our era because we have lost the biblical perspective on the seriousness of our personal, self-induced separation from God, the origin and root of all our sins.

Contemporary Christians also live, even yet, in a highly spiritualized, theological world, which believes that anything material can at best symbolize but never convey the activity of God. That point of view is quite contrary to the biblical picture, of course. Human language and water can serve God's saving purposes, also for an infant, and they do so because He has selected them for that task. Finally, Baptism is God's loving and re-creating action in our behalf, a gift to us, a part of His Gospel. It does not express His Law, which demands something from us. Therefore, God may use this sacrament in accomplishing His intent, the reestablishment of a saving relationship between God and His human creature, also when the creature is still an infant.

To be sure, the biblical writers and preachers did call for repentance and faith in their adult readers and hearers in connection with Baptism, for Baptism aims at the restoration of the original vertical relationship in our lives. On the human side that means that we will be turned away from the other sources of identity, security, and meaning in our lives, and that we will be turned back to the trust which marked Adam's and Eve's relationship with the Creator. The human side of the vertical relationship, namely trust, becomes possible only when God has restored His side of the relationship. He holds the initiative. He can exercise that initiative and create the relationship even where the psychological factors which make faith intelligible to us are not apparent to us. (But an adult's failure to call upon Jesus' name [Acts 4:12] and rejection of Him indicates the absence of the vertical relationship.)

Jesus never did command the Baptism of infants specifically; He only commanded the Baptism of the whole world (Matt. 28:19). But, as Ole Hallesby points out, He did command adults to repent and become as little children to enter the kingdom of God (Matt. 18:3), and He did insist that one must receive the kingdom of God as a little child would (Luke 18:17): "But the opponents of Infant Baptism say that the children must become like us adults; then they, too, will be permitted to enter the kingdom of God."[13] Hallesby goes on to argue that God is Lord of our whole lives. He does not cease to be God of the adult when the adult sleeps or is unconscious. Our relationship with God does not depend on our conscious faith and its pious thoughts. It depends on God's sustaining power, which in the conscious adult does maintain faith and its psychological components in stronger or weaker levels of consciousness. Thus, in our vertical relationship, through Baptism

> God brings about by supernatural means a living connection with the unconscious part of our person. Before the conscious life of the child awakens, God touches its unconscious life with His life-giving Spirit ... and this is what happens to the infant in Baptism. This little slip of humanity is thereby put into living relationship with God.[14]

Furthermore, in addition to God's need to incorporate His fallen people back into His household and the infant's need to have the vertical relationship of life restored as soon as possible, Paul recognized the church's need to incorporate within itself the whole human life, not just life which has met certain psychological or physical qualifications. Thus, Paul viewed Baptism as a continuation of circumcision (Col. 2:11), the means whereby God incorporated ancient Israelites into His people. The church must baptize, Werner Elert observes, because the practice of baptizing infants is essential to its own life in service to God. God has commanded the church to baptize, and Baptism is the means and demonstration of the church's growth.[15]

It will, of course, be argued that many are baptized who show nothing but contempt for their baptisms throughout their conscious, adult life. On that basis some conclude that Baptism must not have any genuine effect. Gerhard Forde notes that this line of argument confronted Martin Luther in the 16th century and that the reformer concluded that

> changing Baptism is no remedy for the fact that Baptism can be abused. It is not Baptism that needs to be changed, it is we ourselves. That is why, basically, Baptism comes first. First God acts and His action makes us what we are. The very "first-ness" of it destroys the man who seeks to put himself first—the old Adam. That is the theological reason for keeping infant Baptism.[16]

Indeed, Baptism is not the problem, grace is. After richly describing God's conditionless grace in Romans 3–5, Paul posed the inevitable question: Should believers sin more so that grace can be richer yet (Rom. 6:1)? His answer is Baptism. Because we are baptized, we do not act like that (Rom. 6:1–11). That may be an unsatisfactory answer on the basis of our experience, but it is the answer that Paul gives for the dilemma of sin under grace. It is an answer of the distinction between Law and Gospel.

If adult baptism, or "believer's" baptism, is understood as *my* act, then it can just as easily be undone as done. The power remains in my hands to disengage or uncommit myself if my relationship depends on my committing myself to God. That is true because I remain the author of the relationship, not the creature of a loving Creator. I remain god in my life.

Certainly the baptized can defy God. This is true of those baptized as infants and of those who thought their adult baptisms were means by which they committed themselves to God and did not know that Baptism is God's commitment, His expression of His promise, to us. We can never successfully resolve the question of why some are able to defy the baptismal promise and others are preserved by God in the renewed vertical relationship which He bestows. The question of why some are finally saved and others are not, in the specific form regarding the varying effects of Baptism, is related to that insoluble question of the origin of evil, of why or how the good and almighty Creator can permit evil to exist.

When the believer encounters the question, "Will my baptism save me?" the answer must be, "Why do you want to know?" If the questioner is trying to find security in and from which to commit sin and be safe, the answer must be, "You cannot hear properly anything about your baptism. Baptism is part of the Gospel, and the Gospel is unintelligible to the arrogant sinner, who seeks some security in the midst of sin." If the questioner asks because of His uncertainty regarding God's gracious disposition toward His chosen people, the answer must be, "Yes, God promised there to be your God, and in the midst of every temptation to doubt and to defy, God is present, wanting to forgive, intent on strengthening you, determined that you shall not fall out of His hand."

Baptism as a Tool for Christian Witness

God's gracious intervention into human life through Baptism offers a great deal to the Christian witness; tragically for the effectiveness of our witness, we often ignore this. For those who have been baptized and who have fallen away, Baptism can be used as a starting point for Christian conversation. Whatever the sinner has done with or to life, God's promise still stands. The analogy of a gift which a father has given and the child has chosen to forget or ignore can provide a basis of discussion of the significance of our hearers' baptisms in a life which has grown parched due to the blockage of the flow of baptismal water. The gift, perhaps in a bank account or a stock portfolio, remains the possession of the child but is of no practical use because the child has not responded to the gift with any kind of acknowledgement. Thus, God's baptismal promise stands, the believer must point out, as a continuing invitation to come home and a perpetual assurance of the Father's love.

Baptism gives assurance simply because it stands outside our power and control. It is God speaking to us. It is God acting as Re-creator in our lives. For unbelievers or new believers, torn apart by their own inadequacies, guilt, impotence, and shame, Baptism, as understood biblically, clearly points away from our strengths and powers to God's strength and power, and it delivers us, like little children, into the hands of God as He fashions His new kingdom for Himself. For the alienated and estranged, the lonely and isolated, Baptism is the birth certificate which incorporates them into a new family, a family whose Father always has a place at the Supper table for all His children.

God undoubtedly chose or formed Baptism as the means to incorporate people into the body of His Son, restoring original relationships and granting new life, because of the universally clear significance of water. Christian witness can capitalize on Paul's imagery of drowning and burial in baptismal water and resurrection from that watery grave. The believer will find useful the analogy of the cleansing properties of water when addressing those who feel that they have fouled their lives with their own filth. The testimony of a God who waters the earth with His own blood and who waters the lives of His people with Baptism gives assurance that the Creator goes about the business of sustaining His creation, also His new creation, and gives it growth. For the baptismal pattern of death and rebirth is repeated in the daily life of repentance, as God turns us away from doubt and defiance and death back to life in communion with Him, and with His people. The Author of life did command that the process of making disciples embrace baptizing. The process of making disciples must certainly also arise from our understanding of Baptism and must also speak of the significance of God's gracious intervention in our lives through Baptism.

TEACHING THEM ... THE GOSPEL IS THE POWER OF GOD

The baptized must be taught so that the human side of the vertical relationship, trust in the Creator, may be developed in the normal, maturing human creature, a being so constructed by God that he or she functions psychologically. The whole human creature as designed by God—with a functioning mind, emotions, and will—is the object of God's re-creating Word.

Making His People Salvation-Savvy

God transforms us through His creative word as it takes form in human language. He has expressed Himself and borne testimony to His saving actions in our behalf in the unique form of the Holy Scriptures. God has authoritatively placed His message for us in the Holy Scriptures through a process only once labeled—and never explained in terms of its mechanics—in the Bible: in 2 Timothy 3:16 He reveals that He has "breathed" or inspired the Holy Scriptures. Those who do not understand that God has selected elements of the created order to do His work try to discount and deny sections of Scripture which do not fit neatly into their scheme of interpretation of life. But God was able to inspire His chosen servants not just to say and write holy things. Indeed, He used human language to report His acts and His intentions from the inspired perspective of normal human creatures, who wrote in the midst of specific cultural situations, in a variety of literary forms and expressions. God took chosen individuals and made their words His, as He used them in His plan for redeeming and restoring His people (2 Peter 1:21).

Believers approach the Scriptures knowing that every word which they dare to speak for God must be evaluated in the light of the authoritative written Word of the Bible. But accepting biblical authority means that we read what God did inspire in the terms of the situation in which He inspired it, in the eighth century before Christ or in His own time. It does not mean that we become sovereign over the text and bend it into what we want to think or want it to say on the basis of modern presuppositions and perspectives. C. S. Lewis rejects a reading of the Bible "as any other piece of human literature" if that means

> reading it without attending to the main thing it is about; like reading Burke with no interest in politics, or the Aeneid with no interest in Rome. That seems to me to be nonsense.

At the same time Lewis affirms that God's Word did become human language of the sort we speak and write every day.

> But there is a saner sense in which the Bible, since it is after all literature, cannot be properly read except as literature; and the dif-

ferent parts of it as the different sorts of literature they are. Most emphatically the Psalms must be read as poems; as lyrics, with all the licenses and all the formalities, the hyperboles, the emotional rather than logical connections, which are proper to lyric poetry. They must be read as poems if they are to be understood; no less than French must be read as French or English as English. Otherwise we shall miss what is in them and think we see what is not.[17]

Of course, there is no way to prevent people from finding in the Bible whatever they think God should or must have said. However, we believe that God speaks in the warp and woof of human history, in concrete situations, and we believe that human language and history have meaning which can be ascertained, quite accurately if not in every detail. Because of this we will concentrate on determining what that meaning is, in the context in which God inspired it. For instance, St. John must chuckle and laugh at the naiveté of modern Christians who try to impose a literal interpretation on his Revelation, which he framed in the apocalyptic genre familiar to his contemporaries. The translation of the biblical message into modern thought must begin on the basis of the ancient text, not on the basis of modern presuppositions. It must move from the ancient text to the modern presuppositions and perspectives, rather than arise out of the modern and return to the text only as a mine which yields no more than malleable support for our own ideas.

That means that we not only recognize the uniqueness of the specific genres and pieces of which the Bible is composed but also that we understand the Bible as a unit, a unique body of literature which in its specific literary forms and units (books) still makes up one whole.

Holy Scripture does not consist of individual passages; it is a unit and is intended to be used as such. As a whole the Scriptures are God's revealing Word. Only in the infiniteness of its inner relationships, in the connection of Old and New Testaments, of promise and fulfillment, sacrifice and law, law and gospel, cross and resurrection, faith and obedience, having and hoping, will the full witness to Jesus Christ the Lord be perceived.[18]

God inspired the Scriptures for that purpose: to make you wise for salvation through faith in Christ Jesus (2 Tim. 3:15). More broadly conceived, God uses the Scriptures to inform and reprove, to correct and train His people (2 Tim. 3:16). The result of the impact of the Scriptures on human life is that God's people may be complete, mature, righteous as they were in Eden, equipped for every good work which God had designed in all our relationships (2 Tim. 3:17). The thrust of the whole of Scripture leads us to the cross and empty tomb of Jesus of Nazareth. Because the Scriptures have carried His message, presence, and salvation across the ages to us through the Holy Spirit's activity and because they are designed to actualize His presence in our world, Jesus and the Bible cannot be separated.

> *The Scripture itself must ... be regarded as also belonging to the center* [of redemptive history]. The fact that these books were written in the apostolic age was at a later time necessarily included in the redemptive happening of the mid-point. The result of this was that from the second half of the second century the entire apostolic age was regarded as the time of the unique *foundation* of the Church, and that this foundation, which, to be sure, already belongs to the post-Easter present period, was nevertheless still understood as an event of the mid-point itself. The apostles, and the New Testament Scripture traced back to them, thus received a place in the unique event at the mid-point, although on the other side they already belonged to the unique events of the period of the church.[19]

The Christian witness perceives the task of witnessing to God's saving work in Jesus Christ is intimately and inextricably tied up with the study of the Scriptures. Believers then also read the Scriptures not to master their content as would a literary scholar but rather to master the message which, as witnessing disciples, they will use for the conversion and restoration of lost and defiant people to disciples who trust and love and fear Him in every part of their lives. This is the way the inspired writers composed their works, and this makes it easy to read the works in that fashion.

> The evangelist who wrote down the "document" presupposed ... that no future reader of his words could read them without receiving from them life or death, and the evangelist hoped that he would receive life (cf. John 20:30f.). As he wrote, the plan and

every detail without exception was controlled by this presupposition. Consequently, a particular passage tells of an outward act of Jesus, for the whole life of Jesus was outward acts, but linked therewith is the message, for Jesus was the Redeemer of the world—that is to say, the Redeemer of every reader, of every hearer, until the end of the world. To preach [or to witness informally] is "to bring what has already happened into history and to proclaim it before the whole world" until the "deed" comes to be "the use of the deed" (or the Word), until "reconciliation" comes to be "a message of reconciliation" (see 2 Cor. 5:19).[20]

Witness Rises from the Scripture

When witnessing disciples take the Scripture in hand, they have grasped the place where the message that meets the sinner's central need sounds forth; that is, that creative Word from which our creative life flows—God's Word, Christ became flesh. In dealing with this power of God, packaged in the Bible as it is, the believer must realize that this creative Word speaks to us out of the words of the biblical page. Since the words of the Bible are packed with this creative power, we will listen to them without demanding such a comprehension as would free us from the need to listen afterwards to other particular passages. Every desire to put ourselves above the Word instead of under it, to master the Word instead of allowing it to master us, implies a failure to see that God creates by His Word and that we are the ones being created anew.[21]

Perceiving that, however, the witnessing disciple will delight in the Word of the Lord, always delving into it with one eye on the needs of those who call out in despair from the surrounding culture for a new—to be sure, the genuine—source of identity, security, and meaning. Through immersion in the thought processes of the inspired writers, the witnessing believer will experience a transformation of his or her own though processes. Aarne Siirila describes the phenomenon with a glance at Martin Luther:

> In becoming steeped in the sacred writings Luther feels such a loosening of the tongue and such an integration of words to new contexts as to thrill him to the depths of his being. Fountains burst forth from which flow living waters to break down the fateful watershed which had separated the stream of words into two

channels, the language of faith and the language of everyday life. This "Pentecost experience," the experience of language made whole, brings him to see in a new light the sacred writings which had opened the fountains. He sees that these writings are themselves the result of the same kind of discovery of such springs of life. He begins to see behind the writings the faces of the writers. Through the Scriptures he is drawn into the company of living men.[22]

Contemporary Christian witnesses will never experience the unique opportunity for witnessing the saving events and actions of God which the prophets and apostles were inspired to record in a unique activity of the Holy Spirit. Nonetheless, since we have been given the message of the prophets and apostles made more sure (2 Peter 1:19) by the completion of God's saving plan on resurrection morn and Pentecost Sunday, we can share this message confidently, as witnesses designated for our day by the Holy Spirit. By rubbing the shoulders of our minds with those whom the Spirit so used in the Lord's day, while maintaining perceptive contact with our own world, we will grow in our ability to serve as the Spirit's means for loosing the creative power of the Scriptures in the lives of those around us.

Increasing familiarity with the Bible also bestows courage for Christian testimony upon those who quake at the prospect "because I wouldn't know what to say." A firmer knowledge of the Word of God is not the only answer to that shaking within us, but it certainly helps. In addition, the biblical Word has the only approach and answers for the dilemmas of human doubt and defiance against God.

How shall we ever help a Christian brother [or the despairing unbeliever] and set him straight in his difficulty and doubt, if not with God's own Word? All our own words quickly fail. But he who like a good "householder ... bringeth forth out of his treasure things new and old" (Matt. 13:52), he who can speak out of the abundance of God's Word, the wealth of directions, admonitions, and consolations of the Scriptures, will be able through God's Word to drive out demons and help his brother.[23]

We approach the Scriptures and their re-creative power recognizing that we have been called to build bridges between the inspired Word and the twisted and perverted world in which our neighbors live. Martin Luther insisted that the voice of the Gospel must come alive in our mouths as we speak "the living voice of the gospel," and he did so not just because he lived in a semiliterate culture, a society which still depended largely on oral communication. He did so because he knew that the Scriptures can be quite easily misinterpreted if an arrogant or secure sinner stumbles upon the Gospel and uses it as a license for sin or if a despairing sinner reads it as only another condemnation of the Law and God's wrath.

God's message comes to us as a message of wrath and a message of mercy. The function of the witnessing believer is to bring the condemnation of the Law and the terror of God's wrath to bear on the secure sinner, so that the sinner may abandon all other sources of security, meaning, and identity. The witnessing disciple's function also embraces the task of bringing the despairing sinner to a faith which trusts, loves, and fears God above all things. Faith is the primary goal of Christian witness, for it is the essence of the vertical relationship which God created between Himself and His human creature.

THE RIGHTEOUSNESS OF GOD
THROUGH FAITH IN JESUS CHRIST

The world is filled with various brands of faith. Faith makes the world go around; it sustains human existence. Without faith that there is someone, something, or some idea to secure human existence against all that threatens it, life collapses. Without faith that my life has meaning and that I have an identity, I will die. Without faith I will, consciously or unconsciously, will myself to die. The human approach to establishing security, meaning, and identity involves knowledge of a person or an object or an ideology, and an emotional commitment to that person, object, or ideology, to its reliability as a source for security, meaning, and identity. Every human being has constructed some faith to keep life going. If a person's current faith breaks an axle and can no longer bear the weight of life, another faith must be found.[24]

The Psychological Side of Faith

God created human creatures as psychological beings, with rationality and emotion, and He created us to function in relationship to Him as such psychological beings who think and know, who feel and are moved by affections. Indeed, as we view faith in the true God from His perspective, we should not fall into the trap of regarding faith merely "as a psychological process and hence as a work [of our own]. It is defined exclusively by the one in whom it believes and to whom it relates itself."[25]

From our perspective faith takes shape in knowing and feeling, in grasping God's Word about Himself and in being committed to that Word and its content, the Word made flesh. Nonetheless, faith is not simply knowledge and commitment as they reside in me. Regin Prenter defines faith as "a movement which never stops ... a constant movement away from myself to Christ." This means faith is more than just a psychological quality. It is the human side of our relationship with God, the means by which Christ, through the Holy Spirit, reorients our lives away from ourselves toward Himself and then back to our neighbors and their needs. It is the product of the Holy Spirit's bringing us to Jesus through the Word and through His turning our minds and hearts to understand and be committed to the Word and Jesus.[26]

Because Christian faith rests in knowledge of and commitment to a person, it differs from those faiths which find their object in one's own money or prestige or in a cause or ideology, whether the Marxist dialectic or narcissistic "rugged individualism." Because the Christian faith rests on the person of the Creator and Lord of life, it differs from those faiths which hope in political messiahs or personal favorites.

> The real and theologically relevant effect and concretion of the biblical faith in God the Creator is belief in God as the supreme judge of the whole world, of all peoples, and of all individuals ... according to the Old Testament, faith in the Creator does not really mean the disclosure of an ultimate ground of being. This faith in creation is not concerned with retracing the chain of causality all the way back to the first cause, or with proving the existence of an unmoved mover of the cosmos. Rather, such faith proclaims an absolute Lord over this world.[27]

That Lord who judges the original creation after its fall has also revealed Himself as the Lord of life and the Re-creator who rescues and restores fallen human creatures to Himself, to trust in Himself. God bestows this knowledge of Him and how He accomplished that as an inextricable element in the faith which is the human component of the vertical relationship.

Faith Rests on the Promise

Such faith rests, by its very nature, on the promise which God delivers in His Word. The relationship between the Word and our faith demonstrates how God does relate to us and how He causes us to relate to Him. His

> revelation does not take place merely on the event side of an external history. It is not just what we usually call the mighty acts of God. It also takes place as appropriation, as the hearing and understanding which overcomes hardening (Matt. 13:15; Acts 28:17; etc.) and opens deaf ears. It is closed to the wise and prudent, i.e., to the initiative of intellectual work (Matt. 11:25–27). ... Second, this experience that takes place to us and in us, this entry into our consciousness as we may now put it, makes it apparent that faith is something that has been effected.[28]

Some Christians define the Gospel altogether too narrowly when they limit it to the work of Christ on the cross and out of the tomb. It includes the Holy Spirit's work through the means of grace, as He sanctifies us in faith through Word and Sacrament as well.

Above all, faith is the relationship with God which God establishes on His end of the vertical dimension of our lives. However, it is also—and we use the term primarily in this way—the human response to God's promise of life in Jesus. Faith is most often understood as the trust and reliance which take psychological form in us, as the psychologically functioning beings God shaped us to be in Eden. This trust and reliance are created when the re-creative Holy Spirit moves our minds and emotions to experience God's love as it comes through the Word made flesh, through the Word announced in the Scriptures, and through the Word announced from the mouths of His people.

What then is the relationship between faith and experience? Why do you want to know? The question must be answered from several perspectives. Witnessing believers will recognize that the call to faith, love, and trust in God cannot be effective if our hearers have little or no inkling of what faith, love, and trust mean on a human level. To the bruised and bedraggled, effective Christian witness begins by establishing a relationship in which trust and love are demonstrated and taught convincingly. In a society falling apart, believers must develop strategies for carrying out the exhausting task of teaching the concepts of trust and love through endless, never-ceasing examples of these concepts. It is too much for one person to undertake alone. Christian witness must be practiced by tag-teams. Believers must trade off demonstrating how love and trust works in the lives of those who have not a clue as to what human life at its best might be like. For people who have grown up without love and apart from an atmosphere of trust, there may never be complete repair. We must avoid judging such people's spiritual state on the basis of their psychological state. The Word of God brings peace, even when the damaged people of this fallen world grasp it in faith in various ways psychologically. For some, indeed, psychological healing does come more completely, as a result of the Gospel's claim upon their lives. For faith does experience joy and peace which comes from realizing that God loves us, died for us, and rose for us, so that he might give us new life, the life which He designed for us in Eden. The believer can have confidence, and feel that confidence, in the almighty Father, whose promise of protection and peace for His children cannot be effectively challenged or destroyed by the power of evil.

Nevertheless, because faith is "the assurance of things hoped for, the conviction of things not seen" (Heb. 11:1), because our sin still perverts our mind's perception of reality and separates it decisively from the reality which God has established in His re-creative Word of absolution, faith experiences a continuing conflict, opposition, and call to doubt in this life. After years in Romanian prisons the modern confessor Richard Wurmbrand can write, "Faith can be put in two words: 'though' and 'yet!' In the book of Job we read, 'Though the Lord slay me, yet I will trust Him.'"[29] This means that faith not only grows with the experience of the presence of

God in the body of Christ which speaks His Word and conveys His love in its actions; faith also grows in spite of and in confrontation against our experiences of our own defiance of God and denial of His lordship. Faith grows as it endures experiences under the impact of evils for which we are not at all or not fully responsible. Witnessing believers will be aware, therefore, that both their own faiths and the faiths of those whom Jesus has recently claimed for Himself will experience the assaults of Satan and every power of evil, as they fight to retain control over the lives they have been dominating.

Faith under Assault

"Faith is by nature always under assault. It exists in the Nevertheless. It is faith against something as well as faith in something. It is achieved only as the enduring of the trial."[30] Old systems of security and meaning and new identities arise to challenge the God who has re-created us in Jesus Christ. They cleverly exploit the young believer's years of practice and training in leaning upon them rather than finding identity and security in Jesus. They suggest to the older disciple that it may be time for a change to a new identity, to seek a form of security which will deal better with evil than does the way of the cross of Christ.

In these conflicts the believer will recognize that experience must be subordinate to the Word of the promise. God's Word frames and establishes reality. Thus, when "the new creation which takes man out of his self-enclosed being and his riveting to the phenomenological," to the "realities" of evil in this world, the believer experiences the "struggle between the spiritual man and the natural man [which] never ends. The end of the struggle remains an eschatological promise (Rom. 7:24f.; 1 Cor. 13:12; 15:57)." This struggle arises from within us as well as from external temptations; "it arises on the field of faith itself, for the believer himself is also, in personal union, a subject of experience and rational reflection. ... The believer himself is the field of battle."[31]

Rational doubts may arise to combat the assurance we have that God has remade us through forgiving our sins. But doubts may also arise from our inability emotionally to accept God's forgiveness.

It is always easier to believe the Gospel about God, that He forgives us, than it is to believe the Gospel about ourselves, that we are forgiven and have real life. In the face of evidence that our faith is not real, God's Word comes to assure us that the reality which He creates is more real than the experiences and feelings which we encounter as we look inside ourselves.

Can a Christian, for instance, lose his temper quickly, or can a person who loses her temper quickly be a real Christian? Why do you want to know? If you are seeking to excuse a bad habit which hurts those around you, if you would like to retain and nurse that habit, then the Law must be proclaimed which condemns the practice you would like to keep at the same time your life has been given up in Jesus. On the other hand, C. F. W. Walther observes to those who perceive a need in this question to hear the Gospel,

> you must also remember that a Christian keeps his temperament also after his conversion, such as a quick temper. Hence you cannot say that a Christian is changed from a bear to a lamb in the sense that he lets everybody taunt and malign him and at once forgives them. No, a Christian often has his hands full with his temper. He may even get so angry that he cannot be calmed. Why? Because his temperament got the upper hand. Then you dare not think that such a person will go to hell if he should die that night.[32]

Walther argues that faith continues also through slips into sinful action, such as the flaring of unrighteous anger, because faith remains fundamentally a relationship established by God. This assertion must be understood as the Gospel for broken sinners; if applied to a secure sinner, it would provide a license for sin. In presenting the Gospel to the broken sinner, the witnessing disciple gives assurance that God's love is greater than our sin. Faith may wear thin, may become "stronger" or "weaker," "more faithful" or "less faithful," in psychological terms, but for the broken sinner the Word of God remains strong and faithful, also in preserving the vertical relationship which the Holy Spirit has restored by incorporating us into Jesus of Nazareth.

REPENT AND BELIEVE THE GOSPEL

Christian witness focuses particularly on the beginning of faith, on what today is called "conversion." The task of evangelism or witness, narrowly defined, is often limited to the process through which witnessing disciples build bridges by which arrogant or secure sinners are broken and are brought to the new life, that is, to finding meaning, security, and a new identity in Jesus of Nazareth. This definition should not obscure the fact that within the body of Christ we serve one another also by calling fellow believers to repentance and by absolving them (Luke 24:46) and by supporting them in hours of temptation and doubt with the same Word of the Lord which we use for bringing people to Jesus in the first instance.

As the Holy Spirit goes about the re-creative process in the lives of sinful creatures, He begins by convicting them of sin, of the impact of evil in their lives (John 16:8). When the broken sinner recognizes the helplessness of the fallen human condition, the Holy Spirit proceeds by putting Jesus on display. He portrays God's love in Jesus before the prospective convert through the words and deeds of the witnessing believer (John 15:26; 16:14). This rhythm of Law and Gospel provides the framework in which the process of conversion—and the process of daily repentance in the convert—takes place.

God Alone Converts

The first fact the witnessing disciple must remember is that God alone converts. In the Baptism of infants the Holy Spirit does it with little reference (so far as we know) to the psychological functioning of the child. In adults He operates through Christian witness, using its application of the Word as His instrument and moving in human minds and emotions to turn them around, to re-create them so that they trust in their Creator as He designed them to depend on Him. Wurmbrand describes his own conversion: "I was like the man in the ancient Chinese story, trudging exhausted under the sun, who came on a great oak and rested in the shade. 'What a happy chance I found you!' he said. But the oak replied, 'It is no chance. I have been waiting for you for 400 years.' Christ had waited all my life for me. Now we met."[33] Christ plotted the path and directed my foot-steps as He drew me to Himself.

A great many contemporary Christians who want and try to stress the grace of God fall into the trap laid by our cultural pre-suppositions regarding human responsibility. Particularly since the Enlightenment the strong emphasis on the individual and on indi-vidual responsibility has made it very difficult for North Americans to understand what it means that God is Creator and Re-creator. Because they believe that God's total responsibility for His creatures contradicts total human responsibility for ourselves and our actions, they try to divide responsibility for conversion.

The result is a theology which proclaims salvation by grace but then undercuts it by insisting that a human act of will is necessary before divine grace can become operative. This theology ignores the biblical insistence that, however difficult or impossible it is to fit together logically, God as Creator must hold the whole world in His hands and be in command of it all, and, at the same time, He has given the human creature responsibility to serve Him and to serve others as His image within His structure for human life. That dual view of responsibility may contradict human reason, but it does not contradict our experience of both a sense of responsibil-ity for our own acts and a sense of impotence at creating a truly good life for ourselves.

God Converts Functioning
Psychological Human Creatures

Contributing to this view that human decision-making is involved at the critical point in becoming a disciple of Jesus is the psychological experience of adult converts. They do experience a psychological act, or series of acts: their minds and emotions do accept Jesus as they reject old security systems. They do commit their lives to Him and to His worship and service.

The biblical writers also assume that we function as we have been created by God to function, also in conversion: our minds and emotions continue to perform the functions of accepting the proclamation of the Gospel as true for us and of responding with a commitment of our lives to Jesus as the only true and reliable source of identity, security, and meaning. However, the biblical writers also insist that as Creator, God holds His own creation in His hands. Particularly in His conversion of us from enemies to be His own people, He is active in effecting what seems to us to be our own actions precisely because He created us as psychological beings. God turns our minds and emotions as the Holy Spirit works within us to create trust in the Word which His people bring to those still doubting Him.

Witnessing disciples will lead converts to respond to their proclamation of the Gospel with affirmations that Jesus is their Lord and Savior and with expressions of commitment. But they will not stress this response nor put the burden of conversion upon the convert. Rather, they will strive to make it clear that even the turning of the mind and emotions from false gods to the Creator is a gift from God. God's gracious acceptance of us precedes our acceptance of Him. It frees us to be able to accept Him psychologically as the God who has already given Himself to us as Father. God's unconditional commitment to us precedes our commitment to Him and liberates us to live out that commitment in our daily lives.

Disciples must not only be fully aware of their own roles as no more than the instruments of God's converting power—absolutely necessary instruments, to be sure, but no more than instruments. They thus need have no compulsion to collect a certain requisite number of spiritual trophies to prove their own faith to themselves, God, or others. At the same time they will feel compelled to keep their witnessing skills as polished as possible so that they may be as effective instruments of the Holy Spirit as He will have them to be.

Believers must also be aware that God works with sinners as the human creatures He made them to be, and thus He creates in them and elicits from them the psychological characteristics of the human phenomenon, faith. This means that He leads broken and despairing sinners to react to the knowledge of Jesus of Nazareth, which they receive from Christian witnesses, by psychological acts of acceptance and commitment.

George Forell labels three levels of religious commitment: that on which I accept my religious past as part of my present, that on which I accept a social-moral perspective on life, and that on which

I accept the revelation of the Absolute in a special form. Christians recognize that this third level is commitment to Jesus the Christ as the disclosure of the meaning, purpose, and ultimate destiny of each person in the plane of God. The Bible is the cradle of Christ, proclaiming the faith in those destined to hear. Religious experience is the encounter with the living God in the crucified Messiah. This kind of commitment "is more like selective service; one is drafted. ... Actually the third commitment is not a commitment of man at all. It is rather the confession that God has committed Himself to man, that He has accepted man, though He considers himself unacceptable."[34]

This psychological aspect of faith, acceptance, and the fruit of faith we call commitment could not be present without the power of the Holy Spirit transforming the mind and emotions of the sinner. This fact does not alter the corollary that this Spirit-created faith does accept Jesus as Lord and Savior and that this faith does commit its life to Him. This commitment is more than just an agreement to serve Him externally. It is my Spirit-wrought faith's placing my whole life in Jesus' hand and relying and depending on Him for my identity, security, and meaning.

Christian commitment grows out of a rejection of false systems of identity, security, and meaning, and the Spirit-wrought acceptance of Jesus of Nazareth as the revelation of true identity, security, and meaning in the Creator. Psychological insight into the nature of effective rejection can be gained from those who have studied alcoholism and the psychological means for combating it. They insist that this evil cannot be assaulted effectively with halfway measures. To use the terminology of Harry M. Tiebout, an attitude of *compliance,* which halfheartedly acknowledges the evil of alcoholic dependence but only reluctantly agrees to do something to assist in dealing with one's own alcoholism, cannot effectively confront the disease. Instead, the alcoholic must *surrender* completely and acknowledge that he or she can do absolutely nothing to combat alcoholism's hold. Only then, in reliance on some higher power, can alcoholism be contained.[35] This analysis provides a model for an understanding of Christian combat against the evils which flow from our doubt and defiance.

However, in actual witnessing the disciple must remember that, from the psychological perspective, this total feeling of acceptance and commitment, based on a firm trust in Jesus Christ, does not drop from the skies in one piece. In some new converts the "total" feeling may appear to be present at first, but the struggles of doubt and the temptations to return to old security systems will raise up their ugly heads, and witnessing believers must either ensure their own presence or arrange for the presence of others from the witnessing congregation for assistance against such trials. In other new converts the struggle to gain more assurance of God's love for them will go on for a long time, creeping by millimeters rather than quantum leaps into the feeling of the reality which God has pronounced upon them, that they are secure in His hands by virtue of His re-creating Word. There are indeed "sudden" conversions, in people who may have lived in a worldly perhaps even ungodly way for years. They are suddenly awakened out of this condition, or so it would appear. But in reality this did not come to pass as suddenly as it would seem. Nor did it happen because of the unaided decision of the convert. "It appeared that way only to the consciousness of the one converted. He did not recognize the quiet work which the Spirit had done during all these years in his subconscious life." [36]

The Spirit's work of re-creation proceeds on the basis of the death of the old system of identity, security, and meaning which had supported the unbeliever previously. The Law, in its crushing, condemning, and frustrating force, must turn the secure sinner to despair, or at least to something approaching utter despair, before that sinner can have any desire to be turned to Jesus for security and meaning. Yet physical death comes to those who live in total despair quite quickly, and so the broken sinner who perceives a need for a new security system will still be able to be living because some remnants of the old system are still functioning, however badly. Thus, witnessing believers need not reduce the sinner to utter brokenness but to that point where the condemnation of God's wrath becomes so crystal clear that they desire and know that they must find a new source of identity, security and meaning. Then the broken sinner can hear the Gospel of Jesus with appreciation, and the Gospel will give that broken sinner a sufficient sense of security in Jesus to perceive how truly sinful his or her life had been.

217

Only from the safe haven of Christ's cross could we be bold enough to admit how completely we had doubted and defied the Author of life. Only with new identities as children of God, secure in His household, can we face the fact that we have hated our Creator and Father—and still slip back into defying Him from time to time.

Believers will recognize that those whom the Holy Spirit is converting through them may rest at one of several stages of the ability to confess their own sinfulness and helplessness honestly. The Christian witness will always try to move the breaking sinner to the fullest extent of brokenness possible, at the same time recognizing that the Gospel can be announced and forgiveness pronounced along the way, with the result that the sinner has new courage to face the full horror of past sins. Some may pause at a "semi-pelagian" stage,[37] in which they confess that they need some help from God's grace in Jesus to assist them in righting their own slightly skewed lives. These people are still hanging onto their old security systems, with a heavy investment in themselves, and yet are looking to Jesus for help. Their understanding of their own sinfulness and of the grandeur and totality of the help which God offers them through His own incarnation is woefully incomplete. If the witnessing disciple permits them to remain at that level of belief, they will encounter points in their lives at which they still are leaning on themselves and their lives will collapse under that weight. These semi-pelagians do show some glimmer of interest in the Gospel, and the disciple must use even this small interest to draw the sinner into the Gospel, through its promises, while at the same time must point out that this sinner's doubt and defiance of God are so serious that they have destroyed his or her relationship with God and rendered the creature impotent and guilty before God.

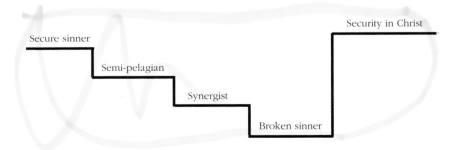

A "synergistic" stage may follow, in which sinners recognize that they are so sinful that God's grace alone can save, but at the same time they still insist that grace is only available if the sinner exercises some responsibility, makes some contribution, by reaching out a hand to grasp God's favor. Synergists are using a psychological description of conversion, specifically of acceptance, as the only, or the ultimate, analysis of this phenomenon, and thus they place the ultimate responsibility for their own conversion on their own shoulders. We can, as a matter of fact, no more make the decision which effects our re-creation than we were able to make some decision to bring about our creation and natural birth. Synergists fail to recognize that the Holy Spirit, in His re-creating power, is effecting the psychological changes in them which they experience with their minds and emotions.

Those who witness must build upon their understanding of God's grace and must stress that a biblical perception of the grace of the Creator includes a rejection of the idolatrous belief that ultimately it is our own psychological act of acceptance which completes the restoration of our vertical relationship—quite apart from any re-creating power exercised by God in and through us.

Finally, believers will assist the convert to perceive the fullness of the biblical teaching regarding the relationship between the Creator and the human creature. The creator creates; creatures depend totally upon their Creator for their existence and for the design of their lives. Thus, any thought of semi-pelagian-style aid which the sinner renders God in the conversion process or the Christian life does not make sense. Neither does any suggestion that God's favor cannot be operative in my life unless I let it be, in the fashion of synergists who may talk about God's grace, but undercut it with their insistence that their decision must ignite the Spirit's fire within their hearts.

The best form for bringing the Word to bear on the life of the fallen with whom we converse is that suggested by the Lord in Luke 24:47. The Holy Spirit uses us to lead people to turn from false gods in repentance, and He uses us to pronounce the presence of God upon our hearers, in the forgiveness of sins or in some other form of the assurance of God's re-creation of the fallen through Christ. If there is a critical moment in rebirth as a child of God, it is imperative that this moment be remembered not as a moment in which fallen creatures commit their lives to God and accept Him as Lord. That critical moment should instead be the gift of God, which comes in hearing His love pronounced decisively upon us. Psychologically, of course, there need be no single, critical moment of conversion. There can be a growing acknowledgement that Christ is at work changing everything in my life.

In dealing with the conversion and re-creation of sinners, witnessing believers face a series of questions regarding the relationship between human responsibility and the re-creative favor of God, which pronounces us righteous without any condition in us whatsoever and then bestows the gift of faith as our reaction to this re-creative pronouncement. They must be answered on the basis of the Christian response, "Why do you want to know?"

"What do I have to do to be worthy of God's grace?" is a frequently asked question in many religions, and the biblical answer is "nothing." Yet many Christians continue to believe that they must at least drag themselves to a sufficiently sincere sorrow over their sin and desire to love Jesus, in order to make God aware that they are in some way or other worthy of God's mercy. When those interested in the Christian faith ask a disciple, "How sorrowful over sin must I be to become a Christian?" the disciple must ascertain why the question is being posed. If potential converts wish to continue to love their sinful way of life, that love must be destroyed, and the disciple must insist that sorrow and death to doubt and defiance are necessary prerequisites for belief in Jesus as Lord and Savior.

If, on the other hand, potential converts feel that they must achieve a certain level of self-deprecation to make themselves eligible for salvation, they should be reminded that contrition, sorrow over sin, is not a cause of our forgiveness or a means of apprehending it. For whatever reason we feel broken by God's Law, God's Word of favor comes to us because He wants to favor us with His mercy, not because we have been sufficiently sorrowful to merit it. In the words of C. F. W. Walther:

> Contrition is not even a good work. The contrition which precedes faith is only something suffered by man. It is anxiety, pain, torment, a being crushed that is produced by God through the

hammer of His law. It is not a fear that man has produced for himself; it is a fear he would like to be rid of but cannot, for God has come upon him with His holy law, from which there is no escape.[38]

Sinners who worry about the sufficiency of their sorrow for paving the way to faith must be taught that God's mercy accepts them before they accept Him, for they need to hear the Gospel which frees them from bondage to their own works. They need to hear that they are His children by His free, adoptive choice, not because they have earned reconciliation with Him through any effort of their own, even their own sorrow.

Those who witness may also encounter the question, "Why can I not believe when I so want to?" Again, they must ascertain the agenda behind the question, the factors of faith or unbelief which prompt it. It may be that faith in Jesus Christ is being held at bay by a refusal to abandon old security systems.

> Are you worried because you find it so hard to believe? No one should be surprised at the difficulty of faith, if there is some part of his life where he is consciously resisting or disobeying the commandment of Jesus. ... If you dismiss the word of God's command, you will not receive his word of grace.[39]

This is a condemning word, designed to bring a sinner yet secure (even if not consciously arrogant) in an old system of establishing identity to death. It may also be that the broken sinner cannot "feel" or "perceive" the presence of faith which is indeed present because he or she is judging the presence of faith on the basis of human emotions or human works rather than on the basis of the promise of God. Walther advised that when good church members ask, "Pastor, I just can't believe, and I feel very bad about it," that the pastor reply, "Would you like to believe?" If the answer is positive, then "let the pastor console the member: 'You are already a believer. just cheer up and wait patiently until God lets the hour of trial pass. Then you will see your faith burst forth full of power and joy.' "[40] The broken sinner needs the support and encouragement of the re-creative Word of God which directs us alone to the power of God's re-creative plan in Jesus.

God begins to convert us through our death to idols. That occurs as we acknowledge the justice of God's condemnation of us for our doubt and defiance, in all their symptoms and forms, and as we recognize that in us there is no good thing anymore. Gustaf Wingren comments on the significance of our recognizing God's judgment:

> By thus affirming the judgment of God, which relates to his entire being, and not just to a part of him, [the believer] ceases from his sinful preoccupation with self. But is such a man not still under judgment, even in his affirmation of God's judgment, in such a way that even his affirmation itself is evil, and therefore to be avoided and denied? To this question there is only one answer—man's assent to God's judgment is not an act of his own which he offers to God, but is God's work in man, by which man comes into full fellowship with God. His true fellowship with God is deepened only when he takes God's judgment upon himself, and is lessened when he sees less in himself to be judged. For God gives life by putting to death and forgives by judging. ... When the Law performs its function of judgment it is serving the Gospel. This work of God under the appearance of its opposite, a work which in its very heart is always the opposite of what it seems, is nowhere so obvious as in the death of Christ.[41]

But we are able to acknowledge the justice of God's ultimate judgment only as we begin to feel secure in His saving hand, through which we cannot slip even though it has a hole in it. This assurance is created in us by the power of the Word, as discussed in the introduction to this volume.[42]

In loosing the Word of power which God gives to us, witnessing believers should remember something of the grammar of Law and Gospel. The Law expresses itself in commands and conditions: this do, and you will be saved. It places the burden of performance upon the human hearer. The Gospel expresses itself in the indicative: Jesus has died and risen to give you new life. This indicative promise takes the burden from the human hearer and places it on Jesus' back. Thus, it is important for disciples to recognize what they are doing when they command belief in Jesus. Lovers do not command the one whom they are wooing to love them; they promise and affirm their own love. Christian witnesses make fools of the bridegroom Jesus when they express His love for the unbeliever in terms of a command, which the unbeliever is powerless to carry out without the Holy Spirit's power. Our bridegroom woos us with His demonstrations and avowals of love. He does so through His promise, His loving self-sacrifice, of which we speak to one another.

Some believers may try to present the Gospel by discoursing on the nature and necessity of faith in Jesus or by trying to stress the importance of acceptance or commitment before discussing seriously the love which God has shown for us in Jesus' death and resurrection. Teaching at the edge of the American frontier in the latter part of the 19th century, Walther used the example of a missionary to Indians, who was killed in ambush after he had made his first presentation to them. It would have been far better, Walther comments, had he spoken of Jesus and His love for the fallen, than had he given a discourse on belief and the necessity or advantage of true faith.[43] The proclamation of the Gospel "does not wait hopefully for faith to appear in a doubting soul but brings faith about where it is lacking (cf. Rom. x.17). It does this by showing forth Christ as He is—and by showing the lost to whom Christ comes and gives Himself who they are."[44] Those who do not understand love and trust out of their personal experience on the horizontal level will not come to love and trust Jesus simply on the basis of our instruction. Those who do know how to love and trust also do not need such instruction, for they will naturally respond to His expression of love for them when the Holy Spirit moves them to believe it.

The witnessing believer will speak both of Christ's coming to us and of the result of His coming, that we are now cleansed, absolved, renewed, indeed, are now new people in Jesus. As such we struggle against infections of our stubborn doubt and defiance. But we are confident nonetheless that we are, above all, forgiven people, empowered by the Holy Spirit to trust, love, and fear our Creator and Father and to go about His assignments, as His restored image, loving those whom He has placed around us and caring for their needs. The conversion process is echoed in the rhythm of daily repentance and its repetition of God's baptismal action. Its goal is that we who recognize that God has saved us through faith in Jesus Christ are thoroughly equipped to live the lives He designed for us in the first place (2 Tim. 3:15–16).

THE BODY OF CHRIST: THE CHURCH

The Creator designed human life to be lived in community; He recognized immediately that it was not good for Adam to be alone (Gen. 2:18). He gathers His people into His body as He restores the horizontal relationships of our lives on the basis of His restoration of our relationship with Himself. The goal of Christian witness is to incorporate broken sinners into the body of Christ, through His baptismal action which takes into Himself their sins and which then bestows upon them His righteousness and innocence. This baptismal action also incorporates the person to whom the believer has been witnessing into the worshiping community, the body of Christ, His church (1 Cor. 12:13).

At the earliest stages of Christian witness, believers often want to shelter their hearers from the problems which arise, even within Jesus' body of the church, when people who are still struggling with sin gather together. There is some wisdom in that in certain instances. Also, the public worship service is designed to bring together the praises of those whose lives are already overflowing with joy in Jesus, and the proclamation of the Word to the worshiping congregation does take different forms than it does when it is being presented to someone outside or at the edge of the faith. Thus, a prospective convert may feel out of place in the worshiping congregation. As a matter of fact, it is unavoidable that the heart of Christian worship will be foreign to those who do not live within the culture of the church. It must be so. They are outside the faith, and they cannot understand what lies at the heart of our enterprise and way of life. The gap between our way of worship and the language and understanding of those around us dare not be exaggerated, but to abolish it is to render the church merely an arm of the unbelieving culture around us. If people have not learned the customs of our family yet, they will, of course, be uncomfortable in our midst. But we must help them make the transition into the family as effectively as possible. Furthermore, in our worship we dare never make the differences matters of merely earthly concerns, hanging onto elements of ecclesiastical culture for their own sake rather than for the sake of the Gospel.

It is certainly very important that the person to whom we witness realizes at the outset that our relationship with God is inextricably connected to living a life of corporate praise as a part of the community of God's people. One of God's most beautiful gifts is our restored ability to express the faith in praise of Him. This ability is important because it helps us realize our identity as children of God. And because the service of praise is a community affair, it reminds us of our identity as siblings of all other Christians. Especially for those who feel impotent in their loneliness or guilty in their estrangement, it is vital to know that God does gather the solitary into families and, as He forgives, gives the desolate a home (Ps. 68:6). This becomes concrete in the worshiping congregation. Christian witness not only articluates God's love; it also opens the lives and homes of individual members for those whom God is seeking among the alienated and forsaken. It incorporates them into the extended family of God in the congregation. Finding that kind of home may indeed even precede making the convert at home in the worshiping community. To be sure, other activities of congregational life may also aid in integrating the new convert into the total parish life. But those who are integrating this person into the congregation must remember that the parish's life centers in the public worship service, not in the youth group or the women's Bible study class or the men's bowling team.

A congregation's approach to Christian witness must also include a conscious dependence on the entire body of Christ in its midst. It may be that one member begins to witness to an unbeliever and sees quickly that another member could far better speak to this person. Believers must practice "tag-team evangelism" in such a case. One witnessing disciple may be able finally to deliver the killing blow of the Law to a neighbor, but the psychological strains of that interchange may prevent this disciple from being able to make the Gospel clear. The first witness must then find a fellow disciple, who is able to articulate and demonstrate God's love in Jesus to the newly broken sinner. In turn, this second witness may find it impossible to walk at the repentant sinner's side through the first months of the new believer's assimilation of a Christlike lifestyle, and a third disciple will have to pick up that assignment, probably with the help of several others. This is simply the way God has designed His church and its outreach to those who are outside it.

The church is indeed His. Many North Americans view their local congregation as a free association of individuals who want and like to be together in their own little group. Yet the church does not belong to its members; they, rather, as individuals and as a congregation, belong to the church's Lord and are directed by His Word.

> The church is called "the church of God" not because at the time of their allegiance men gave themselves this label, but because God has here gathered men and joined them together. Just as the origin of the church was God's deed, so every subsequent membership in the church results from God's deed. Man does not make himself a member of the church, but he is made a member. He does not join the church, but he is received into the church. In this sense Paul spoke of being "baptized into one body" (1 Cor. 12:13) and Luke of "being added" to the church through Baptism (Acts 2:41).[45]

This is not to say that the sociological principles which govern human institutions do not come into play in the life of the church. Members of Christ's body are indeed human; they are restored to true humanity in His sight. That does not result in their abandoning the design for human interaction which God placed in His creation in Eden and which still functions, albeit in flawed fashion, in daily life even under sin.

These two facts about the church must be kept in tension: the church belongs to Jesus, and it functions as a human institution. Indeed, tensions do arise in the Christian community because human principles as understood by fallen and flawed minds sometimes are permitted more than the role of servant; they become masters of the church's design for its own life and thus defy the Lord of the church. Dietrich Bonhoeffer contrasts the community of Jesus' body with the community in which His people lean more on their own wit and wisdom than on Him:

> In the community of the Spirit the Word of God alone rules; in human community of spirit there rules, along with the Word, the man who is furnished with exceptional powers, experience, and magical, suggestive capacities. There God's Word alone is binding; here, besides the Word, men bind others to themselves. ... In the spiritual realm the Spirit governs; in human community, psychological techniques and methods.[46]

226

The tension dare not be resolved by regarding the church in institutional form only in terms of sociological principles and at best only loosely related to the true people of God. Neither can the tension be resolved by abandoning all recourse to insight into the nature of the human creature which may be gained from study of such disciplines as psychology, sociology, and anthropology. We must also remember that these disciplines, even when unbiblical presuppositions do not shape their results, can give us descriptive insights, but never prescriptive directives, into the nature of our hearers and ourselves.

God has placed His church in the midst of His world above all as His image, as a witness to the world of His love. That witness begins with the church's focus on the Creator, expressed in the body of believers in public worship. Viewed from its everlasting dimension, as reflected in Revelation 5:11–14, for example, the Christian community is fundamentally and abidingly a community of faith, expressing this faith in praise which responds to His Word. God serves us with His Word; the church serves Him with praise and obedience. It exhibits itself before the world in a variety of ways, but in its worship the world sees its true focus in the object of worship, the Creator and Re-creator. Worship services are possible because God comes to us in the midst of them in His full power as He releases it in Word and Sacrament.

No Isolated Christians

Several factors in our culture today tend to let people keep their distance from the worshiping community and still deceive themselves into thinking that they are practicing Christians by permitting them electronic contact with the Word. Among the greatest of God's blessings to the church in the 20th century are those which come from technical advancement in communication aids, the radio and the television broadcast and other forms of audio/visual communication, for instance. Such media have significantly aided the church in bringing the Gospel to people who otherwise might never have heard it. Yet, in a culture in which personal relationships seem so difficult to make, in which many seek to avoid others and nurse a sense of alienation as a protective device, we need to be aware of the dangers which can arise if we lose the proper perspective on the network of horizontal relationships which the restoration of our vertical relationship with our Creator also restores.

Our engagement of the Word can, of course, happen in the privacy of our own minds on the basis of some proclamation of the message which God gives us, through the printed page, through some previous conversation, through electronic means. But God did not design us to retreat into cells as Christians. When Jesus urged us to pray in closets (Matt. 6:6), He was attacking hypocrisy, not charting permanent room reservations for His people. It was not good for Adam to be alone, the Creator recognized immediately (Gen. 2:18). So He created human community as a part of His basic design of what it means to be human.

Those who remain in isolation, perhaps because they believe that their spiritual needs can be sufficiently met and their relationship with God sufficiently nourished and cultivated through electronic contacts with the church, are separated from that living voice of the Gospel which hears and diagnoses their own needs from an external, more objective stance. Those whose community of faith is booked up only by radio or television waves are forced to perform spiritual surgery on themselves. The danger of our letting the Law's sharp edge slip and do great damage when we operate on ourselves is great. We would generally not try to remove something from our own eye which threatened to blind us. We would go to an eye surgeon. So also with our sin; the application of God's surgical and healing arts is best practiced within the body of Christ in mutual love, service, and witness.

In our culture, where the error of "rugged individualism" and various forms of narcissistic estrangement rage, it is a sad fact of life that many tragically sealed-off lives can be reached only by the impersonal approach of radio or television. Many who are too afraid to risk any personal confrontation can relax a bit with a radio preacher or permit themselves to listen when the Christian witness is at a safe distance behind a television screen.

Nonetheless, God did not intend us to be alone. Electronic contacts must be only the basis by which people are drawn into the community of believers in their own locales. The church universal is a precious Christian concept, but like our God it must take on real flesh and blood to become clear and meaningful. The church cannot remain wrapped in plastic for easy handling in the plastic casing of the television or radio. It must become real in the griefs and joys of the people of our area to whom God calls us to minister. There is more to Christian community than exerting the effort to turn on the knob or seal the envelope, and there is more to Christian community than enjoying the beautiful color of a mammoth church on screen or the professional music of the well-coiffed pianist and soloist as they smile into the camera.

Christ's Body in the Flesh and Blood of Believers

The Christian community takes form in us as we exert the effort to visit the estranged and lonely person down the street, and to listen in patience and concern when he or she only seems to want to pour out bitter invective about the rottenness of life when we stop by. The Christian community takes on flesh when we intervene unwanted into a life that is not just broken but really messed up, and as we try to mend that life without the cooperation—in the face of the resentment—of the old crank or the young smart aleck who has always given us so much trouble. It is, of course, neater to sit in front of the television, which will not vomit its frustration upon us. Yet the Christian community is truly functioning when found in the pew in which the neighbor who makes noise in the middle of the night exhibits, albeit off-key, his desire to praise God with the sounds of the hymn in which we are joining together. The Christian community becomes real as we can put away the hurt we felt on Friday, when the pastor walked right past us in the grocery store and did not venture to say a word to us, and as we recognize that his call from the pulpit on Sunday for us to love as Christ has loved us is real and heartfelt. God has called us to live together and to serve one another as members of the same body. Christian witness must involve integration into a flesh and blood body of believers. The congregation and groups within it must become a home for the homeless, a hospital for the hurting, a haven for the harried.

We have discussed that power in the proclaimed and read Word and in the formal absolution, which the pastor pronounces as one of the disciples, and a representative of all other disciples, accord-

229

ing to Jesus' command to remit sins (John 20:23; Matt. 18:18). The action of human confession and God's absolution as the Holy Spirit works in the worshiping community repeats His baptismal action. He also conveys the favor of God through His own flesh and blood in the Lord's Supper.

THE BODY OF CHRIST IN THE LORD'S SUPPER

Similar as it is to Baptism in many ways, and thus justifiably linked to it by the church's term "sacrament," the Lord's Supper serves specific functions in the economy of God's re-creative Word.

> The Lord's Supper is repeated, for it is the food and drink of the desert journey. But baptism is not repeated, for it is the crossing of the Red Sea, which only took place once for all. ... Through baptism a person is delivered from the land of slavery and then begins his journey to heaven: the Lord's Supper is "the food of travellers."
> .... Deepest of all, certainly, lies the thought of birth in baptism; birth into life takes place only once. Thereafter one lives the life into which one was born—lives by receiving food. Birth takes place in baptism, which is undergone once for all; food for the journey is offered to man repeatedly in the Lord's Supper."[47]

In the Lord's Supper Jesus approaches us as the banquet speaker and the meal itself; He is chef as well as entree. Those who cannot believe that God has selected elements of His created order to serve as the instruments of His re-creative power have trouble recognizing that He gives His people His own body with the bread of the Lord's Supper and His own blood with its cup of wine (1 Cor. 10:16; cf. 1 Cor. 11:23–26 and parallels). The early church and universal Christendom throughout history have not shared that difficulty in taking the Lord at His word when He said that He was giving His disciples His body and blood. Most Christians, apart from many in the Anglo-American religious ghetto of the past quarter millennium, have recognized that God is present in the body and blood of His fully human and fully divine Son Jesus, also in bread and wine, and that He is so present because He says so.[48]

The disciple will explain carefully the significance of this special form of God's approach to us in the Word conveyed with bread-body and wine-blood to the new convert, and heighten the anticipation of receiving God's assurance of His forgiveness and favor in this sacramental form. At the same time the new convert must not be encouraged to think that the Lord's Supper will work some magic, either in feeling or external effect. The Lord's Supper accomplishes what other forms of the Word accomplish: it expresses the promise and power of God by focusing our attention on His love in Jesus Christ. It forgives, and it strengthens faith.

The Christian witness must make certain that the new convert appreciates what God is saying in the Lord's Supper, where Jesus approaches us as sacrificial lamb and as priest. In its institution (e.g., in Matt. 26) the Lord's Supper was set for all Christians in the context of the celebration of God's deliverance of Israel from Egyptian bondage through the Passover. In the Lord's Supper God smears the blood of His Lamb on the doorways of our lives, marking us as those to whom He will permit no ultimate harm to come. He joins us there in a fellowship meal, which, like the original Passover, is a meal of people ready to depart on a liberating but dangerous journey, to the promised land, for which we are destined because the Lamb's sacrifice has atoned for our sins. His atoning sacrifice is conveyed to us as we receive this body and blood for the forgiveness of our sins. This forgiveness removes our sins further from us than Golgotha is in space and time from the sacramental bestowal of His love on us.[49]

In the Lord's Supper, the convert must be instructed, believers not only receive renewal through the food of the Savior's body; they also die His death to sin once again. Here, too, we experience the preenactment of judgment day while God also reenacts creation day, as He incorporates into us the body and blood of the dying and rising Deliverer, Jesus of Nazareth.

> In the Supper celebration there is concretized, so to speak, the present's entire situation in redemptive history: its simultaneous and particularly close relation to both the mid point and the end. In the Lord's Supper there is a pointing back to the Last Supper of Jesus before His death and to the Easter suppers that were eaten with the Risen One, and there is a pointing forward to the Messianic Banquet, which Christ will eat with His people in the Kingdom of God ... particularly in the Apocalypse of John the Supper is thought of as an anticipation of the Kingdom of God (ch. 3:20).[50]

231

God takes us in Baptism and in daily absolution to judgment and to creation so that we may be reborn to function in human community, joined to other believers in the one loaf of the Supper (1 Cor. 10:17), where Jesus becomes present in a special way to forgive and strengthen His people. At this Father's Supper table, there is always a place for every member of the family, whether new, regular, or strayed. Thus, trust in His forgiveness bestowed through the Lord's Supper transforms the way we live. "The more strongly we emphasize this real presence of Christ with all His benefits, the more clearly we shall perceive the connection between the Eucharist and our service of our neighbor," Gustaf Wingren observes, as he reviews how death and resurrection in Jesus within our vertical relationship, as accomplished through the sacraments, leads to dying to the habits of hell and coming alive to the habits of heaven in the ways we relate to those whom God has placed around us.[51] We cannot walk away from the table of the Lamb, with His words of forgiveness, life, and salvation given us with His body and blood still ringing in our ears, to return to kicking people in the shins. We want to wash their feet instead.

THE BODY OF CHRIST AT PRAISE AND PRAYER

This desire to serve the Lord who has given us all good things in His body and blood first turns us to Him, however, and our response to Him finds a community culmination in the public worship service. As our praise of Him frames the Sacrament, we call it the Eucharist, or the Thanksgiving. Our reaction to God's gift of Himself, as presented in the proclamation of His Word, the pronouncement of absolution, and the distribution of bread-body and wine-blood finds its necessary expression in praise. "We delight to praise what we enjoy because the praise not merely expresses but completes the enjoyment; it is its appointed consummation. It is not out of compliment that lovers keep on telling one another how beautiful they are; the delight is incomplete till it is expressed."[52]

New converts above all will enjoy entering into public worship because their hearts are filled with the excitement and thrill of finding new identity, security, and meaning in life. At the same time new converts, who are still locked in struggle with old systems of security and meaning, will find support and encouragement—though certainly not some kind of magical transformation—in the liturgy. The worship services not only give form to our praise but also teach the Word as they review God's goodness and shape our response to it. The witnessing congregation will recognize how important the discipline and experience of public worship is for the new convert. The congregation will carefully shape its liturgical life to encourage and excite all the members and give them sustenance for the week. It will also carefully cultivate in young believers in its midst an appreciation for the dynamics of worship and will train them to appropriate from it the joy and inspiration which God wants the liturgy to give to His people.

The promise of incorporation into the community of mutual hearing and praise will assist witnessing disciples in making the appeal of the Gospel and its relevance to all of life clear to the hearer. Witnesses should also be sensitive to the potential for testimony to Jesus which arises from the liturgical calendar. The church year rehearses the history of salvation, and believers may use particularly the most important and familiar festivals of God's people to invite those outside the church into its midst. Especially those who have earlier left the church may listen more carefully as disciples approach them in the context of childhood memories of Christmas or Easter to talk of the Lord's incarnation and resurrection.[53]

Believers respond to Jesus' revelation of God's love and to all the many blessings which the Creator gives in daily life in personal praise and thanks as well, and they respond to His Word and to the needs of their own lives and of the world around them in prayer. An important part of the initial instruction of new converts is teaching them how to pray. So many false ideas concerning prayer abound in our religious culture that the task of teaching people how to pray must begin by clearing away these mis-impressions.

Our prayer can never occur prior to God's advance toward us in the Word, and what we have to say to Him is always shaped by His Word and in response to it. Prayer does not provide the all-knowing God with information which He previously did not have at His disposal. It provides instead the opportunity for God to enjoy conversation with His children, who cannot resist chatting with Him and sharing their needs and joys.

Prayer does not offer some special power to those who pray; prayer has no power of its own, such as that of a pagan magical incantation designed to put a hammerlock on God. Prayer rather offers the opportunity for God's children to express their aches and sorrows, their delights and hopes to their loving and beloved Father, confident that He alone exercises the power needed to deal properly with their concerns. Prayer is also not just a therapeutic exercise in which the human being hypnotizes himself or psychologically alters her own state. God puts us in contact with Himself as His Holy Spirit moves us to pray (Rom. 8:15). In prayer the believer comes to God, in response to His call, as a beloved child comes to a loving Father, relaxed in His presence no matter how urgent and exciting the content of the prayer may be. "The child learns to speak because his father speaks to him. He learns the speech of his father. So we learn to speak to God because God has spoken to us and speaks to us. ... Repeating God's own words after him, we begin to pray to him."[54]

Genuine prayer depends on Jesus. It depends first of all on His teaching us how to pray (Luke 11:1).

> The phrase "learning to pray" sounds strange to us. But it is a dangerous error, surely very widespread among Christians, to think that the heart can pray by itself. For then we confuse wishes, hopes, sighs, laments, rejoicings—all of which the heart can do by itself—with prayer. And we confuse earth and heaven, man and God. Prayer does not mean simply to pour out one's heart. It means rather to find the way to God and to speak with Him, whether the heart is full or empty. No man can do that by himself. For that he needs Jesus Christ.[55]

If this is true for seasoned believers, it is certainly true for new converts. In the process of listening to our witness, they will have begun to learn how to hear the Word of the Lord. We must also teach them how to practice the faith in prayerful response.

Second, genuine prayer depends on Jesus as mediator.

> The disciples are permitted to pray because Jesus tells them they may—and he knows the Father. He promises that God will hear them. ... the disciples pray only because they are followers of Christ and have fellowship with him. Only those who, like them, adhere to Jesus have access to the Father through him. All Christ-

ian prayer is directed to God through a Mediator, and not even prayer affords direct access to the Father. Only through Jesus Christ can we find the Father in prayer. Christian prayer presupposes faith, that is, adherence to Christ.[56]

It furthers the growth of the acquaintanceship between Jesus and the converts by leading them into a two-way conversation between themselves and the Trinity.

Prayer expresses faith in Jesus. It does not win merit in God's sight, and, strictly defined as our response to God and not as a combination of that response with meditation on God's Word in which He speaks to us, prayer is not a means of grace. It is not an instrument of the Father's reconciling us to Himself and giving us new life. God is the object of the action of our prayer; we are not. Neither, directly, are those for whom we pray. They are, we pray, objects of God's power and presence, for which we are praying in their behalf. Thus, Jesus objected to public displays of pious religiosity of focusing specifically on prayer (Matt. 6:5–8).

> Prayer is the supreme instance of the hidden character of the Christian life. It is the antithesis of self-display. When men pray, they have ceased to know themselves and know only God whom they call upon. Prayer does not aim at any direct effect on the world; it is addressed to God alone, and is therefore the perfect example of undemonstrative action. ... In the last resort it is immaterial whether we pray in the open street or in the secrecy of our chambers, whether briefly or lengthily, in the Litany of the Church, or with the sigh of one who knows not what he should pray for. True prayer does not depend either on the individual or the whole body of the faithful, but solely upon the knowledge that our heavenly Father knows our needs. That makes God the sole object of our prayers, and frees us from a false confidence in our own prayerful efforts.[57]

Since witnessing believers often use prayer at critical points in their testimony to unbelievers, they must remember what prayer is and what it is not. For their prayers during the course of witnessing will determine to a significant degree the shape and place which prayer assumes in the life of the convert. Above all, the believer must remember that we proclaim people into the faith and God's kingdom; we do not pray them into trust in their Creator—even though our prayers for those to whom we witness and for guidance and assistance in our own witnessing are of utmost importance as well.

THE BODY OF CHRIST IN WITNESS AND SERVICE

Life in the Christian community focuses primarily on God. However, because He designed us also to focus His image on others through our own demonstration and sharing of His love, that focus extends to the whole world. It begins within the church. Through Christian fellowship within a congregation God tends to a wide range of human problems. Basically, Christians are called together to edify one another in the faith, to educate and strengthen others in their trust in Jesus and in the way of life which pours forth from that trust. Because God gives His people, as individuals and as communities, growth through His Word, this internal use of the Word must be diligently cultivated.

God has given His church gifts in the talents of people whom His Holy Spirit moves in order to keep the growth going. The New Testament speaks of a number of gifts to which contemporary Christians apply the term "spiritual gifts" (cf. e.g., Eph. 4:11; 1 Cor. 12:28–30; Rom. 12:6–8). These spiritual gifts must be distinguished from the believer's calling to serve God in home, occupation, society, and even congregation in ways which relate only to the horizontal relationships of our lives. The Holy Spirit uses our spiritual gifts to initiate and strengthen the vertical relationship with God, and they influence and take shape in our horizontal relationships. However, these gifts generally rest upon a natural talent. The Creator's gift of the ability to be sensitive and persuasive differs psychologically very little in an organizer for a secular group and a witnessing disciple. Gifts of the Spirit then incorporate these natural talents into the service of the faith and the Word of Jesus of Nazareth. They are spiritual gifts because they are exercised under the power and direction of the Holy Spirit.

Paul writes to the Ephesians about gifts which are people, and about their Spirit-directed, faith-motivated talents. These gifts are given to the church so that God's saints may be equipped to serve one another and edify the body of Christ (Eph. 4:11–12). The goal of this edification is the unity of faith in knowing the Son of God.

Knowledge of Jesus marks human maturity, for as we are returned to knowing Him, and reach His stature as a human creature, we are returned to Eden. God does not want us tossed to and fro and carried about by every system which teaches some source or other for our identity, security, and meaning. He wants His Word taught purely and confessed boldly against the cunning and craftiness of deceitful human creatures, who peddle the devil's lies against His revelation of the way He created us and our world to be and of the loving regard and concern He has for us (4:13-14). He insists that His message be delivered faithfully, and that means both speaking the truth clearly and unequivocally, according to the inspired Scriptures, and speaking it in love, not just so that we can say that we have spoken it but so that it effectively does its work. This brings the growth which knits Christ's people together in His love (4:15–16).

Especially in contemporary North American culture, where ideological tolerance of every point of view except ideological intolerance is a supreme virtue, witnessing believers need to be conscious of the vital importance of speaking God's Word accurately, reflecting its content and its intent appropriately. This means more than reciting words from the pages of Scripture. It means aiming Law at secure sinners so that they may die to their idols, and it means applying Gospel to broken sinners so that they may come alive through Jesus' forgiveness to His way of life in trust toward God and love toward other human creatures.[58] Within the people of God forces have always been at work to abstract the living Word of God into heresies of one kind or another, into cultural ideologies in biblical dress, which do not bring God's power of re-creation to transform the focus of individual lives from self to God, but instead call these lives to find identity, security, and meaning in the ideology itself, in reliance on the heresy.

> Always and everywhere God's church confronts a wrong church, and divine humanness confronts an idolatrous inhumanness. ... Men are either being integrated into a divine community, the church of God, or being fragmented into groups which destroy the basic web of life, the wrong churches. The divine word and Spirit create in men a texture of life which repairs the damage caused by the denial of life. This texture of grace, this kingdom,

is not made by men. ... It is born out of listening to the giver of life, out of being "hearers of God."[59]

This means that believers must be sensitive to the necessity of pointing out the conflict between certain ideas which our culture takes for granted and the Christian faith. Although we do not make these differences the focal point of our witness, we must be aware that unbelievers will sense the conflict. These cultural values must be commandeered for the Gospel when possible and resisted as temptations to pervert the Gospel when necessary. In opposition to false doctrines and ideologies inside and outside the church, believers must wield the sword which Jesus came to send (Matt. 10:34), not just against the idolatries of interpersonal relationships but also against false proclamations regarding the source of our security and identity in God's gift of Himself to us. His church remains a remnant, and believers must not confuse the movement of people towards it in response to false perceptions of God and what the church has to offer with true conversions to Christ. They must resist those cultural forces which want to kidnap the church and its Gospel, either for secularity or for a false religiosity, even when it comes in Christian dress. Hermann Sasse, facing the onslaught of the Nazi-sympathizing "German Christian" movement, noted that "a religious teaching with which a whole nation agrees—agrees, perhaps, enthusiastically—certainly has nothing to do with the Word of God. For this Word speaks a 'sign which is rejected' "[60] (1 Peter 2:7–8).

The witnessing congregation has been knit together so that it might evaluate its own proclamation of the Word and those of others to determine whether the forgiving and re-creating Word is being announced to the world in the proper fashion, a fashion which will genuinely meet human need. Christian witness always takes place within the tension of the need to draw sinners into the family of faith and the need to resist the temptation to draw them in the easy way, under false pretenses. Congregations dare never evaluate their outreach strategies according to a false concept of quality—making sure every jot and tittle are in place—versus quantity—"numbers for numbers' sake." Instead, we must recognize that no one has a perfect faith. For those who come into our midst, we will be a hospital for the sick, the broken, those just beginning to recover from their sinful way of life. Their understanding and expression of the faith will necessarily be incomplete and often ragged and torn. With all the patience and persistence of the Good Shepherd we will tend and nurture them.

Knit together and secure in Jesus' love, a love exhibited in the incorporation of His people into the body of His death and resurrection, and into the body of His church, we serve one another's needs in a wide variety of areas—spiritual, emotional, and physical. Because we are secure in Jesus' love, we can risk what He has given us to serve fellow Christians. "The physical presence of other Christians is a source of incomparable joy and strength to the believer. ... The prisoner, the sick person, the Christian in exile sees in the companionship of a fellow Christian a physical sign of the gracious presence of the triune God."[61] Witnessing disciples sometimes forget the importance of their presence as well as their words, but for the alienated and the impotent, facing evil alone, simply the presence of someone who cares enough to spend time and invest concern, if explained as arising from Jesus' love, can be the most effective witness to God's intervention in our behalf. The Christian community and the activities of its members within the context of congregational life demonstrate and renew God's plan for human life in community.

The Gospel produces restoration to human community and its commitments. Thus,

> the Christian community is not a spiritual sanitarium. The person who comes into a fellowship because he is running away from himself is misusing it for the sake of diversion, no matter how spiritual this diversion may appear. He is really not seeking community at all, but only distraction which will allow him to forget his loneliness for a brief time, the very alienation that creates the deadly isolation of man. ... Let him who cannot be alone beware of community. ... Let him who is not in community beware of being alone.[62]

Effective Christian witness does not merely provide a haven from the world but rather cultivates growth in human maturity, through faith in Jesus, so that the guilty and the ashamed, the alienated and the impotent, may no longer be like children tossed to and fro but may instead stand strong against the deceitful winds which would twist life and take away both truth and love.

The community exists to venture forth into the world which surrounds it with Jesus' love and His truth. The worship and edification which the Christian enjoys in the community equips and inspires him or her for service in God's world. In a congregation in which I once served a figure of Jesus with outstretched, inviting arms was removed from the chancel when the altar in which it was encased was replaced in remodeling. The statue was placed over the exit from the nave, and thus it assumed another appropriate stance. At the altar Jesus invites us to receive Himself in the Sacrament and to come to Himself in response to the Word. As the congregation leaves public worship now, Jesus invites its members into His world to serve within the structure He established for human life in Eden, even though the world has damaged that structure in various ways.

> ... The church is the nation of God's children called out of the world and the nation of prophets, priests, and kings sent out into the world, The church lives in the world in an elementary double movement of life: as being summoned by God out of the world again and again and as being sent back to the world again and again. Both movements belong inseparably together. Both have their center in the worshiping assembly.[63]

The re-created disciple goes forth into the world to practice a piety which lives and flows from faith. Faith's new perception of the reality which proceeds from God's Word transforms the way in which life is lived. "The most important ethical contribution of the Christian congregation does not lie in the area of appeals to action but in the area of interpretation of life."[64]

This interpretation of life rests upon the conviction that we need not be in bondage to our own deeds, relying on them as means by which we obtain true life, genuine security, and meaning. The righteousness which Jesus is and bestows upon us through His liberating Word and our trust in that Word is indeed a better righteousness exceeding that of the very pious religious leaders of Jesus' time (Matt. 5:20, 46–48).

> But the disciple had the advantage over the Pharisee in that his doing of the law is in fact perfect ... because between the disciples and the law stands one who has perfectly fulfilled it, the one

> with whom they live in communion ... This righteousness is therefore not a duty owed, but a perfect and truly personal communion with God, and Jesus not only possesses this righteousness, but is himself the personal embodiment of it. He is the righteousness of the disciples. By calling them he has admitted them to partnership with Himself, and made them partakers of His righteousness in its fullness.[65]

As the disciples of Jesus go forth into His world, their attitudes, and thus their actions, are shaped by their confidence that Jesus has exchanged their unrighteousness for His righteousness. Confident that they may relax in the presence of their Father, they need not be tense about whether they are using people around them to ingratiate themselves with their Father. They can concentrate on the needs of the neighbor because God has concentrated His love on them. If we believe that our identity and our security will be affected by the way we treat the neighbor, we will always regard our neighbor with one eye looking at God and the other at ourselves. Only when faith rests secure in Jesus' hand can we truly function as God designed us to function, as the image of God which pours out its love, care, and concern on the fellow human creature without any regard for self at all.

> For Paul's imperatives always refer back to what has already happened to me. They are not oriented to a future form of existence which is still to be achieved. They relate to a determination of existence which is already past, and they insist that I for my part now do what has already been done on me. You are risen with Christ—seek then those things which are above; you are dead with Christ—mortify then your members (Col. 3:1ff.).[66]

Because natural human religions, those which fashion gods in their own image, all stress the importance of what we do as a source for our own security and meaning in life, the witnessing believer must make certain that the new convert understands that works are fruits of faith, not its cause, that God is pleased with us as His own infants before we can do any works which please Him at all. Our hearers must be led to understand that the question "do Christians have to do good works?" is a "why do you want to know?" question. If the question is asked in the hope that grace frees the Christian from living a life as God's image, reflecting His love and care, then the answer is "yes" to the secure or arrogant sinner who nurses such defiant hopes. If the question is asked in anxiety over the proper number of good works needed to maintain one's status as Christian, then the Gospel must be enunciated: God loves us and pledges Himself to us totally apart from our works, and our relationship with Him has been restored to its original right and righteous form solely by the work of Jesus and our trust in His saving message (Rom. 3, esp. v. 28).

As a matter of fact, there is no way to discuss the Christian life without the potential of making it sound like a condemnation. "The Christian ought," or "the Christian should," or even "the Christian is" or "does" will all pronounce judgment on the person who has failed to do what should or ought to have been done, or who has not achieved the standards enunciated in "the Christian is" or "does." Even the disciple cannot escape that accusation of the Law as we discuss the shape or performance of our lives. We can only take refuge in the Gospel of Jesus' forgiveness. Having taken such refuge from the Law's condemnation, we can freely address the neighbor's need with Jesus' love because we are safe in that love ourselves.

Christian witness profoundly alters the lives of those who come to believe our message. It moves them from death to life, from one culture to another, from one way of life—a way of death—to the true way of human living. Christian witness does so through the power of a Word that not only bestows God's gift of identity as His child but also provides psychological motivation for the daily Christian life. Changes in the pattern of daily living flow naturally from the changes in perception and motivation which faith effects.

Faith Produces Works

Faith moves us to return to the natural human actions which God designed and implemented in Adam and Eve through a number of motivating factors. First, faith recognizes that God is a good and loving Lord. In sin we regard His will as our enemy, for we perceived Him only in His Law and felt His condemning and curbing wrath against us. Jesus has introduced us to God as a loving Father, as a friend who has expressed His love in His creative and in His re-creative activity in our behalf. We can follow God because He has become incarnate in Jesus of Nazareth, and we perceive now that it is fun to follow God. Just as a toddler delights in chugging along behind Daddy, doing what Daddy does, so we find delight in following our Father in the person of His eternal Son, Jesus. Bonhoeffer describes the way Matthew (Levi) experienced it:

> Follow me, run along behind me! That is all. To follow in His steps is something which is void of all content. It gives us no intelligible programme for a way of life, no goal or ideal to strive after. It is not a cause which human calculation might deem worthy of our devotion, even the devotion of ourselves. What happens? At the call, Levi leaves all that he has—but not because he thinks that he might be doing something worthwhile, but simply for the sake of the call. Otherwise he cannot follow in the steps of Jesus. This act on Levi's part has not the slightest value in itself, it is quite devoid of significance and unworthy of consideration. The disciple simply burns his boats and goes ahead. He is called out, and has to forsake his old life in order that he may 'exist' in the strictest sense of the word. The old life is left behind, and completely surrendered. The disciple is dragged out of his relative security into a life of absolute insecurity (that is, in truth, into the absolute security and security of the fellowship of Jesus), from a life which is observable and calculable (it is, in fact, quite incalculable) into a life where everything is unobservable and fortuitous (that is, into one which is necessary and calculable), out of the realm of the finite (which is in truth the infinite) into the realm of the infinite possibilities (which is the one liberating reality). Again it is no universal law. Rather it is the exact opposite of all legality. It is nothing else than bondage to Jesus Christ alone, completely breaking through every programme, every ideal, every set of laws. No other significance is possible, since Jesus is the only significance. Beside Jesus nothing has any significance. He alone matters.[67]

We embrace this Jesus and His Father as the loving Creator whose wisdom is reflected in the life-style of Jesus and in the structure for human life which He made clear in that life-style. We recognize that God is Father and Creator by living as the image of His love, which reflects our conviction that He is our Lord.

Second, the believer acknowledges God's goodness in His restoring righteousness through His Word, in the flesh, proclaimed, in absolution, and the sacraments. In reaction believers cannot help but give thanks. God's goodness is so great that it elicits an automatic expression of gratitude. That thanksgiving finds its form in seeking ways to please God, who is already pleased with us for Jesus' sake. Thus, these thankful acts of pleasing do not bring God into our orbit but are means by which we express our appreciation for His bringing us into His own orbit. Thankful faith transforms our old style of life:

> Faith, thankfulness, and patience bind men to God in such a way that they may continually be created, moulded, and formed by God's hand and remain living creatures with "gentle and submissive hearts." Faithlessness and ingratitude create a gulf between God and man in such a way that man becomes hardened, pushing aside the hands of the Creator—he "flees from His hands"—and by this rejection is at the one time both dead and evil.[68]

We become good and alive through God's re-creative pronouncement of righteousness upon us, and we demonstrate our life and goodness, gifts from God, by embodying His goodness and life for others.

Third, God's gift in Jesus elicits a trust in Him which can dare to risk what He has given us in our efforts to carry His love to others. We trust that He who has supplied life to us can be trusted to give aid and support if we surrender time or possessions or other gifts to meet the needs of those whom He has placed within our reach. Faith relies on God to supply what is lacking because we take what He has given us to use for other purposes than we had at first intended for His gifts. If God will not replace these gifts, He will open up ways for us to live without them.

Fourth, God's gift of Christ's righteousness means that believers are willing to submit to Him in afflictions, for the sake of the neighbor's need. Faith's perspective recognizes that we no longer need to be caught up in our search for security and meaning. Instead, we can feel secure and find meaning even in those circumstances and situations which the world counts as evil and interprets as judgment. Faith knows that God has implemented His desires for His people successfully by living in such a way that the world labeled Him most unsuccessful. His way of life embraces self-sacrifice and self-surrender; He succeeded in and by suffering, submission, and service.

Faith perceives that in affliction God works genuine success, that out of the midst of trouble, tragedy, trial, and tribulation God's triumph emerges. Faith thus goes forth in the full confidence that Jesus' pattern of self-sacrifice and self-surrender can and will "work" for those whom He has given crosses to bear as a mark and as the means of His association with us and for us under the burden of evil.[69]

Fifth, Christians enjoy doing the work of God because they realize that it gives witness to God's love and forms an important part of their testimony to the Father who has reclaimed and re-created them.

> Men do not see the disciples but their good works, says Jesus. And these works are none other than those which the Lord Jesus Himself has created in them by calling them to be the light of the world under the shadow of the cross. ... If the good works were a galaxy of human virtues, we should then have to glorify the disciples, not God. But there is nothing for us to glorify in the disciple who bears the cross, or in the community whose light so shines because it stands visibly on the hill—only the Father which is in heaven can be praised for the "good works." It is by *seeing* the cross and the community beneath it that men come to believe in God. But that is the light of the Resurrection.[70]

Witnessing disciples cannot separate the articulation of the message of Jesus from their testimony in deeds and attitudes of love.

Therefore, in discussing motivation for the Christian life, as well as the motivation for conversion, disciples will resist the temptation to believe that "the Gospel is fine in its place but sometimes you have to get practical,"[71] because nothing is more practical for moving people to the love of God than His Good News for us in Jesus Christ. "If one feared a severe illness—hence has regarded oneself as biologically irreparable—the good news the physician brings is the renewal of the person as a functioning being. No moralistic exhortations, appeals, or proclamations are needed. One is simply made active through the assurance that one is healthy."[72] This is the kind of Good News the Gospel of Jesus is: people who believe it cannot help but be turned to Him so that they may live in and for Him.

The Structures of Human Living

The life which faith in Jesus motivates finds its structure in that which God designed in Eden for the care of both His human creatures and His entire world.[73]

Faith recognizes that life takes place in the situations of home, occupation, society, and congregation, and it proceeds to orient life toward the responsibilities of those situations, perceiving those responsibilities as assignments or callings from God. Christians reflect God's image in loving and serving all who are needy, forgiving enemies, praying for all, and being willing to suffer wrong. "Love is the inner willingness to do and bear all that is required by vocation [the responsibilities of each of our situations, not just of occupation], but does it gladly and without resistance. Indeed it willingly exceeds what is called for."[74]

> Thus a Christian finds himself called to drab and lowly tasks, which seem less remarkable than monastic life, mortifications, and other distractions from our vocations. For him who heeds his vocation, sanctification is hidden in offensively ordinary tasks, with the result that it is hardly noticed at all that he is a Christian. But faith looks on simple duties as tasks to which vocation summons the man; and by the Spirit he becomes aware that all those "poor, dull, and despised works" are adorned with the favor of God "as with costliest gold and precious stones."[75]

The works of vocation are entirely reasonable and natural, corresponding to the needs of the present hour. At the same time, they lack characteristics which invest them with a visible aura of sanctity; hence, they clash with natural feeling about religion.[76] Believers trust that they are secure in Jesus' hand and that their lives have meaning because of what they are, God's children, rather than what they do. Therefore, they have no problem in relaxing in God's presence and going to work in front of other people with such ordinary acts of piety as changing diapers, washing dishes, raising hogs and baking bread, teaching, visiting the imprisoned and the elderly or helping the neighbor paint a fence. They proceed with the tasks at hand and need not feel tense when conflicts between the claims of competing responsibilities arise.

In making those often very difficult decisions on how to act in specific circumstances, the believer relies on human observation of how those situations are structured and how those responsibilities are exercised in order best to show divine love, although such observations often twist the proper perception of God's structure. The believer relies decisively on God's commands, which, as they curb our sinful desires and accuse us of breaking God's plan for human life, also give us guidance in faithful decision making. In some instances believers must do more than just determine whether alternative courses are good or evil. In life as we have twisted it we must sometimes make choices between two or more goods or two or more evils. Disciples will not be immobilized at such a point by fears of doing the wrong thing. Instead, they will ask for the Holy Spirit's guidance and proceed in full confidence that God is at work in us and guiding us, *and* that God will forgive wrong decisions and do His will in spite of us when we are wrong.

Above all, believers will seek to determine the proper course for their actions by turning to Jesus, who is both the motivating and liberating basis for their Christian living and is also the perfect embodiment of the principles or structure which He established in creating human life.

> The example of Jesus, both in its ethical rigor and in its unconditional forgiveness, is the key ingredient in building a Christian fellowship [and, we might add, an individual life of discipleship]. Jesus is the pattern for everyday actions. No one needs to go to school or to be a deep thinker to follow His example. The deed lies hidden and waiting in human existence, and it can be carried out even by one who is illiterate. No one has yet followed perfectly the example of the crucified one. His example is always an *impossible* ideal. Yet the one who falls short still meets in Jesus the model for action, the one who affirms and accepts the failing person and offers unconditional forgiveness.[77]

Jesus' model for our lives reminds us that God designed human life to love and that in a world twisted by sin love takes away the form of suffering in many instances. His kind of love we call *agape,* the Greek word which we interpret as that love which seeks not its own but abandons itself in offering love, care, and concern to others.[78] As we turn to those around us in our horizontal relationships, this *agape* is "not motivated by pragmatic interests, by the usability or social productivity of the neighbor. It is motivated by his alien dignity, by what he means for God."[79] We see in our neighbors the needs of Jesus, and we respond as Jesus' lips, eyes, hands, and feet. For the Holy Spirit who makes us the temple of God must rely on our bodies to do His work.

Agape, as God channels it through us, is directed at specific individuals and groups, not at humanity in general. We must be prepared to do good to all, but we actually do good to specific neighbors. Jesus did not say that the neighbor was anybody and everybody but was a beaten stranger by the side of the road (Luke 10:30). Among those individuals whom we are to love are even those who exhibit hostility and hatred toward us.

> By our enemies Jesus means those who are quite intractable and utterly unresponsive to our love, who forgive us nothing when we forgive them all, who requite our love with hatred and our service with derision, "For the love that I had unto them, lo, they now take my contrary part; but I give myself unto prayer" (Ps. 109:4). Love asks nothing in return, but seeks those who need it. And who needs our love more than those who are consumed with hatred and are utterly devoid of love? ... Christian love draws no distinction between one enemy and another, except that the more bitter our enemy's hatred, the greater his need of love.[80]

The genuine love God has for us and which extends even to our enemies ought not be confused with being nice at every point. Our neighbors, like ourselves, combine both good and destructive desires. Hence, the neighbor's cry to us may include something we must stand against decisively. We must sift and separate that which supports life from that which can despoil it even though we run the risk always of making wrong judgments.[81] Particularly in Christian witness this task of separating what our hearers want from what they need may try our wisdom and our patience. We must cultivate a sensitivity to God's will and to the other person's need which enables us to stand firm against wrong desires and yet show love and concern for the person. Also in Christian witness we proceed according to the Lord's dictum that we act toward others in the way in which we want them to act toward us: no psychological tricks, no manipulation.

Because we love even our enemies, because we love people in ways in which they do not want to be loved, because we love people by joining them under the burdens of the evils which they suffer through great fault or through no fault of their own, we also suffer. Only God Himself could suffer in our place and atone for our sins with His own suffering. But God sends us forth to bear the crosses of others with them (Mark 8:34–35 and parallels), even as He joined us to suffer with us as well as for us. His coming together with us under evil provides the model for our risking suffering and daring to place ourselves under the evil burdens of those around us.

> Only as the Christian community permits itself to undergo a continuous crucifixion to the world can it be *in* the world as the friend of those who are crucified. Apart from that, it always ends in a theology and an ethic of glory. For it imagines that it has something to bring, something to give, something that will enable *it* to master the situation. Real solidarity with those who suffer recognizes that their condition is our own: we are all beggars together. The possibility of *community,* which is the aim of Christian social ethics, is given at that point of recognition, and nowhere else. True community exists only at the foot of the cross.[82]

This suffering which cannot be separated from Christian living not only serves the neighbor's immediate needs. On the one hand, it points the one who is suffering toward the perfect exhibition of God's love which is to come and, on the other hand, aids us in putting to death the selfishness which would keep us from reaching out from ourselves to those in need. Christians do not glory in their own suffering; they are hardheaded realists, who know that evil is not good but evil, even when God uses it for His good purpose. Therefore, we do not

> idealize submissive and passive suffering as is the case with the traditional "imitation of Christ." Suffering-thinking is creative and stretches toward the future. It is not afraid to face violence and destruction, that which in the form of death ultimately confronts everything human. The crucifixion and resurrection of Jesus show that death does not have the last word, that the word of life breaks through and tears apart the web made out of the knowledge of good and evil, that life springs forth and shatters the artificial worlds built on the knowledge of good and evil.[83]

This grasp of life under the cross is an "exercise in thinking according to the rhythm of crucifixion and resurrection, the death of the old and the springing forth of the new."[84] At the same time, within me, the crosses which I bear for my neighbor help put to death my old self.

> The old man is characterized by wrath, envy, greed, laziness, pride, unbelief, and such obvious sins, which manifestly constitute an encumbrance on vocation and one's neighbor. When the demand of vocation and of neighbor is laid upon the old man, he is made amenable. These sins are repressed and give place to a gentle and patient new man, who receives his life from God's hand. In daily activity baptism is realized as a daily repentance. Thus the Christian is both old and new man, not only in relation to God's judgment, God's forgiveness, but also in his encounter with vocation and neighbor. He is still the old man, insofar as the encounter irritates him, and new man when the encounter takes place with inner calm and joy.[85]

This inner struggle means that Christian love is not an untroubled spontaneity in any psychological sense. The devil retains a hold on us as long as we live; and divine love must make its way through a sinful medium wherein obstacles and resistance are encountered. In every self-sacrificing act we do for the neighbor, the old self asks what it will gain from this sacrifice. It follows that all good appears psychologically to be something commanded. In new creatures the breakthrough of the Law occurs in God-given freedom. Yet from our point of view, it presents itself as straightforward obedience to commandment, because free, creative action must make its way directly against opposition from the body of sin. We are aware that we obey gladly, albeit in the face of resistance.[86]

The implications of this understanding of Christian piety and daily life for Christian witness are clear. First, disciples dare never suggest that what they offer in the new life in Jesus is a bed of roses, an experience of never-ending blessing. They offer instead death, often painful death, to old loves and old gods, and they offer a continuing struggle against evil within themselves and against evils which are afflicting the lives of others.[87] James commended the example of the prophets to his readers. Their patience in suffering provides a model for all those who take comfort and find power in the Lord precisely in the midst of suffering. That is simply the way the Lord could use them most effectively, they found, as do contemporary disciples. In such situations, James urged, there should be no grousing, no grumbling, no grudges. Suffering is never pleasant, but we are confident that God is still Lord even in the evil day, and that His love is sure even in the visitation of His wrath. Therefore, we can find joy and peace, security and a sense of relaxation, in the midst of the trauma and turbulence of the struggle against evils. Christian witness equips new converts to perceive peace and rest in the context of trouble and tribulation.

Believers also help hearers to refine their expectations regarding their hesitation about sufferings, and about their inability to follow the Lord without reservations and regrets at times. Christian faith does not work psychological magic. Believers are often conscious that old fears still arise and that on occasion they shrink back from Jesus' call to serve. The Gospel enables us to bear crosses, not to avoid them. Jesus bestows peace in the midst of troubles, not in such a way that they vanish but rather so that we can cope with them and contain them. Thus, if we fail to be realistic about the stormy course on which Satan leads Jesus' disciples—particularly new disciples—as they leave Satan's grasp, then we will only be setting our hearers up for a fall.

Christians Live, Making Disciples

This life, in which the sanctifying power of the Holy Spirit in Word and Sacrament daily renews and restores faith in the Father, expresses God's love in countless ways, meeting innumerable physical and emotional needs. Above all, the life of the disciple is a life which engages in making others disciples as well. Christian living is so caught up in God's Word, of which it is a product, that it cannot help but spread and share that Word. In the midst of all responsibilities in our situations at home, on the job, in our society, and in the worshiping congregation, the Good News of Jesus of Nazareth bubbles over and out. For

> the Church exists for the sake of the unredeemed who are outside it. This is its raison d'être. If instead it exists only for the sake of its members, it will be in continual conflict with its indwelling Lord. For Christ is the "light of the *world*." The Church is therefore to stand open to all mankind, her light is to be the light of the world, and the salt in her is to be the salt of the earth. The door which stands open to all mankind—to all unredeemed mankind—

251

is baptism, the gateway through which those who are outside enter in and the act by which the Church "multiplies greatly" from Pentecost on and adds new stones to the building.[88]

Thus, disciples are to be engaged in searching for those who are imprisoned by false security systems and to search for ways to bring them to dependence on their Creator in true discipleship, through Baptism and teaching, through repentance and the forgiveness of sins.

Jesus commanded and commissioned us to witness to His love and to forgive sins (Matt. 28:18–20; Luke 24:46–48; John 20:23; Matt. 18:18). We search for the lost sheep of our world primarily because God has found us, and we cannot suppress our delight and joy at this Good News. Telling a child a secret is a contradiction in terms, and the children of God reflect in their lives and words the same enthusiasm for their Father as little children do—except when the deceiver convinces us that for some reason we should fear to speak His name or we do not need to testify to His saving work.

God has bound Himself to us and to our witness in order to complete the task of re-creating people in the image of His Son. There is no other name given among us by which we can be saved (Acts. 4:12). God could make His words appear mysteriously scrawled across a wall or boom them from the heights of Sinai (Dan. 5:5–30; Ex. 19:3–24), but since He has said it all in Christ, His Word comes through our words, for He has called us to convey His message from Scripture into the lives of others.

We speak for Him. We can do so because He is our Father. We do not speak for ourselves as Christian witnesses: we do not need to, for He has already spoken for us in pronouncing us His forgiven children. Believers are always tempted to make an idol of their church and their own activities in the church. It can happen that witnessing believers erect an altar of their own evangelistic activity and evaluate their own worth in God's sight on the basis of how well they witness or, worse yet, how many "converts they make." In so doing we replace our Lord as the center point of our lives with our own talking about Him. Our efforts to testify of Him displace Him as that which gives us security and meaning. Such idolatry merits God's judgment and renders God's call to witness ineffective in many instances. His calling us to Himself, to worship

Him alone and to find in Him alone our identity, security, and meaning is the only basis for His call to us to testify to His saving work.

His call comes to us in many situations in our lives. There are guilt-ridden, anxiety-beset, lonely, shamed, despairing people hiding behind many a closed door. There are people waiting for a knock, waiting for someone to burst in upon them and rob them of their guilt and anxiety and alienation—hoping against hope that someone will come to deliver them. Such people may or may not size up a specific evangelistic caller as the kind of person they can trust with their problems when the caller comes to knock on their door and ask to talk about life, its source, and its goal. For those who need such an intervention from a stranger, however, it is imperative that the church "knock on doors." Formal evangelism programs must be an ongoing part of the witnessing congregation's activities.

Yet many more people are just as much in need of deliverance from lives of death and are already living on the very doorsteps of believers. Indeed, the destructive work of the Law can be done by Christian witnesses who confront broken sinners directly or break fragile sinners in one or more unarranged conversations, without prior preparation of the hearer on the part of the witness's part. The destructive task of breaking the sinner is done more easily when the unbeliever encounters the Christian's explanation of the reality of God's judgment—in whatever form it falls upon him— when that Christian is a friend, neighbor, family member, fellow-worker. When that Christian is a familiar person, he or she will be recognized as trustworthy because a longer period of acquaintance has shown him or her to be someone reliable, worth turning to in times of trouble, perhaps on the basis of a life that appears relaxed and resilient.

In some cases we may have to wait months or even years— and endure some mocking, kidding, or reviling of our faith and way of life in the meantime—for that moment of crisis when God's wrath finally begins to make itself felt in a hurting way, when God's judgment finally begins to become visible, to an acquaintance or friend. This may finally happen at our initiative, through our bold and decisive diagnosis, or it may happen because of circumstances beyond our control.

The wait is worthwhile. Without the crisis of the threat of death to a loved one or to oneself, without the loss of the prestigious job, without the feeling of failure or the sense of shame or the realization of guilt, our smug brother-in-law or our cocky colleague at work may well not be able to catch any glimpse at all of the reality of his ruined life, in spite of all our pointing. But if at that critical juncture in his life, when the first thread frays and what had seemed like a seamless cloak for life begins to unravel, no one will be able to speak of the realities of God's message in as effective a way as can a trusted relative or friend or neighbor. This does not, of course, mean that the Christian will never pull a thread on his own, by pronouncing God's judgment upon the person who perceives no threat to his self-contained existence. In either case it is easier for our friends and neighbors to listen to us when they perceive life beginning to unravel and to grasp from our lives the Word of life.

The situations for the Christian witness to God's wrath arise in the context of our daily callings or responsibilities, in the situations where God has positioned us and given us assignments to perform for our families and communities. The time for the Christian to announce God's judgment on a life lived apart from Him is the very time when God brings us together with a life that is turning sour for our neighbor. Different techniques and different approaches are required, depending on whether our friend's life is broken and he knows it, or whether his life is broken but he does not realize it. The time for witness either arises out of crisis or provokes a crisis which demonstrates the need for liberation and for re-creation. The more skilled Christian witnesses become in intervening in crises with means of support, the more skilled they will be in meeting the needs of friends in such crises, and thus the more powerful will be their presence and their ability to discuss the reality of sin and the promise of God's favor in the midst of a life gone off the mark.

Believers must always be wearing God's mercy on their sleeves, as they live lives which proclaim new life both in deeds which support neighbors in crisis and in words explaining the reality of God's love to those broken by crisis. It happens where Christians are called to minister: front doors in a canvas area; our own homes, where we forgive sins against each other and our God with Christ's Word of peace; our neighborhoods, where we cheer, comfort, and mend lives torn apart by the run-of-the-mill tragedies which bring tears, terror, and trauma to the ordinary folks next door; our places of employment, where guilt can hang heavily or shame can permeate deeply. In every situation of our lives God wants us to be on the lookout, searching for lost and erring sinners.

This search demands sensitivity to all the dimensions of humanity and its brokenness under sin. Those who witness must always analyze how best to approach an individual hearer, in terms of the several dimensions which constitute our approach to identity, security, and meaning: the cognitive, the moral, the emotional, and the communal. All human efforts to forge security and meaning in any of these areas fail;

> ultimately they reveal that there is no way from man to God, neither by reason or morality nor by emotion or community. ... the proclamation of the Gospel in a pluralistic world means ultimately that the men and women engaged in the serious, exhilarating, and inescapable process of world construction and world maintenance must be allowed to experience again and again that in spite of the failures of our cognitive systems, our moral codes, our emotional experience and expressions, and our communal search for identity, God is with men; He has chosen to be with them in the midst of the failures and frustrations of their many reality-defining agencies.[89]

Within any witnessing congregation some disciples will better be able to address cognitive objections to the faith and set forth the Word of promise in detailed explanations; others will better be able to approach those with difficulties in their emotional relationship with themselves, or in their communal relationships with others. All witnessing disciples should work on cultivating sensitivity and skill in dealing with each of these areas, but some will have stronger gifts to deal with certain areas rather than others.

As the witnessing congregation and individual disciples look about them to chart their own territory in which to concentrate their witness, two elements must be kept in tension. The first is the fact that God's commission sends us, His people, to the whole world. Jesus could not rest satisfied with the few who had heard His call and followed. He shrank from the idea of forming an exclusive little coterie with his disciples. Unlike the founders of the great religions, He had no desire to withdraw them from the vulgar crowd and initiate them into an esoteric system of religion and ethics. He had come, he had worked and suffered for the sake of all his people. But the disciples wanted to keep him to themselves, as they showed when the young children were brought to him, and on several occasions when he was accosted by beggars on the roadside (Mark 10:48). The disciples had to learn that Jesus would not be hemmed in by them in his service. His gospel of the kingdom of God and his power of healing belonged to the sick and poor, wherever they were to be found among the people. God's beloved people had been ill-treated and laid low and the guilt belonged to those who had failed to minister to them in the service of God.[90]

In tension with this universal command to make disciples stands a second factor, the specific gifts and the limited resources which we as individuals and as local congregations have at our command. We cannot bring the Gospel to the entire world, and much pious talk about the world can actually divert us from the specific individuals or groups whom God has placed at our doorsteps. We may be tempted at the same time to shape our view of the mission which God puts before us according to the standards of this world, not according to God's standards. We may persuade ourselves that we minister best to people of our own socio-economic situation or racial or ethnic background. The social sciences would support that judgment, and we are tempted to take their descriptive observations of human interaction as prescriptive. We thereby deny the power of the Gospel to cut through human prejudice, and we vitiate that power because we cater to our own social instincts. Already in the early church this problem had to be addressed (James 2:1–7).

Certainly disciples will recognize that they are by natural talent and personal disposition better equipped and situated to approach some unbelievers rather than others. But if a congregation makes its natural collective predisposition into an exclusive program and so tailors its evangelism outreach to avoid those who do not fit into "Our Savior's congregation," they are shutting up the power of God which the Holy Spirit has poured into them. That can only end in explosion, for the Spirit's power wants to get out in the whole world, as it lies within our reach. The judgment of God hangs over those Christians who have preferred to "save our kind" rather than the Savior's kind, the poor, the imprisoned, the lonely, those not able to contribute most to the congregation of God's people but whose lives He nonetheless regards as precious.

The Christian witness also lives with another tension, that which arises in the difficulty of gauging approaches and strategies for witnessing in specific situations. The great variety of unbelief in our culture contributes to this tension (as does the difficulty in distinguishing secure from broken sinners) in sorting out correctly the times to speak God's message of wrath and the times to speak His message of mercy. Disciples need to step back to observe themselves and determine what kind of profile they are projecting as they testify to the world about them. Is our model that of God's knights or posse, charging into people's lives, brandishing the sword or pistol of the Law? Or is it that of someone reaching over a cliff to lift a stray, seared sheep from the thornbush into which it tumbled because it went its own way? We must be careful that our models for personal witness are determined by the Lord, not by our own cultural values and patterns. We must be conscious of the way we project ourselves and of the way in which we make basic decisions regarding specific approaches with the Word to individuals.

As we approach those outside the faith with the condemning message of God's wrath and the vivifying message of God's mercy in Jesus of Nazareth, we need to marshal the Word and our insights into the personalities and personal spiritual needs of those whom we are addressing. The disciple never moves beyond the tension between speaking the Word purely and effectively and rephrasing it so that it can be understood in our culture. Nor do we move beyond the tension involved in determining when the secure sinner has been broken and when that sinner remains not just slow to learn but actually resistant to God's Law.

> This is the biggest problem of the ministry: how can it proclaim the Gospel about Christ crucified and risen without diminishing it, but how at the same time can it deal patiently with the varying reception which it receives and with its slow growth among men?

None should be excluded from the Christian community who has even the slightest grasp of the Gospel, but correspondingly those who have no more than a passing acquaintance with the Gospel have no right to affect or alter the greater part of the whole, for this greater part, the whole Gospel, belongs to the Church and not to the individuals within it.[91]

We do not resolve this tension, but we are able to live with it gladly when we keep our eye on Jesus rather than on our own performance of the witnessing task, when we proceed with confidence that His power in His Word, not our "getting it right," makes disciples. We dare never be indifferent to conveying the Word correctly and properly; we dare never depend on our conveying of the Word in that manner either to justify ourselves or to convert our hearers, both of which are tasks which the Holy Spirit performs. We dare never use Him as a license to be sloppy in preparation or proclamation, yet God's love and favor, as well as our confidence in the Word's power, relax us so that we can throw off the immobilizing tension of such problems and thus witness joyfully, to—and in—our heart's content.

This is possible because we are confident that He is always with us.

CONCLUSION

Peace to Those Whom He Sends

UNTIL THE CLOSE OF THE AGE

The disciples received a commission which had a promised termination. Time as we experience it will end. Biblical Christians reject the ancient idea that time rolls around a giant circle and brings good or bad fortune with it as it rolls. They also reject the contemporary evolutionary view which discounts beginnings and endings. The biblical writers trace the history of God's creation from its origin in His Word through His decisive intervention in the Word made flesh into the story of the church, commissioned as it is to spread the Gospel and to gather disciples into itself.[1]

Believers in our day are conscious, as believers in almost every age of the church have been, that the signs of the end promised by the Lord are appearing in our day (Matt. 24:3–14). Those who trust in Jesus as their Lord and Savior realize that whether or not the end comes quickly, they still stand in God's favor. They do not abandon the responsibilities of their situations but would plant trees and harvest grain even if they did have advance warning that tomorrow would be the Day of the Lord. They do not hope for some earthly utopia, in which they can enjoy seeing God wreaking vengeance upon their enemies, for they love their enemies. They do not desire a reward of this-worldly pleasure but only the peace of their restored relationship with their Creator. Nor do they desire to have advance information regarding the last day, which Jesus Himself could not claim.

The last day has *already* decisively occurred in their lives, in the judgment worked upon their sinfulness in Baptism and daily repentance. The day of the Lord's liberation has already made its mark on believers as they were incorporated into the body of His resurrection and its righteousness. The future culmination of God's restoration of His people to their true humanity has not yet taken place for those who remain on earth; nevertheless, the action of God in pronouncing them His and re-creating them in His Son's image has already decisively turned them from evil and death to the Author of life. They have already realized the promised benefits of the reconciliation of His sons and daughters to Himself.

RECEIVE THE HOLY SPIRIT AND FORGIVE SINS

Jesus' assurance of His presence with His disciples in Matthew 28:20 has frequently been applied to all areas of Christian living, and He certainly is present with us in whatever we do. His assurance of this continuing presence was given in the context of the Great Commission (Matt. 28:20). Disciples can take special comfort from the Lord's promises that He will be with them as they go forth to make disciples among those who do not depend on Him nor have lives determined by His re-creative and forgiving Word. As Jesus met His disciples a few weeks earlier, on the evening of His resurrection day, He had pronounced peace upon them as He sent them forth in the world to speak His word of judgment and His word of forgiveness under the power of the Holy Spirit (John 20:19–23). Christian witnesses rely on His presence and His peace as they articulate and demonstrate His love in the midst of the world.

He is also present with those Christians who are reluctant to witness. To those who dodge the opportunities to exercise the responsibilities for witnessing which He offers, He gives the gift of forgiveness, which brings the peace to enable us to relax and leave behind our tensions over testifying of His love. Many of those tensions result from our fears of not saying the right thing, not being able to provide all the right answers, not stating the Gospel as clearly as we might.

We excuse ourselves from speaking for God, as He has designed and commissioned us to do, with a variety of reasons which seem plausible. In essence this only reveals that we do not feel fully secure in our identities as God's children. We tell ourselves we do not want to represent God poorly in front of those who do not know Him, for we would thus embarrass Him and alienate our potential hearers. As a matter of fact, that betrays more of a lack of confidence in ourselves, not only in how we might appear before the unbelievers but also in our appearance before God. It may be true that speaking the Word poorly is worse than not speaking at all in some instances, but we must also remember that Paul relied on the Word's power rather than on his own rhetorical skill (1 Cor. 2:1–5). From a purely psychological standpoint, we witness effectively from our vulnerability. Those who seek information or philosophical expertise are looking for someone who seems to know all the answers. Those whose lives are tattered and torn are attracted to us, not because we are holier or smarter than they, but because we share the vulnerability of the lost and fallen in a world of sin. It is precisely in our vulnerability that we make the most effective witness to many in today's world.

Some questions which will arise in the course of our Christian conversation will be embarrassing, both for us and, from a human standpoint, for God, for they will relate to the origin and existence of evil. Those urgent questions cannot be answered in a logically satisfying way, and the witnessing believer must be prepared to meet those questions in all honesty regarding our lack of final answers. To that honesty we join a demonstration of care and love which puts the origin of specific evils behind our hearers to the greatest extent possible as we aid them in coping with the present and facing the future in and through that peace which comes as we pronounce Jesus' forgiveness.

There are other questions which I may not be able to answer when an unbeliever confronts me with them, but which are indeed answerable in one way or another. Because Christian witness takes place within the context of the witnessing congregation, I can face the possibility of such questions because I know others from my congregation will be able to pick up on my contacts and continue to testify of Jesus' love when my own gifts fail to serve in some specific instances.

Some questions will be posed which I am able to answer on one level or another, the cognitive or moral, for example, but which do not seem to satisfy even though they make sense on that level. In such instances the witnessing disciple must be sensitive to the emotional and communal hurts of the hearer, which may be crying out for healing so loudly that the correct and proper cognitive or moral answers cannot be heard. Often such approaches will also require that the individual witness bring others into the situation for a more formidable assault on the evils which are imprisoning the hearer.

In many cases the excuse that the Christian puts forth, "I just do not know enough to be an effective witness," may be correct. It is a problem that is quite easily solved, however. Every witnessing congregation provides opportunities and resources for study of the Word and growth in it. Every believer has access to means by which he may better assess the world around him and communicate more sensitively with its people. No witnessing believer will ever have all the answers. Often we think that the people to whom we witness will be able to offer more formidable objections to our testimony than they can, or that they will demand an uncommon degree of knowledge. Nonetheless, confidence for Christian witness grows not only out of trust that God the Holy Spirit's presence sustains and guides us to do well (and forgives us when we fail). It grows also out of knowing that both our command of God's Word and our ability to demonstrate His love are sufficiently strong, so that most hearers will not overwhelm us with their problems or their objections to our message. The study of the Scriptures and the church's continuing reassessment of how best to apply the biblical message in the contemporary setting is vital for effective communication of God's message and for the confidence to be engaged in that task.

The message consists of two fundamental parts, the Word of condemnation which must be addressed to secure sinners, and the Word of forgiveness and re-creation, which must be addressed to broken sinners. God's presence in our world continues to be revealed in His wrath and His mercy. Our testimony regarding God's attitude toward His human creatures under the impact and influence of doubt and defiance must begin by analyzing whether those with whom we speak are secure or broken. We must further analyze what sort of security system they are clinging to or stuck in, and how we may best hone God's Law to be that particularly sharp arrow which will pierce their hearts. The use of God's message of wrath against human defiance as a club with which to beat sinners will first make them angry and alienated. It is the long and hard way to bring them to death with their false systems of security and meaning.

Likewise, if we are to bring the healing power of the Gospel to cure the broken sinner, we must be able to pick that strain of the vaccine of Jesus which meets the particular form of the sin-sickness plaguing this sinner. We must be able to put the vaccine of our Lord's death and resurrection into the vein, not just under the skin. As the people to whom we witness reveal the agendas of their lives and pose the questions which bedevil them, we must be prepared to ask, "Why do you want to know?" and be prepared to meet their agendas and respond to their questions, rather than to questions and agendas with which we feel comfortable or for which we have prepared answers.

Such witnessing agility is possible for us when we are able to relax with our God, because we know He stands by us no matter what, and with ourselves, because we know that we can call on a formidable arsenal of approaches at our own command and a variety of backup within our congregation.

Carrying both God's message of wrath and God's message of mercy also requires that we be able to live with the seeming embarrassment of reversing ourselves as the sinner before us changes from secure to broken or from broken to secure. If our stern word of condemnation or our pointed observation regarding the inadequacy of an old, false security system breaks the secure sinner, we must lay aside God's Law and speak the Gospel: that nothing can pluck the repentant sinner from the hands of God (Rom. 8:38–39). But if this sinner quickly resolves that the Gospel provides a license for sin, we must return to the message of God's wrath without hesitation and without any reason for embarrassment. As a matter of fact, we have no reason to be embarrassed. We have not changed the message which we have for a specific kind of human sinner. It is the human creature before us who has changed.

Witnessing disciples may grow weary, discouraged, and disgusted if it seems that our hearers are playing us and God for suckers as they repent and then slip back into old, sinful habits and attitudes. Our Lord does not, of course, give us any prescription for the 491st time that sinner returns appearing to be broken, but He does command that the first 490 times we again reassure him or her of forgiveness (Matt. 18:21–22). That the 490th application of the Gospel will employ a more effective means of harnessing the power of Jesus' death and resurrection for this sinner's life than did the first, we can only hope. But it must still be the unadulterated and unconditional Gospel of the mercy and love of the God who died and who began breathing again on the third day.

Finally, Christian witness seems difficult because it continually involves such judgments, our own estimates, of whether the sinner is secure or broken and of how the Word of God can best be applied. We need to be so conscientious that we never stop trying to sharpen our skills and our knowledge of both the society in which our hearers have been shaped and the Word of Christ in the Scriptures.

We also need to live in the Gospel with confidence in God's love, forgiveness, and acceptance when our judgment is wrong. The Holy Spirit will take our frail estimations and our frail words and do His work not because of us but even, when He must, in spite of us. Christian witness is really possible only for those who do believe the Gospel and trust the re-creative power and love of God in Jesus Christ.

Notes

Introduction

1. George W. Forell, *The Proclamation of the Gospel in a Pluralistic World* (Philadelphia: Fortress, 1973), 6.
2. J. M. Stephens, *The Process of Schooling: A Psychological Examination* (New York: Holt, Rinehart, and Winston, 1967), 35.
3. See pp. 64–69.
4. Helmut Thielicke, *The Evangelical Faith*, trans. Geoffrey W. Bromiley (Grand Rapids: Eerdmans, 1974, 1977), I, 27.
5. This twofold aspect of doctrine or teaching—content and application—was stressed by the 16th-century reformers. See Peter Fraenkel, "Revelation and Tradition: Notes on Some Aspects of Doctrinal Continuity in the Theology of Philip Melanchthon," *Studia Theologica,* XIII (1959): 97–133. Cf. the strong statement of this point in C. F. W. Walther, *Law and Gospel,* trans. Herbert J. A. Bouman (St. Louis: Concordia, 1981), 13.
6. C. S. Lewis, *Reflections on the Psalms* (New York: Harcourt Brace Jovanovich, 1958), 1.

Chapter 1

1. Werner Foerster, *"Exestin, exousia,"* *Theological Dictionary of the New Testament,* ed. Gerhard Kittel, trans. Geoffrey W. Bromiley (Grand Rapids: Eerdmans, 1964–72), II, 566.
2. Ibid., 566–67.
3. See Chapter 3.
4. This is the definition of Martin Luther in his Large Catechism, *The Book of Concord,* ed. Theodore G. Tappert (Philadelphia: Fortress, 1959), 365–68. See also Gustaf Wingren, *Creation and Law,* trans. Ross Mackenzie (Edinburgh: Oliver and Boyd, 1961), 51. Originally published by LiberFörlag CWK Gleerup in Lund.
5. Arthur Miller, *Death of a Salesman* (New York: Viking, 1949).
6. Alvin Toffler, *Future Shock* (New York: Bantam, 1970), 285.
7. Helmut Thielicke, *The Evangelical Faith*, trans. Geoffrey W. Bromiley (Grand Rapids: Eerdmans, 1974, 1977), I, 325–26.
8. Carl Gustave Jung in "Psychotherapists or the Clergy," *Psychology and Religion: West and East, Collected Works* (New York: Pantheon, 1958), II, 334, as quoted in Hans Küng, *Does God Exist?* trans. Edward Quinn (New

York: Doubleday, 1980), 317.

9. See the discussion of the personhood of God in Francis A. Schaeffer, *He Is There and He Is Not Silent* (Wheaton: Tyndale, 1972), 1–20. Cf. Karl Heim's discussion of the search for "natural animation" in the organic world, *Christian Faith and Natural Science* (New York: Harper and Row, 1953), 91–95, and his chapter on "Belief in the Personal Nature of God," 2–18. *Christian Faith and Natural Science* originally published by SCM Press Ltd., London.

10. Thielicke, *Evangelical Faith*, I, 107–11.

11. Dietrich Bonhoeffer, *Creation and Fall: A Theological Interpretation of Genesis 1–3, Temptation* (New York: Macmillan, 1959), 13.

12. C. S. Lewis, *Reflections on the Psalms* (New York: Harcourt Brace Jovanovich, 1958), 78.

13. Bonhoeffer chose Charles Darwin (1809–82) and Ludwig Feuerbach (1804–72) as arch-examples of the materialism of the 19th century.

14. Bonhoeffer, *Creation and Fall*, 46.

15. Gustaf Wingren, *Credo: The Christian View of Faith and Life*, trans. Edgar M. Carlson (Minneapolis: Augsburg, 1981), 51.

16. See J. N. D. Kelly, *Early Christian Doctrines* (New York: Harper and Row, 1960), esp. 22–28; Oscar Cullmann, *Christ and Time: The Primitive Christian Conception of Time and History*, trans. Floyd V. Filson (London: SCM, 1962), 51–61; and Cullmann, *Salvation in History* (New York: Harper and Row, 1967), 24–28.

17. Lewis, *Psalms*, 78.

18. Thielicke, *Evangelical Faith*, II, 96.

19. Robert Frost, "Death of a Hired Man," *Complete Poems of Robert Frost* (New York: Holt, Rinehart, and Winston, 1958), 58.

20. Martin Luther's explanation to the First Commandment in his Small Catechism, *Book of Concord*, 342.

21. Lewis, *Psalms*, 80ff.

22. Wingren, *Credo*, 51. See also Helmut Thielicke, *How the World Began: Man in the First Chapters of the Bible*, trans. John W. Doberstein (Philadelphia: Muhlenberg, 1961), 110–11.

23. Wingren, *Credo*, 124.

24. Heim, *Christian Faith and Natural Science*, 77.

25. Ibid., 52.

26. Gustaf Wingren, *Luther on Vocation*, trans. Carl C. Rasmussen (Philadelphia: Muhlenberg, 1957), 137–43, 185–87.

27. Ibid.

28. Small Catechism, explanation to the First Article of the Apostles' Creed, *Book of Concord*, 345.

29. Merton P. Strommen, *Five Cries of Youth* (New York: Harper and Row, 1979), 24, citing the study of Peter Benson and Bernhard Spilka as well as his own work.

30. Arend Th. van Leeuwen, *Christianity in World History: The Meeting of the Faiths of East and West*, trans. H. H. Hoskins (New York: Scribners, 1964), 135. Van

Leeuwen offers an extensive analysis of the relationship of biblical and Greek thought patterns.

31. The synergism of much of modern American theology will be discussed in Chapter 4.

32. Toffler, *Future Shock,* 319. See the extensive and provocative analysis of modern American society produced by Christopher Lasch, *The Culture of Narcissism* (New York: Warner, 1979). Although the popularity of the term has faded, perhaps because Lasch's analysis of us is too awful to hold in focus, the fact of its grip on North American society remains.

33. B. F. Skinner, *Beyond Freedom and Dignity* (New York: Knopf, 1971).

34. Bonhoeffer, *Creation and Fall,* 13, 15.

35. Schaeffer, *He Is There and He Is Not Silent,* 2.

36. Karl Menninger, *Whatever Became of Sin?* (New York: Hawthorn, 1973), 178.

37. Christopher Lasch argues that "the contemporary climate is therapeutic, not religious. People today hunger not for personal salvation … but for the feeling, the momentary illusion, of personal well-being, health, and psychic security." See *Narcissism,* 33.

38. Ernest Becker, *The Denial of Death* (New York: The Free Press, 1973), 89.

39. Toffler, *Future Shock,* 321.

40. Bonhoeffer, *Creation and Fall,* 38.

41. Thielicke, *Evangelical Faith,* I, 91. C. S. Lewis' argument for a freedom of the will which possesses a kind of independent stance between good and evil is inadequate. See *Mere Christianity* (London: Collins, 1952), 48–53.

42. Thielicke, *Evangelical Faith,* I, 339.

43. Küng, *Does God Exist?* 124.

44. See Chapter 2.

45. *Newsweek,* 14 December 1981, 94.

46. Thielicke, *Evangelical Faith,* II, 6.

47. Rudolf Otto, *The Idea of the Holy,* trans. John W. Harvey (London: Oxford University Press, 1923).

48. Cited by Küng, *Does God Exist?* 94.

49. Cullmann, *Salvation in History,* 25–26; *Primitive Christian Conception of Time and History,* 52.

50. Schaeffer, *He Is There and He Is Not Silent,* 78.

51. Ibid., 64.

52. Gerhard O. Forde, *Theology Is for Proclamation* (Minneapolis: Fortress, 1990), 147–90.

53. George W. Forell, "Eucharistic presence as the key to theological understanding," *Festschrift für Franz Lau zum 60. Geburtstag* (Göttingen: Vandenhoeck und Ruprecht, 1967), 95–97.

54. See Thielicke, *Evangelical Faith,* II, 55–56.

55. Ibid., I, 194–95; II, 34–35.

56. Aarne Siirila, *Divine Humanness,* trans. T. A. Kantonen (Philadelphia: Fortress, 1970), 99.

57. C. F. W. Walther, *Law and Gospel,* trans. Herbert J. A. Bouman (St. Louis: Concordia, 1981), 15–17.

58. Thielicke, *Evangelical Faith,* II, 188.

59. Ibid., II, 192–98; and Walther, *Law and Gospel,* pp. 55–59.

60. Ludwig Feuerbach, *Das Wesen des Christentums* (1841), *The Essence of Christianity* (New York: Harper, 1957), 13–14, 22–43, 108.

61. See especially Walther von Loewenich, *Luther's Theology of the Cross,* trans. Herbert J. A. Bouman (Minneapolis: Augsburg, 1976), 22–24, 27–50.

62. See Walter R. Bouman, "Piety in a Secularized Society," in *Confession and Congregation: Resources for Parish Life and Work,* ed. David G. Truemper (Valparaiso: Valparaiso University Press, 1978), 65–67.

63. Heim, *Christian Faith and Natural Science,* 126–39; Schaeffer, *He Is There and He Is Not Silent,* 37–88. Cf. Arthur F. Holmes, *Faith Seeks Understanding* (Grand Rapids: Eerdmans, 1971).

64. Gustaf Wingren, *Gospel and Church,* trans. Ross Mackenzie (Philadelphia: Fortress, 1964), 82.

65. Thielicke, *Evangelical Faith,* II, 309.

Chapter 2

1. Karl Menninger, *Whatever Became of Sin* (New York: Hawthorn, 1973), 5.

2. Ibid., 13.

3. Ibid., 17.

4. Douglas John Hall, *Lighten Our Darkness: Toward an Indigenous Theology of the Cross* (Philadelphia: Westminster, 1976), 98–100.

5. Christopher Lasch, *The Culture of Narcissism* (New York: Warner, 1979), 21, 69–70.

6. Gustaf Wingren, *Credo: The Christian View of Faith and Life,* trans. Edgar M. Carlson (Minneapolis: Augsburg, 1981), 44.

7. John E. Keller, "The Realities of Original Sin in Clinical Pastoral Counseling," Third Concordia Academy, Wartburg Theological Seminary, Dubuque, Iowa, Aug. 12, 1975.

8. Helmut Thielicke, *How the World Began: Man in the First Chapters of the Bible,* trans. John W. Doberstein (Philadelphia: Muhlenberg, 1961), 145.

9. Wilhelm Dantine, *Justification of the Ungodly,* trans. Eric W. and Ruth C. Gritsch (St. Louis: Concordia, 1968), 68–69.

10. Kenneth F. Korby, "Naming and Healing the Disorders of Man," in *Confession and Congregation: Resources for Parish Life and Work,* ed. David G. Truemper (Valparaiso: Valparaiso University Press, 1978), 8.

11. Dietrich Bonhoeffer, *Creation and Fall: A Theological Interpretation of Genesis 1–3, Temptation* (New York: Macmillan, 1959), 104–05.

12. Ibid., 66.

13. Aarne Siirala, *Divine Humanness,* trans. T. A. Kantonen (Philadelphia: Fortress, 1970), 31.

14. Menninger, *Whatever Became of Sin,* 19.

15. John Milton, *Paradise Lost* (1667; New York: Norton, 1975); see, for example, I.36, 7; XII.25, 264.

16. Gustaf Wingren, *Creation and Law,* trans. Ross Mackenzie (Edinburgh: Oliver and Boyd, 1961), 50. Originally published by LiberFörlag CWK Gleerup in Lund.

17. Bonhoeffer, *Creation and Fall,* 82.

18. Wingren, *Creation and Law,* 51.

19. Menninger, *Whatever Became of Sin?* 88.

20. Wingren, *Creation and Law,* 150–51.

21. Hannah Arendt, *Eichmann in Jerusalem: A Report on the Banality of Evil* (New York: Viking, 1964), 231.

22. Ernest Becker, *The Denial of Death* (New York: The Free Press, 1973), 51–52, citing Maslow's judgment that this insight was Freud's "greatest discovery."

23. Lasch, *Culture of Narcissism,* 179.

24. Walter R. Bouman, "Piety in a Secularized Society," in *Confession and Congregation,* 70; cf. Becker, *Denial of Death,* 47–66.

25. Becker, *Denial of Death,* 196.

26. Bonhoeffer, *Creation and Fall,* 70–71.

27. Wingren, *Creation and Law,* 115.

28. Gustaf Wingren, *Man and the Incarnation: A Study in the Biblical Theology of Irenaeus,* trans. Ross Mackenzie (Philadelphia: Muhlenberg, 1959), 57–58.

29. Bonhoeffer, *Creation and Fall,* 75–76.

30. Ibid.

31. Korby, "Disorders of Man," 8.

32. Ibid., 9.

33. Wingren, *Credo,* 75.

34. Helmut Thielicke, *The Evangelical Faith,* trans. Geoffrey W. Bromiley (Grand Rapids: Eerdmans, 1974, 1977), II, 9–10.

35. Bonhoeffer, *Creation and Fall,* 78.

36. To use Melanchthon's phrase in the Apology of the Augsburg Confession, *The Book of Concord,* ed. Theodore G. Tappert (Philadelphia: Fortress, 1959), 112–13.

37. Thielicke, *Evangelical Faith,* II, 200–01.

38. Alan Paton, *Too Late the Phalarope* (New York: Signet, 1953), 5.

39. Francis Schaeffer, *He Is There and He Is Not Silent* (Wheaton: Tyndale, 1972), 32.

40. Gerhard O. Forde, *Where God Meets Man: Luther's Down-to-Earth Approach to the Gospel* (Minneapolis: Augsburg, 1972), 31.

41. J. N. D. Kelly, *Early Christian Doctrines* (New York: Harper and Row, 1960), 8–9. C. S. Lewis offers a biblically inadequate view of the created freedom of the will which places the human creature in a neutral position between God and Satan, able to choose between them. See *Mere Christianity* (London: Collins, 1952), 48–53.

42. Hall, *Lighten Our Darkness,* 104.

43. Ibid., 111.

44. Augsburg Confession, Art. XIX, *Book of Concord*, 40–41.

45. Schaeffer, *He Is There and He Is Not Silent*, 27–28.

46. Archibald MacLeish, *J.B.* (Boston: Houghton, Mifflin, 1958), 15.

47. Werner Elert, *Der Christliche Glaube*, 5th ed. (Hamburg: Furche, 1956), 285.

48. Ibid., 286.

49. I am indebted to Dr. Robert C. Schultz for the initial provocation resulting in the discussion that follows, even though I may have taken this material in directions he did not intend in his paper, "Loss and Rediscovery of the Confessional Doctrine of Original Sin: Orthodoxy, Enlightenment, Pietism, and the Confessional Reawakening," Third Concordia Academy, Wartburg Theological Seminary, Dubuque, Iowa, Aug. 12, 1975.

50. Hall, *Lighten Our Darkness*, 23–24.

51. Becker, *Denial of Death*, 84–85; cf. Lasch, *Culture of Narcissism*, 138.

52. Alvin Toffler, *Future Shock* (New York: Bantam, 1970), 95–96.

53. Lasch, *Culture of Narcissism*, 64–65.

54. Merton P. Strommen, *Five Cries of Youth* (New York: Harper and Row, 1979), 42–43.

55. Hans Küng, *Does God Exist?* trans. Edward Quinn (New York: Doubleday, 1980), 322.

56. Karl Heim analyzes this modern secularity in *Christian Faith and Natural Science* (New York: Harper and Row, 1953), see esp. 16–17.

57. George Forell, *The Proclamation of the Gospel in a Pluralistic World* (Philadelphia: Fortress, 1973), 44–45.

58. Wingren, *Credo*, 74.

59. See Lasch's chapter, "Changing Modes of Making It: From Horatio Alger to the Happy Hooker," *Culture of Narcissism*, 106–33.

60. Strommen, *Five Cries of Youth*, 16–19.

61. Ibid., 23–24.

62. Robert C. Schultz, "Therapy and Absolution: Issues of Healing and Redemption," *Confession and Congregation*, 42.

63. Ibid.

64. Menninger, *Whatever Became of Sin?* 114, a quotation from an unnamed professor at the University of Wisconsin.

65. C. F. W. Walther, *Law and Gospel*, trans. Herbert J. A. Bouman (St. Louis: Concordia, 1981), 164.

66. C. S. Lewis, *Reflection on the Psalms* (New York: Harcourt Brace Jovanovich, 1958), 24.

67. Wingren, *Credo*, 66–71.

68. Korby, "Disorders of Man," 10.

69. Bouman, "Piety in a Secularized Society," 71.

70. Lasch, *Culture of Narcissism*, 87, shows the particular terror which aging has for the narcissist. Cf. Wingren, *Creation and Law*, 75.: "Death does not come upon

me instantaneously and suddenly, on a certain date, but draws near to me in everything which diminishes my vitality."

71. Becker, *Denial of Death,* ix.

72. Dylan Thomas, "Do Not Go Gentle into That Good Night," *The Poems of Dylan Thomas* (New York: New Directions, 1971), 207–8.

Chapter 3

1. See J. N. D. Kelly, *Early Christian Creeds* (New York: McKay, 1960); and *The Athanasian Creed* (New York: Harper and Row, 1964).

2. Dietrich Bonhoeffer, *Christ the Center,* trans. John Bowden (New York: Harper and Row, 1960), 85–88, 102–04; Kelly, *Early Christian Doctrines* (New York: Harper and Row, 1960), 139–40, 115–19, 158–60, 223–51, 119–23; Kelly, *Early Christian Creeds,* 231–62; Kelly, *Athanasian Creed,* 70–90. Against adoptionistic misinterpretation of certain New Testament texts, see Edmund Schlink, *The Doctrine of Baptism,* trans. Herbert J. A. Bouman (St. Louis: Concordia, 1972), 22.

3. Bonhoeffer, *Christ the Center,* 78–85; Kelly, *Early Christian Doctrines,* 141–47, 197–98, 289–95; Kelly, *Early Christian Creeds,* 332–37; Kelly, *Athanasian Creed,* 70–90.

4. Bonhoeffer, *Christ the Center,* 88–92; Kelly, *Early Christian Doctrines,* 310–30; Kelly, *Early Christian Creeds,* 323, 329; Kelly, *Athanasian Creed,* 94–98.

5. Bonhoeffer, *Christ the Center,* 88–92; Kelly, *Early Christian Doctrines,* 330–43; Kelly, *Early Christian Creeds,* 308–09, 333–36, 348–50; Kelly, *Athanasian Creed,* 103–08.

6. I use the translation "sharing of characteristics" instead of the usual "communication of attributes" for the dogmatic term *communicatio idiomatum.*

7. John Calvin, *Institutes of the Christian Religion,* ed. John T. McNeill, trans. Ford Lewis Battles, in Library of Christian Classics XX (Philadelphia: Westminster, 1960), I, 494–503.

8. Oscar Cullmann, *The Christology of the New Testament,* trans. Shirley C. Guthrie and Charles A. M. Hall (Philadelphia: Westminster, 1963), vii–ix.

9. See, for example, Marshall McLuhan, *Understanding Media: The Extensions of Man* (New York: McGraw Hill, 1964), essay 1, "The Medium is the Message."

10. Martin Luther also stressed this distinction of Jesus' work; see Marc Lienhard, *Martin Luther's Christologisches Zeugnis,* trans. Robert Wolff (Göttingen: Vandenhoeck und Ruprecht, 1980), 64; Ian D. Kingston Siggins, *Martin Luther's Doctrine of Christ* (New Haven: Yale University Press, 1970), 156–64.

11. Oscar Cullmann, *Salvation in History* (New York: Harper and Row, 1967), 110–11.

12. William Barclay, *Jesus As They Saw Him: New Testament Interpretations of Jesus* (New York: Harper and Row, 1962), 20–37, discusses these and other passages, including some with difficulties in establishing the original text. Cf. Cullmann, *Christology of the New Testament,* 306–14. *Jesus As They Saw Him* originally published by SCM Press, Ltd., London.

13. Barclay, *Jesus As They Saw Him,* 408–20. Werner Foerster and Gottfried Quell, "Kyrios," *Theological Dictionary of the New Testament,* ed. Gerhard Kittel, trans.

Geoffrey W. Bromiley (Grand Rapids: Eerdmans, 1964–72), III, 1041–46, 1058–81.

14. Cullmann, *Christology of the New Testament,* 234. He notes, for example, the use of Is. 45:23 in Phil. 2:10–11 and of Ps. 102:25ff. in Heb. 1:10ff.

15. Ibid., 195–99; Foerster and Quell, *"Kyrios,"* TDNT III, 1047–58.

16. Walter Künneth, *The Theology of the Resurrection,* trans. James W. Leitch (St. Louis: Concordia, 1965), 131.

17. Rudolf Kittel, *"Eikon,"* TDNT II, 395–96; Barclay, *Jesus As They Saw Him,* 388–94.

18. Vincent Taylor, *The Names of Jesus* (London: Macmillan, 1962), 129–30; Barclay, *Jesus As They Saw Him,* 316–19.

19. Cullmann, *Salvation in History,* 279.

20. Barclay, *Jesus As They Saw Him,* 319–20.

21. H. Kleinknecht, O. Proksch, R. Kittel, *"Logos,"* TDNT IV, 77–91, 91–100, 124–36; Barclay, *Jesus As They Saw Him,* 421–29; Cullmann, *Christology of the New Testament,* 249–69. Cf. Oskar Skarsaune, *Incarnation: Myth or Fact?* trans. Trygve R. Skarsten (Saint Louis: Concordia, 1991).

22. Werner Elert, *Der Christliche Glaube,* 5th ed. (Hamburg: Furche, 1956), 119.

23. Gustaf Wingren, *Man and the Incarnation: A Study in the Biblical Theology of Irenaeus,* trans. Ross Mackenzie (Philadelphia: Muhlenberg, 1959), 96–98.

24. Elert, *Christliche Glaube,* 316–17.

25. Siggins, *Luther's Doctrine of Christ,* 54–55.

26. Gerhard Friedrich, *"Prophetes,"* TDNT VI, 841–48; Cullmann, *Christology of the New Testament,* 13–50; Barclay, *Jesus As They Saw Him,* 229–39.

27. Siggins, *Luther's Doctrine of Christ,* 86.

28. Barclay, *Jesus As They Saw Him,* 163–68; Taylor, *Names of Jesus,* 131–33.

29. Barclay, *Jesus As They Saw Him,* 404–07.

30. Gustaf Wingren, *Gospel and Church,* trans. Ross Mackenzie (Philadelphia: Fortress, 1964), 47–51.

31. Ibid., 51. Cf. F. F. Bruce, *The New Testament Documents: Are They Reliable?* (Downers Grove, Ill.: InterVarsity, 1960).

32. Cullmann, *Christology of the New Testament,* 55. Cullmann notes that in the intertestamental period some Jewish literature indirectly identified the Servant with the Messiah by ascribing to the Messiah the epithets of the Servant. See Cullmann's treatment of the entire Servant motif, 51–82; and Barclay, *Jesus As They Saw Him,* 160–86.

33. Cf. 1 Cor. 15:3–5; 11:23; Rom. 8:32–34; Gal. 1:4; 2:20; Eph. 5:2; 1 Tim. 1:6; Titus 2:14, which may also employ the "handing over" image of the Septuagint translation of Is. 53:12. The Septuagint uses the same word for sin and sin-offering, and it is also possible that 2 Cor. 5:21 and Rom. 8:3 reflect Is. 53:10, in which the Servant makes Himself a sin offering. Phil. 2:6–11 also reflects Isaiah's description of the Suffering Servant.

34. Charles Dickens, *A Tale of Two Cities* (1859).

35. Markus Barth, *Was Christ's Death a Sacrifice?* (Edinburgh: Oliver and Boyd, 1961), esp. 10–27.

Notes

36. Siggins, *Luther's Doctrine of Christ,* 119–20.

37. Cullmann, *Christology of the New Testament,* pp. 83–107; Barclay, *Jesus As They Saw Him,* 346–57.

38. Barclay, *Jesus As They Saw Him,* 301–15.

39. Helmut Thielicke, *The Evangelical Faith,* trans. Geoffrey W. Bromiley (Grand Rapids: Eerdmans, 1974, 1977), II, 406. Cf. Wilhelm Dantine, *Justification of the Ungodly,* trans. Eric W. and Ruth C. Gritsch (St. Louis: Concordia, 1968), 86–88.

40. Barclay, *Jesus As They Saw Him,* 338.

41. Ibid., 334–38.

42. Wingren, *Gospel and Church,* 58.

43. Walter R. Bouman, "Piety in a Secularized Society," *Confession and Congregation: Resources for Parish Life and Work,* ed. David G. Truemper (Valparaiso: Valparaiso University Press, 1978), 73. Ralph W. Quere provides helpful charts for understanding and organizing biblical materials which facilitate one's witnessing to Jesus' rule as vicar and victim in *Evangelical Witness: The Message, Medium, Mission and Method of Evangelism* (Minneapolis: Augsburg, 1975), 57–65, 152–55.

44. Cullmann, *Christology of the New Testament,* 109–36.; Barclay, *Jesus As They Saw Him,* 93–159.

45. Thielicke, *Evangelical Faith,* II, 421–22.

46. Cullmann, *Christology of the New Testament,* 239–45; Barclay, *Jesus As They Saw Him,* 9–28.

47. Barclay, *Jesus As They Saw Him,* 269–72.

48. Ibid., 284–91.

49. Ibid., 325–28.

50. Künneth, *Theology of the Resurrection,* 61.

51. John Warwick Montgomery, *History and Christianity* (Downers Grove, Ill.: InterVarsity, 1965), esp. 79–80. See also Paul L. Maier, *First Easter: The True and Unfamiliar Story* (New York: Harper and Row, 1973).

52. Gustaf Wingren, *The Living Word: A Theological Study of Preaching and the Church,* trans. Victor C. Pogue (Philadelphia: Muhlenberg, 1960), 119–36.

53. Gustaf Wingren, *Credo: The Christian View of Faith and Life,* trans. Edgar M. Carlson (Minneapolis: Augsburg, 1981), 123.

54. Künneth, *Theology of the Resurrection,* 97.

55. Wingren, *Credo,* 121. See also Quere, *Evangelical Witness,* 54–56, 150–51.

56. Wingren, *Man and the Incarnation,* 82–87, 125.

57. Cullmann, *Christology of the New Testament,* 166–81. Cf. Paul's use of this image in 1 Cor. 15:45–49, and the possibility that it stands behind Phil. 2:6–11 as well.

58. Cullmann, *Christology of the New Testament,* 137–92, esp. 140–42, and 270–305; Barclay, *Jesus As They Saw Him,* 68–92, 43–67.

59. Dantine, *Justification of the Ungodly,* 87.

60. Barclay, *Jesus As They Saw Him,* 201–08.

61. Siggins, *Luther's Doctrine of Christ,* 162.

62. Barclay, *Jesus As They Saw Him,* 187–200.

63. Ibid., 258–62.

64. Ibid., 384–87.

65. Ibid., 273–77.

66. Ibid., 253–57.

67. Peter Sholtes, "They Will Know We Are Christians by Our Love," in *Hymns for Now* I (Chicago: The Walther League, 1967), from "Hymnal for Young Christians" by F. E. L. Publications, Ltd.

68. Siggins, *Luther's Doctrine of Christ,* 109–10.

69. Gustaf Aulen, *Christus Victor: An Historical Study of the Three Main Types of the Idea of Atonement,* trans. A. G. Hebart (New York: Macmillan, 1951), 96.

70. Ibid., 133–42.

71. Wingren, *Man and the Incarnation,* 120.

72. Ibid., 53–54.

73. C. S. Lewis, *Reflections on the Psalms* (New York: Harcourt Brace Jovanovich, 1958), 10.

74. Dantine, *Justification of the Ungodly,* 78–79.

75. See George H. Williams, *Anselm: Communion and Atonement* (St. Louis: Concordia, 1960); R. W. Southern, *Saint Anselm and His Biographer: A Study of Monastic Life and Thought 1059–c. 1130* (Cambridge: University Press, 1963), 77–121; John McIntyre, *St. Anselm and His Critics: A Reinterpretation of the Cur Deus Homo* (Edinburgh: Oliver and Boyd, 1954).

76. Southern, *Anselm and His Biographer,* 92–93.

77. Gerhard O. Forde, *Where God Meets Man: Luther's Down-to-Earth Approach to the Gospel* (Minneapolis: Augsburg, 1972), 42.

78. Helmut Thielicke, *How the World Began: Man in the First Chapters of the Bible,* trans. John W. Doberstein (Philadelphia: Muhlenberg, 1961), 256–57.

79. Dietrich Bonhoeffer, *Psalms: The Prayer Book of the Bible,* trans. James H. Burtness (Minneapolis: Augsburg, 1970), 58.

80. Dantine, *Justification of the Ungodly,* 101–02.

81. Douglas John Hall, *Lighten Our Darkness: Toward an Indigenous Theology of the Cross* (Philadelphia: Westminster, 1976), 149–50, 121.

82. Thielicke, *Evangelical Faith,* II, 383–85.

83. Ibid.

84. Martin Luther, *Lectures on Galatians, 1535, Chapters 1–4,* vol. 26 of *Luther's Works,* American Edition, trans. and ed. Jaroslav Pelikan (St. Louis: Concordia, 1963), 279.

85. Künneth, *Theology of the Resurrection,* 155.

86. Georg Fohrer, Werner Foerster, *"sozo,"* TDNT VII, 970–98.

87. O. Proksch, F. Büchsel, *"luo and compounds,"* TDNT IV, 329–35, 340–56.

88. Forde, *Where God Meets Man,* 16–17.

89. See Siggins, *Luther's Doctrine of Christ,* 138–39.

90. Forde, *Where God Meets Man,* 37.

91. Thielicke, *How the World Began,* 179.

92. Wingren, *Man and the Incarnation,* 49–50.

Notes

93. Francis Schaeffer, *He Is There and He Is Not Silent* (Wheaton: Tyndale, 1972), 11.

94. Siggins, *Luther's Doctrine of Christ,* 137; Friedrich Büchsel, *"katallasso,"* TDNT I, 254–58.

95. Wingren, *Man and the Incarnation,* 106.

96. Wingren, *Credo,* 69.

97. Gottlob Schrenk, *"dikaioō,"* TDNT II, 211 (see further, 192–225). Cf. Elert, *Christliche Glaube,* 468–70.

98. Dantine, *Justification of the Ungodly,* 84–109.

99. Friedrich Wilhelm Kantzenbach, "Christusgemeinschaft und Rechtfertigung. Luthers Gedanke vom fröhlichen Wechsel als Frage und unsere Rechtfertigungsbotschaft," *Luther* 35 (1964), 34–35.

100. Dantine, *Justification of the Ungodly,* 81.

101. Gerhard O. Forde, *Theology Is for Proclamation* (Minneapolis: Fortress, 1990), 30–37, 147–86.

Chapter 4

1. J. N. D. Kelly, *Early Christian Doctrines* (New York: Harper and Row, 1960), 255–63; and *Early Christian Creeds* (New York: McKay, 1960), 338–44.

2. C. S. Lewis, *Reflections on the Psalms* (New York: Harcourt Brace Jovanovich, 1958), 39–40.

3. Dietrich Bonhoeffer, *Christ the Center,* trans. John Bowden (New York: Harper and Row, 1960), 54.

4. Regin Prenter, *Spiritus Creator,* trans. John M. Jensen (Philadelphia: Muhlenberg, 1953), 141.

5. Bonhoeffer, *Christ the Center,* 54.

6. Dietrich Bonhoeffer, *The Cost of Discipleship,* trans. R. H. Fuller (New York: Macmillan, 1959), 8; Edmund Schlink, *The Doctrine of Baptism,* trans. Herbert J. A. Bouman (St. Louis: Concordia, 1972), 31–35, 45–46; Gustaf Wingren, *Gospel and Church,* trans. Ross Mackenzie (Philadelphia: Fortress, 1964), 60–61.

7. Wingren, *Gospel and Church,* 11.

8. Schlink, *Doctrine of Baptism,* 44.

9. While some might claim that these passages do not explicitly refer to Baptism, it is clear from all we know of the apostolic church that they could be referring to nothing other than Baptism by the phrase "water and the Word": "The expression 'baptism,' like the expression 'washing of water with the word' (Eph. 5:26), they have taken to be a figurative expression. But this is in direct opposition to all sound methods of interpretation. The churches which received these epistles had only one washing. And when the author uses this term with the definite article, the washing, no reader could think of anything else but the washing of Baptism. And if the author had had another washing in mind, he would have had to indicate it." Ole Hallesby, *Infant Baptism and Adult Conversion,* trans. Clarence J. Carlsen (Minneapolis: Augsburg, 1924), 13.

10. Schlink, *Doctrine of Baptism,* 54–56.

11. Bonhoeffer, *Cost of Discipleship,* 208–9; cf. Schlink, *Doctrine of Baptism,* 65–72, 82–105.

12. Bonhoeffer, *Cost of Discipleship,* 230–31.

13. Hallesby, *Infant Baptism and Adult Conversion,* 22–23.

14. Ibid., 34, 38–39, 46–47.

15. Werner Elert, *Der Christliche Glaube,* 5th ed. (Hamburg: Furche, 1956), 447; Schlink, *Doctrine of Baptism,* 72–81 (on infant baptism in general, see 130–66).

16. Gerhard Forde, *Where God Meets Man: Luther's Down-to-Earth Approach to the Gospel* (Minneapolis: Augsburg, 1972), 78.

17. C. S. Lewis, *Reflections on the Psalms,* 3–4.

18. Dietrich Bonhoeffer, *Life Together,* trans. John W. Doberstein (New York: Harper and Row, 1954), 50–51.

19. Oscar Cullmann, *Christ and Time: The Primitive Christian Conception of Time and History,* rev. ed., trans. Floyd V. Filson (London: SCM, 1962), 171. See also Cullmann, *Salvation in History* (New York: Harper and Row, 1967), 99–114; Elert, *Christliche Glaube,* 119.

20. Gustaf Wingren, *The Living Word: A Theological Study of Preaching and the Church,* trans. Victor C. Pogue (Philadelphia: Muhlenberg, 1960), 65.

21. Ibid., 70.

22. Aarne Siirila, *Divine Humanness,* trans. T. A. Kantonen (Philadelphia: Fortress, 1970), 99.

23. Bonhoeffer, *Life Together,* 55.

24. Thus, trust forms the basis of Erik Erikson's psychological analysis of the stages of human life, see e.g., his *Childhood and Society* (New York: Norton, 1950).

25. Helmut Thielicke, *The Evangelical Faith,* trans. Geoffrey W. Bromiley (Grand Rapids: Eerdmans, 1974, 1977), I, 129.

26. Prenter, *Spiritus Creator,* 88.

27. Wilhelm Dantine, *Justification of the Ungodly,* trans. Eric W. and Ruth C. Gritsch (St. Louis: Concordia, 1968), 63.

28. Thielicke, *Evangelical Faith,* II, 38–39.

29. Richard Wurmbrand, *In God's Underground* (New York: Bantam, 1968), 80.

30. Thielicke, *Evangelical Faith,* I, 25.

31. Ibid., II, 51.

32. C. F. W. Walther, *Law and Gospel,* trans. Herbert J. A. Bouman (St. Louis: Concordia, 1980), 156–58.

33. Wurmbrand, *In God's Underground,* 11.

34. George W. Forell, *The Proclamation of the Gospel in a Pluralistic World* (Philadelphia: Fortress, 1973), 15–19.

35. See the articles by Harry M. Tiebout, "Surrender Versus Compliance in Therapy with Special Reference to Alcoholism," *Quarterly Journal of Studies on Alcohol* 14 (1953), 56–68; "The Act of Surrender in the Therapeutic Process. With Special Reference to Alcoholism," Ibid., 10 (1949), 48–58.

36. Hallesby, *Infant Baptism and Adult Conversion,* 49.

37. Pelagius, an early fifth-century monk, taught that people can take the initial steps toward salvation by their own efforts, apart from the assistance of divine

grace. The term "semi-pelagian" is applied to the position which teaches that, in varying degrees, grace and human effort both contribute to the reconciliation between God and the sinner. The Protestant Reformation decisively rejected these views, but there has crept into much of modern Protestantism a view which, while insisting on "grace alone," also insists that the human will must cooperate with the Holy Spirit in accepting grace if the individual is to be saved.

38. Walther, *Law and Gospel*, 126–27.

39. Bonhoeffer, *Cost of Discipleship*, 57.

40. Walther, *Law and Gospel*, 106.

41. Gustaf Wingren, *Creation and Law*, trans. Ross Mackenzie (Edinburgh: Oliver and Boyd, 1961), 73–74. Originally published by LiberFörlag CWK Gleerup in Lund.

42. See Elert, *Christliche Glaube*, 116, 119.

43. Walther, *Law and Gospel*, 133.

44. Wingren, *Gospel and Church*, 29.

45. Schlink, *Doctrine of Baptism*, 72–73.

46. Bonhoeffer, *Life Together*, 32.

47. Wingren, *Living Word*, 160.

48. Bonhoeffer, *Christ the Center*, 54–56.

49. Thielicke, *Evangelical Faith*, II, 393–96.

50. Cullmann, *Christ and Time*, 155–56; and *Salvation in History*, 259–60.

51. Wingren, *Gospel and Church*, 15–17.

52. Lewis, *Reflections on the Psalms*, 95.

53. Cullmann, *Salvation in History*, 313.

54. Dietrich Bonhoeffer, *Psalms: The Prayer Book of the Bible*, trans. James H. Burtness (Minneapolis: Augsburg, 1970), 11.

55. Ibid., 9–10.

56. Bonhoeffer, *Cost of Discipleship*, 145.

57. Ibid., 146–47.

58. Walther, *Law and Gospel*, 26–32.

59. Siirila, *Divine Humanness*, 66.

60. Hermann Sasse, *Here We Stand*, trans. Theodore G. Tappert (New York, 1938; St. Louis: Concordia, n.d.), 43.

61. Bonhoeffer, *Life Together*, 19–20.

62. Ibid., 76–77.

63. Schlink, *Doctrine of Baptism*, 78; cf. Bonhoeffer, *Cost of Discipleship*, 232–33.

64. Gustaf Wingren, *Credo: The Christian View of Faith and Life*, trans. Edgar M. Carlson (Minneapolis: Augsburg, 1981), 41. See also Thielicke, *Evangelical Faith*, I, 192; and Wingren, *Gospel and Church*, 53.

65. Bonhoeffer, *Cost of Discipleship*, 113.

66. Thielicke, *Evangelical Faith*, I, 191.

67. Bonhoeffer, *Cost of Discipleship*, 49.

68. Gustaf Wingren, *Man and the Incarnation: A Study in the Biblical Theology of Irenaeus,* trans. Ross Mackenzie (Philadelphia: Muhlenberg, 1959), 58.

69. See Robert Kolb, "God Calling, 'Take Care of My People': Luther's Concept of Vocation in the Augsburg Confession and Its Apology," *Concordia Journal,* 8 (1982), 10.

70. Bonhoeffer, *Cost of Discipleship,* 107–08.

71. The ironic observation of my faculty colleague at Concordia College, Saint Paul, Minnesota, Jeffrey Burkart.

72. Wingren, *Credo,* 68.

73. See 22–23; 27–29; 40.

74. Gustaf Wingren, *Luther on Vocation,* trans. Carl C. Rasmussen (Philadelphia: Muhlenberg, 1957), 64.

75. Ibid., 73.

76. Ibid., 229.

77. Wingren, *Credo,* 104.

78. Gottfried Quell, Ethelbert Stauffer, *"agapao," Theological Dictionary of the New Testament,* trans. Geoffrey W. Bromiley (Grand Rapids: Eerdmans, 1964–72), I, 21–55; cf. Bonhoeffer, *Life Together,* 32–39, 90–109.

79. Thielicke, *Evangelical Faith,* II, 252.

80. Bonhoeffer, *Cost of Discipleship,* 132–33.

81. Wingren, *Credo,* 59.

82. Douglas John Hall, *Lighten Our Darkness: Toward an Indigenous Theology of the Cross* (Philadelphia: Westminster, 1976), 152.

83. Siirila, *Divine Humanness,* 99.

84. Ibid.

85. Wingren, *Luther on Vocation,* 55; cf. Bonhoeffer, *Cost of Discipleship,* 151.

86. Wingren, *Luther on Vocation,* 204–05; cf. Bonhoeffer, *Psalms: Prayer Book of Bible,* 47.

87. Bonhoeffer, *Cost of Discipleship,* 79.

88. Wingren, *Gospel and Church,* 10–11.

89. Forell, *Proclamation of Gospel in Pluralistic World,* 13.

90. Bonhoeffer, *Cost of Discipleship,* 179.

91. Wingren, *Gospel and Church,* 122–23.

Conclusion

1. On the biblical understanding of time and history, see Oscar Cullmann, *Christ and Time: The Primitive Christian Conception of Time and History,* rev. ed., trans. Floyd V. Filson (London: SCM, 1962), and his *Salvation in History* (New York: Harper and Row, 1967).

Library of Congress Cataloging-in-Publication Data

Kolb, Robert, 1941–
    Speaking the Gospel today : a theology for evangelism / Robert Kolb. — Rev. ed.
        p.   cm.
    ISBN 0-570-04258-5
    1. Evangelistic work—Philosophy. 2. Lutheran Church—Doctrines.
I. Title.
BV3793.K64   1995
269'.2—dc20   95-20239